ON MAGIC & MIRACLES

ON MAGIC & MIRACLES

A THEOLOGICAL GUIDE TO DISCERNING FICTIONAL MAGIC

MARIAN A. JACOBS

B&H PUBLISHING®
BRENTWOOD, TENNESSEE

Printed in the United States of America

979-8-3845-0126-8

Published by B&H Publishing Group
Brentwood, Tennessee

Dewey Decimal Classification: 231.73
Subject Heading: MIRACLES—CHRISTIANITY / MAGIC / FANTASY

Cover design and illustration by David Wardle.

1 2 3 4 5 6 • 28 27 26 25

This book is dedicated to my Realm Makers family whose sub-creations glorify God and increase faith.

Acknowledgments

I am overwhelmed with gratitude for the village of people God provided to make this book possible. First, I would like to thank my husband for his constant support, feedback, philosophizing, and encouragement. Tim, you are my other half in more ways than one, and I wouldn't be the person or the writer I am without you. To my children, your excitement and hunger for wisdom inspire me to keep going in moments of discouragement. To the rest of my family and especially Melissa and Mom, thank you for always cheering me on and putting up with me talking too much about demons.

I am so thankful to the team at B&H who worked to help me get this book out into the world. A special thank you to Clarissa Dufresne—you are an amazing editor and a joy to work with. To Madison Trammel at B&H Academic, thank you for taking the initial interest in this project and helping me get connected. I would also like to thank my agent Steve Laube for being such a supportive mentor.

I am grateful for my amazing friends for all your support, inspiration, and encouragement to keep writing through some hard seasons of life. Thank you to Lorehaven—Laura, Stephen, Josiah, Eli, Zack, Ticia, Daniel, Andy, Jenneth, Jessica, Jasmine, Lacy, Parker, and the rest of the team. You guys are an endless source of wisdom and help in times of trouble. Thank you to my other Realmie friends, especially Brianna and Cathy, for your prayers and support. I am also incredibly grateful to my church family—Stacy, Mike, the Millers, and my small group. Your tireless prayers sustained me for many months. And lastly to Caryn and Georgia for your constant encouragement.

To my alpha readers, Tim and Shannon, for putting up with my sloppiest writing and half-formed thoughts. This book wouldn't be what it is without you. Thank you to my beta readers, Mike, Jasmine, and Stephen, for your invaluable insight and encouragement.

Although I don't know most of you personally, I would like to thank the many former New Agers and occultists who bravely made your testimonies public. Your incredible faith in Jesus amidst some of the worst storms in life bolstered my own faith and served as a constant source of inspiration.

Finally, I want to thank God for his unceasing, guiding presence. There were many times I became overwhelmed with new information or couldn't figure out how to connect the dots in my head. The Lord was always there teaching me—through a sermon or his Word—whenever I cried out for help. He was also my comforter and protector during times of spiritual warfare. Without God as my shield, I would not have been able to finish writing this book.

Contents

Introduction

I grew up on a steady diet of science fiction and fantasy movies in the 1990s. From Disney princesses to Jim Hensen's *Labyrinth* to the original Star Wars trilogy—speculative films were the bread and butter of our home. I didn't become a reader until well into middle school. Once I discovered fantasy literature, I slowly grew into both a reader and, eventually, a writer of speculative fiction.* I was aware of the controversy surrounding Harry Potter at the time, but I didn't think that it had anything to do with me. Other Christians seemed to think children would want to become a witch if they read about fictional magic. But nothing sounded more distasteful to me than real witchcraft. Saved at a young age, I believe God protected me from any temptation toward the occult.

Whenever I saw a mixture of New Age and fantasy knickknacks displayed in shops, I felt simultaneously drawn to the dragon figurines as well as repulsed by the more spiritual items sitting next to them on the shelf. I would often walk away from those displays with lingering grief and even guilt. Although I knew almost

* Speculative fiction refers to all science fiction, fantasy, and their many subgenres.

nothing about the occult or alternative spirituality, the cool dragons somehow felt tainted by association with the "healing" crystals, sage bundles, and burning incense. As an adult, I'm able to discern the difference between individual products and not feel any guilt over purchasing something that was merely sitting next to occult items. Yet as a child, not purchasing any of it, including the dragons, was what made my developing conscience feel safe.

Children aren't the only people who have a developing conscience. This is a process Christians go through all our lives as God sanctifies us in different ways. Even as adults, we continue to wrestle through how to best filter the content we watch or read. How can we tell if a certain book or film is more like a simple dragon figurine or an occultic Ouija board? Some of you picked up this book thinking it would help you discern which, if any, fantasy novels are appropriate for your children. Perhaps you're a fantasy reader yourself, but the topic of magic in fiction is still confusing. Others of you may not read fantasy, but you're still interested in learning about what Scripture says regarding magic and miracles. Doesn't the Bible say magic is an abomination in Deuteronomy 18:9–12? And yet many Christians love The Chronicles of Narnia and The Lord of the Rings—fantasies that contain magic. Even some of the most robust theologians are confused about the reason why Aslan's Deep Magic is widely accepted in the church when Scripture uses strong language in opposition to magic. How can we teach our children to discern fantasy when we aren't sure how to do it ourselves?

Most of the time, those who feel free to read and watch stories about fantasy magic use the reason that "it's just a story; it's not real." This defense shows that they understand there's often a difference between fantasy magic and occult magic even if they don't always know why or where to draw the line. It also shows that even if they're not fully aware of what they're saying, the idea that something is "just a story" and not real life speaks to the intrinsic awareness we have that stories are usually filled with metaphors and layered meaning that reveal something about reality beyond the basic movements of the plot. For example, *The Lion, the Witch and the Wardrobe* is not just a story about four children and a lion who fight an evil queen in another world. It's a story about forgiveness, the gospel, and the ultimate authority of Christ who defeats our accuser through painful and humiliating self-sacrifice.

However, "it's just a story" is also an insufficient answer to the question of whether depictions of occult-like magic in a fantasy book could pose a threat to a reader. Stories are not merely entertainment but one of the most powerful ways mankind processes and accesses truth as well as lies. Studies show that through the fictional experiences of others, we grow in empathy and insight into the mind, joys, and sufferings of someone different from ourselves.[1] That emotional connection can be used to turn our hearts and minds toward or away from truth depending on the story. "Guard your heart" (Prov. 4:23) is not only something to be aware of when interacting with others; it's also essential when choosing which stories to invest in and which characters to empathize with.

Due to the empathy stories rouse in us, it's not an insignificant question to ask if a book or a sympathetic character could influence someone into joining the occult. Yet despite some believers feeling confident in their answers that it either will or will not be a temptation, proof of either side has yet to be seen. And if there is a difference between fantasy magic and occult magic, what is it? How can the Bible help us answer this question when it doesn't speak explicitly to how we should engage with fiction and media?

When I first set out to find the answers to these questions, I thought I would pull back a drape to expose a painting on the wall. Instead, I found a doorway to another world. I discovered the answers to my questions, but I also found something far better. As I explored this new-to-me realm of magic and miracles, I wanted nothing more than to belong there for eternity with the Ancient of Days. More than ever before, I desired to know Christ—to have the most profound intimacy with him this earthly realm could afford me.

In this book, you'll learn about the theology of magic and gain practical tools to apply to stories and games. But more than that, I want you to fall on your knees and worship Christ the moment you walk through that portal with me. Jesus is the ultimate Word of power and King over all things in both the heavenly and earthly realms. "For everything was created by him, in heaven and on earth, the visible and the invisible, whether thrones or dominions or rulers or authorities—all things have been created through him and for him. . . . For God was pleased to have all his fullness dwell in him, and through him to reconcile everything to himself, whether things on earth or things in heaven, by making peace through his blood, shed on the cross" (Col. 1:16, 19–20). Even in a study of supernaturalism and fiction, everything comes back to the authority and majesty of Christ.

Laying the Foundation

Many books on Christian discernment are able to delve straight into their primary topic in the first chapter. The foundation is usually laid. You'll find I wasn't able to do that with this book. With the near total lack of discussion or scholarship on magic in the church today, a large portion of this book may feel like a preamble. Many of the resources I found on the topic of the theology of magic were liberal leaning, nearly out of print, or from a different branch of Christianity than my own. We have a lot of ground to cover before we can dig into literature and fictional magic systems. Instead of a foundation to build a house, we have only an empty lot with a bunch of weeds and briars.

Because of that, we are going to start on the theology of supernaturalism and what that has to do with fantasy magic. The reason for this is threefold. First, we already have a great many Christian books, websites, and YouTube channels dedicated to analyzing films and stories from a Christian perspective. I have no desire to add to that growing list with this book. Second, the topic of magic and miracles has been egregiously overlooked in the past, and the church is in desperate need of a recalibration in regard to the theology of the spiritual realm and the occult. That recalibration will have a weighty impact on how we think about fictional magic.

Third, I want to teach you how to fish, not just serve you a plate of poached salmon. My goal is not to detail every type of magic ever practiced or fictionalized. Instead, I want to give you the foundational principles you'll need to engage with fictional magic on your own. I will give examples, but for the most part, I want you to walk away feeling as though you can use Scripture to discern the nuances of fictional supernaturalism by yourself. At the end of this book, you should have a new tool bag, not a mental list of what books, films, or games to avoid.

If you're tempted to skip ahead to the more applicable parts of this book for quick answers, please don't. Have patience as we lay the foundation for our house. Like any good foundation, it all points back to Jesus. Without a complete understanding of what magic has to do with Christ and his upside-down kingdom, I guarantee you that you either won't understand the application or you'll inadvertently misuse it.

Since the topic of supernatural theology is so rarely discussed, there will certainly be new information. Some of it may be shocking and force you to question what you've been taught or whether you should consider me a reliable source. When that happens, stop and investigate God's Word. Read, pray, and seek the guidance of the Holy Spirit. No book is perfect outside of inerrant Scripture, and this one is no exception. The beauty of encountering the thoughts and research of other believers on topics such as the theology of magic is not that their words are perfect or authoritative but that coming into contact with new ideas forces you to go back to the Bible and read with new questions in mind. It's my desire that you would do that alongside the reading of this book so you might gain new insights in your own study of Scripture.

Discernment Notes

When discussing books as examples, I've left footnotes on the content of the story. In order to discuss a wide range of magic systems, I cite examples from books I normally wouldn't read and do not recommend. It can be difficult to know whether or not a book is appropriate for you or your child without online discernment guides, so please be sure to check my notes. Just because I discuss a book or film doesn't mean it's appropriate for everyone (or anyone). I didn't leave the same notes for films since those are available online at IMDb.com under the "Parents guide" or at Pluggedin.com. For reviews of other fantasy books written by Christians that I didn't discuss, see Lorehaven.com.

PART ONE

A THEOLOGICAL FOUNDATION OF MAGIC & MIRACLES

Chapter 1

Magic or Miracle?

From The Lord of the Rings and The Chronicles of Narnia to more modern stories like Harry Potter, Christians have been debating the issue of fictional magic for decades. We've formed distinct sides of whether Christians should read fantasy magic, both of which contain a generous number of humble, biblically minded believers as well as dogmatic extremists. These factions have written more articles and books arguing their point than most would ever care to read, largely about Harry Potter. There are a great number of fantasy stories containing magic, but J.K. Rowling's series has received the most attention in recent years due to its worldwide popularity.

It may seem as though popular media is responsible for an increase of fictional magic that many believers find dangerous. Yet Christians have produced fictional stories that portray magic in a positive light for hundreds of years despite clear scriptural commands regarding witchcraft. Oral traditions and fairy tales, as well as medieval works by Christians such as the Arthurian legends (twelfth century), *The Canterbury Tales* (fourteenth century), and *The Faerie Queene* (sixteenth century), are just some examples of early Christian fantasy involving magic.

Even though the fantasy genre didn't begin with J. R. R. Tolkien and C. S. Lewis, they wrote faith-filled fantasy that sent cultural shock waves around the world. Some of the biggest influencers of the fantasy genre before the nineteenth and twentieth centuries were George MacDonald's *Phantastes*, Carlo Collodi's *Pinocchio*, Lewis Carroll's *Alice's Adventures in Wonderland*, H. Rider Haggard's *She: A History of Adventure*, and Bram Stoker's *Dracula*. But once Tolkien published the first serial epic fantasy, The Lord of the Rings, the genre exploded. Today, fantasy is one of the most popular genres of fiction, expanding beyond books into film, television, board games, and video games.

The Lord of the Rings may have had the most dramatic influence on fantasy's popularity, but The Chronicles of Narnia was a close runner-up.[1] While Middle Earth broke ground with world-building and "sub-creation" (the act of creating in imitation of God's creation), Narnia set a high bar for the marriage of magic and Christianity at the Stone Table.[2] Tolkien wrote of "The Secret Fire"—God's power of creation. He also stated in *The Silmarillion* that the good "wizard," Gandalf, was one of the Maiar—a kind of angel.[3] But it was Lewis who blatantly referred to theology—specifically to the gospel—as the "Deep Magic" and an "incantation" in *The Lion, the Witch and the Wardrobe*.[4]

> "It means," said Aslan, "that though the Witch knew the Deep Magic, there is a magic deeper still which she did not know. Her knowledge goes back only to the dawn of time. But if she could have looked a little further back, into the stillness and the darkness before Time dawned, she would

> have read there a different incantation. She would have known that when a willing victim who had committed no treachery was killed in a traitor's stead, the Table would crack and Death itself would start working backward."[5]

This reflects quite a different view of magic than many Christians possess. Lewis likely wasn't the first fiction author to use the word *magic* this way, but with the fire he and Tolkien kindled for fantasy, Aslan's speech—both surprising and beautiful—resonated with readers in a new and profound way. The Narnia books have sold more than one hundred million copies, have been translated into forty-seven languages, and have been adapted into multiple films.[6] The popularity and impact of this classic series can't be overstated.

Although some Christians aren't fans of Lewis's Deep Magic, it hasn't sparked even a fraction of the outrage that Harry Potter has. In an Internet search, I counted at least ten books dedicated to tracing biblical themes in the Harry Potter series, such as John Granger's *Looking for God in Harry Potter*.[7] Another search brings more critical titles such as *Harry Potter and the Bible: The Menace behind the Magick* by Richard Abanes.[8] Critics of Harry Potter have fought for the Christian community at large to reject the series and most other forms of supernaturalism in the fantasy genre. Despite efforts made by some Christians to encourage others to see fictional magic as an issue of Christian freedom, author J.K. Rowling received hate speech, slander, and even death and bomb threats from believers.[9] The primary concern was that Harry would be an easy gateway into the occult. CBN's Linda LaFond states: "But because Wicca, New Age, and the occult have infiltrated mainstream culture in recent years, it is easy for unsuspecting children who want to learn more about Harry's world to find occult books, Web sites, and chat rooms. Christians are concerned that children will find the attractiveness of Harry Potter an easy entrance ramp to researching witchcraft without realizing the demonic reality behind it."[10]

Such caution against fictional magic is not restricted to Harry Potter but has been said about many other fantasy books and films. Harry Potter specifically presents a conundrum for Christians and not just because of his incredible popularity. Rowling said in 2007 that she grew up Anglican and is a member of the Church of Scotland.[11] Her books present a compelling combination of overt gospel themes within a large and fascinating world containing both fictional magic and some occult-like practices. Christians are understandably confused.

Former witch, Kristine McGuire, speaks openly about her early fascination with the occult and her journey to Christ in her book *Escaping the Cauldron: Exposing Occult Influences in Everyday Life*. When asked what her thoughts were on Harry Potter, she acknowledged that the books do contain some depictions of occult practices. She eventually drew this conclusion: "The real issue, to me, is whether an interest [in the occult] exists before reading the books or seeing the movies. Truthfully, the average reader or moviegoer will probably never be enticed toward witchcraft because of Harry Potter."[12]

Is she right that Harry Potter is only dangerous if someone has a previous interest in the occult—or as Lewis calls it, "spiritual lust"?[13] If so, are there other fantasy books, movies, or games out there that are more dangerous? How can we discern which are safe and which aren't? And what are we to think when great Christian men like Lewis and Tolkien included magic in their fiction, but the Bible clearly states that such things are evil? Surely there's a difference between the "Deep Magic" of Aslan in *The Lion, the Witch and the Wardrobe* and the wand-waving in Harry Potter? But if so, what is it? Can we distinguish between "good magic" and "evil magic" when choosing books for ourselves or our children?

The problem only deepens for writers of fantastical fiction attempting to spin stories like these same heroes of old. Lewis and Tolkien were Oxford professors, highly educated in classical philosophy, and dedicated theologians in their own right. How can the laymen of our modern churches hope to discern the use of fictional magic without a similar understanding of philosophy and theology? How do we know when it's appropriate to use the word *magic* and when to avoid it?

C. S. Lewis may not have initiated a linguistic flattening of all supernaturalism into the word *magic*, yet I believe he played a large role in furthering it as a modern literary umbrella term for all supernatural occurrences including miracles, superpowers, the Force from Star Wars, and more. If you pick up a modern fantasy book now, the "magic" within its pages could refer to anything from occult magic, superpowers, innate magical gifting, science as magic, and more. Such a wide literary scope is undoubtedly influenced by the works of Lewis and Tolkien. With these stories fresh in the minds of modern readers and moviegoers, how can we possibly discover the true nature of "good" and "evil" supernaturalism? Before we analyze specific books and films, we'll first discuss the chasm that has formed between the words magic and miracle historically and how those words appear in Scripture.

What Is Magic?

Broadly speaking, modern Christians often think all magic is evil and against God's law, whereas miracles are events God ordains.

More specifically, some Christians believe the difference between "good" and "evil" supernatural events in Scripture is that magic entails use of incantations and spells, interpretations of omens, and more. Others have proposed that occult magic needs a tightly controlled environment and methodology whereas Jesus is able to perform a miracle anywhere at any time.[14] Some make the argument that all magic, even magic found in Scripture—like Pharaoh's magicians turning their staffs into serpents—is simply an illusion.*[15] Yet the Bible never states nor implies that magic isn't real. People sometimes pretend to have psychic powers, but those who are genuine in their commitment to the occult are not illusionists nor sleight-of-hand magicians. We will discuss whether magic is real in the following chapters.

For now, it's important to turn our focus away from magical methods such as the use of spells, crystals, or wands. The real distinction between magic and miracles doesn't lie primarily in the method but in its source—God or Satan—and its intended goals—to glorify God or the individual magic user. Other contextual clues surrounding supernaturalism include the setting of the event within Christ's upside-down kingdom and a person's heart posture.

Divination, necromancy, and so on originate with Satan and demons (or fallen "spirits"), and what Christians typically consider "miracles" originate from God and seek to glorify him. In fact, the Bible sometimes presents mirrored events in which we see the

---

* "The three sign miracles that we're considering—the staff turned into a serpent, the water turned to blood, and the invasion of the frogs—have in common the fact that all of them were duplicated by Pharaoh's court magicians. Perhaps 'counterfeited' is a more accurate word, because what they did was more likely deceptive sleight of hand. However, Satan can empower his people to perform 'lying wonders' (2 Thess. 2:9–10; Matt. 24:24; Rev. 13:11–15), and that may have been the source of their power."

same or similar activities from both God and demons—something I refer to as "mirrored magic." Former witch, Julie Lopez, says, "The Enemy doesn't create—he copies."[16] For example, in Exodus 7–8, Pharaoh's magicians mimic Moses's "signs and wonders" by turning staffs into serpents, turning water into blood, and conjuring frogs. Passages like these need to be interpreted with care to discern whether the magic is real and what difference exists between Moses and Pharaoh's magicians. We'll discuss this event in-depth in chapter 3.

Although Satan can mimic God's miracles, the contexts surrounding these different events are nothing alike. Even more confusion arises through a modern misunderstanding of the nature of magic in the practice of Christian witchcraft. This syncretist practice continues to grow in tandem with the New Age occult despite the clearly stated warning against drinking "the cup of the Lord and the cup of demons" in 1 Corinthians 10:21.* Products such as prayer tarot cards and "Holy Spirit" Ouija boards are now available for purchase online. In *Ritual Magic for Conservative Christians*, Catholic priest and occultist, Brother A. D. A., argues that magic is a historical Christian practice, and he provides a system for its use.[17] When McGuire was in the throes of syncretism, she found many others who shared her beliefs and practices. "One day, on a whim, I searched the internet for *Christian witch*. My jaw dropped when I saw the results. There were thousands of websites devoted to my quest. Here was evidence of other people forging their own magickal path while holding onto Jesus. I wasn't alone!"[18]

Exploring every variation of witchcraft or Christian-pagan syncretism is beyond the scope of this book. Yet being aware of its

---

* Syncretism is the practice of merging differing or opposing religious, cultural, or ideological beliefs into one.

existence is important. As we continue to look at the way these matters impact how we discern the world's buffet of fictional magic, it's not essential to have an exhaustive knowledge of paganism and witchcraft but a functional understanding of its foundational principles. We'll discuss whether the New Age occult poses a legitimate threat in chapter 4.

Indefinable Supernaturalism

The relationship between magic and miracles has been debated throughout church history. While we tend to use different words for *magic* and *miracles*, that distinction isn't always clear in Scripture. Catholic theologian Gustavo Benavides explains this divide well: "In order to account for religious activities that ordinarily would be considered magical but that must be kept apart from such risky association, Christianity distinguished between 'magic' and 'miracle'—the first having to do with activities that are either fraudulent or demonic, and the second with the divine overruling of the divinely established natural order.[19]

Historically, these distinctions have been widely misunderstood. Even now, we can't seem to agree on how to define magic. In his essay "Magic in Early Christianity," David E. Aune comments on the difference between magic and miracles along similar lines as Benavides: "The popular distinction between magic and miracle has it that the latter is more "religious" than the former. In reality, the magic/miracle dichotomy is not only an artificial distinction which presupposes an unambiguous difference between magic and religion, it also appears to have little value in interpreting the evidence available to us from the Graeco-Roman period."[20]

Although Aune doesn't distinguish between good and evil supernaturalism, he's right about the superficial distinction of the language as well as our poor grasp of the historical data. In the modern church, we seldom understand the cultural context of the early church—the framework of magic and the supernatural in the Greco-Roman and ancient Near Eastern mind. We live in a post-Enlightenment era as born and bred *materialists*.* This kind of "materialism" doesn't refer to a social label of shallow desire for wealth and possessions. It's the belief that only physical matter exists and everything is explainable by natural occurrences. This is why it's also called "naturalism."

Materialism is common among modern atheists who not only reject the existence of God but of any spiritual entity or realm such as heaven. Although Christians reject atheism, we still often function as materialists in other ways and even analyze Scripture through this lens without realizing it. Our resistance to believing in the existence of magic and our tendency to interpret the Bible as anti-supernaturalists are two ways Christians partially hold to materialism. It's like rot hiding under the soil and infecting the blooms in our theological garden. Perhaps the brightest spots of the garden are less infected and better tended. But those shadowy places beneath the heavy canopies and in the dark corners where we put "unimportant" doctrines on supernaturalism—those places are teeming with spores, and all the plants are on the verge of death.

Materialism was not a commonly held philosophy in the ancient world. For Hellenistic Jews, "magical-miracle" was a

* The Enlightenment (or "Age of Reason") occurred in seventeenth and eighteenth centuries which introduced Modernism and made an idol of reason and science apart from supernaturalism. The effect was the prolific philosophy of materialism (or naturalism) that still influences our culture today.

category, revealing the difference between the two which was, at times, indiscernible to them.[21] It's possible this confusion eventually led to the Colossian heresies of legalism and mysticism that Paul addresses in Colossians 2:4–23, as well as the Pharisees' accusations that Jesus was performing miracles by the power of demons (Matt. 12:22–32; Mark 3:20–30). The Pharisees might as well have called Jesus a magician if they truly thought his signs and wonders were empowered not by the Holy Spirit but by a fallen spirit.*[22]

In his book, *Hellenistic Magic and the Synoptic Tradition*, theologian John M. Hull examines various perspectives of magic in the Hellenistic period. In these views, magic is defined either by specific methodology, rituals, or any supernatural act mediated by humans or objects, and neglecting the dichotomy of demonic or divine origins. In that age, miracles were seen as something that came directly from God *or* pagan gods without a human mediator.

The first-century Jewish historian Josephus attempted to draw a stronger distinction between magic and miracles in response to his contemporaries who conflated them. From the point of view of Moses, Josephus wrote: "I assert that the deeds wrought by me so far surpass their magic and their art as things divine are remote from what is human. And I will show that it is from no witchcraft or deception of true judgment, but from God's providence and power that my miracles proceed."[23] Josephus's desire to distinguish

* "The belief that Jesus was a magician is an ancient one. It goes back at least as far as the middle of the first century, as is shown by the Beelzebub story in Mark. During the early Christian centuries, it is found in a variety of traditions and became from time to time a subject of warm debate. Jewish tradition attributes Jesus' miracles to his magical power and he is said to have been executed as a sorcerer. The Jewish objection to the healings on the Sabbath was therefore, according to this tradition, not the sabbath activity itself but the magical techniques used by Jesus."

between witchcraft and God's providence was not always recognized by first-century Jews.

Hull said that the "Hebrew attitude to nature and history is such that everything is pregnant with magical-miracle."[24] He goes on to explain how some of the Israelites may have perceived miracles in Exodus as "a battle by one [magician] against less potent ones"* and "a contest of magic.[25] They also likely viewed prophecy as being delivered in a "magical manner."[26] More interesting still, Hull links the creation account with the ancient concept of "magical-miracle" because God created the universe by speaking words of power in Genesis 1:1: "It is not easy to make a clear distinction between magic and miracle. The fundamental miracle of biblical thought is the creation of the world. . . . The magical association was expressed most clearly in the idea of creation by means of a word of power."[27]

What was the word of power? The specific syllables God spoke? God is spirit (John 4:24) and did not speak audibly or with a physical body. His spoken word is anthropomorphic or analogous so we can comprehend some aspect of the mystery and power of his ability to create with a mere word, breath, or thought. Jesus is the Word of power—the Logos. He is the one given all authority in heaven and on earth (Matt. 28:18). Jesus was in the beginning with God, "and the Word was with God, and the Word was God. He was with God in the beginning. All things were created through him, and apart from him not one thing was created that has been created" (John 1:1–3). Jesus is the ultimate Word of power. His name, as a spoken word, has authority because our eternal king "is before all things, and by him all things hold together" (Col. 1:17).

---

* Hull's unedited statement reads: "A battle by one *thaumaturge* against less potent ones" (emphasis added). A thaumaturge is a magician or person who works miracles.

With this cultural and historical context in mind, what can we say magic is at its core? Baptist theologian T. Witton Davies asserts the answer is religion: "All magic is incipient religion, for it is an appeal to spirits believed to be more powerful and wise than man, and the methods employed to secure what is desired are no other than applications to the goodwill of the beings consulted."[28] In Davies's book, *Magic, Divination, and Demonology among the Hebrews and Their Neighbours*, he makes a case that demonic magic and divination are deeply religious modalities that mimic Jewish and Christian practices. We'll spend time discussing *mirrored magic* at length in chapter 5.

Davies's insistence that magic is religious (and, therefore, spiritual) is essential to our understanding of both magic and religion. Its importance to religion has been long overlooked among Christians and theologians to our great detriment. In the ancient Near East and first century, paganism and occultism were dominant practices. It was the basis for their religious life, which deeply impacted their relationship with Israel. However, we spend little to no time attempting to understand the pagan occult and their supernatural methods of worship—namely sorcery, divination, necromancy, and more.

Consider how Daniel was counted amongst the "wise men" of Babylon (Dan. 2). This group included magicians, mediums, and astrologers. They were deeply religious and acted in a similar role as Pharaoh's priestly magicians in Exodus 7. Daniel was one of them due to his wisdom, spirituality, and being gifted with supernatural abilities such as interpretations of dreams and visions. The fact that his power came from the Hebrew God and not their demon gods made no difference to the Babylonians until they witnessed the far greater power of Daniel's God (Dan. 3:24–30; 4:28–37; 6:19–28).

Even more obvious is the fact that magic, or demonic supernaturalism, can only be achieved through appeals to fallen spirits. At its very core, sorcery is spiritual and, therefore, religious in nature.

The religious context of demonic magic and divination that Davies noted is also essential for our understanding of magic since moderns often don't perceive the connection between the two unless being trained for the mission field. In Western society, magic is only fictional whimsy and frivolity. It's unfathomable to imagine how these things could possibly relate to religion. To modern Christians, the concept of magic seems entirely irrelevant to our faith and understanding of the Bible. The real tragedy here is less in the loss of understanding the supernatural and more in the fact that the church has become so influenced by materialism that we sometimes unknowingly divorce our own spirituality from our lived Christianity.

In his book, *The Case for Miracles*, Lee Strobel lists a number of definitions of miracle from theologians and philosophers before giving his favorite by Richard L. Purtill: "A miracle is an event (1) brought about by the power of God that is (2) a temporary (3) exception (4) to the ordinary course of nature (5) for the purpose of showing that God has acted in history."[29] This is a great definition, but there are many other religions—pagan religions included—that refer to supernatural events as "miracles" that aren't from God. Even within an exclusively Christian context, it's too broad for our literary purposes.

The best definition of magic I have found is by Davies, who says, "Magic may be briefly defined as the attempt on man's part to have intercourse with spiritual and supernatural beings, and to influence them for his benefit."[30] Although this is adequate for most uses, for our purposes we can be more specific about the intended goals and heart posture of the magic user. In order to understand why someone would draw a correlation between magic and miracles and to be able to apply these to fantasy magic, we need to narrow the scope of our definitions. We will be primarily looking at supernatural events mediated through humans, animals, and objects, as opposed to unmediated direct acts of God or other spirits.* Within mediated supernatural actions, I'll designate what distinguishes between *demonic* and *divine* acts.**

The following definitions aren't exhaustive or intended to replace those previously held but to merely aid this conversation about magic, miracles, and fantastical fiction. Neither Scripture nor fiction uses these terms with such precision or exclusion. Yet as we continue to examine these throughout the remainder of this book, we need to be specific about what types of supernaturalism we're focusing on.

> **Divine supernaturalism:** A supernatural act mediated by a person, animal, or object in submission to God's authority over nature, through the power of the Holy Spirit, for the sake of God's glory, the spread of the gospel, and our eternal joy.

---

* Although we need to separate these for the sake of this discussion, keep in mind that demons don't have power in and of themselves. All power is God's power. The small measure demons have, has been allotted to them by the will of God (Job 1:12; Isa. 45:7). But what Satan means for evil, God means for good (Gen. 50:20).

** In chapter 2, we will discuss the "divine council" of God which includes angels and demons. Although other spirits besides God are considered "divine," I'll be using it as a label in the popular sense of the word (for Yahweh alone) for practicality and because I enjoy alliteration (i.e., *demonic* and *divine*).

> **Demonic supernaturalism:** A supernatural act mediated by a person, animal, or object that subverts God's authority over nature, through the power of fallen spirits, for the sake of power, secret knowledge, and/or self-aggrandizement.

Supernatural events occur when a spiritual entity that resides in the spiritual realm causes something physical to act beyond its nature. *So that which is supernatural is also spiritual, but not all that is spiritual is supernatural.* For example, it's a spiritual reality when God speaks with angels and demons. But that isn't supernatural. Many things happen in the spiritual realm that don't interact with the physical world at all. When a spirit in the unseen realm moves a physical object, the object is acting beyond its nature because it's being propelled by a nonphysical force and superseding the laws of nature. Without spirits and the spiritual realm, the supernatural is impossible. Therefore, everything that is supernatural must also be spiritual.

Humans are both spiritual and physical beings. Since we aren't exclusively spiritual entities and don't reside in the spiritual realm, we don't have the authority or ability to cause supernatural events. However, our intellectual soul—that which is spiritual—cries out for the spiritual reality we can't see. We long for that which our modern society often refuses to acknowledge exists. A portion of that innate longing is for the supernatural and for the God who wields such power. We shouldn't assume that a child who pretends she has superpowers or magical abilities is always acting against God's commands or being tempted by "spiritual lust."[31] Instead she may be displaying a good, human desire for God and his authority over nature through play—a small act of what Tolkien calls "sub-creation."[32] Her soul is crying out for more than what her five senses tell her of the world—for a God who can do all things. In the same way, it wasn't wrong for Elisha to ask for a double portion of Elijah's spirit—double his supernatural abilities—after Elisha's mentor was gone (2 Kings 2:9).

Lewis's concept of spiritual lust doesn't universally apply to just anyone who desires to engage with supernaturalism. In its simplest form, a desire for the supernatural is good and an expression of sub-creation. Yet lust is rooted in envy—in desiring to possess something or someone that doesn't belong to you. Longing for the supernatural and the expression of that in play and the creation of stories is not necessarily lust; it's a subconscious working out of our spiritual selves and our desire for an eternity where heaven and earth are reunited as they once were in Eden. The distortion of "spiritual lust" occurs when we envy and take supernaturalism for ourselves when God hasn't given it to us, as though we are divine. Instead of *sub-creation in submission to God's will*, it attempts to *cocreate as though equal with God.*[*33] At its core, spiritual lust for the supernatural is demanding, selfish, and prideful. It trades knowledge of God and his divine supernaturalism for worldly enlightenment and demonic powers. Spiritual lust says, "I can reach into the spiritual realm by my own power and authority and take whatever I like."

As we continue to discuss the possible existence of magic, keep in mind that all forms of magic were historically practiced in a religious setting and are meant as application to spiritual entities that have long deceived people into believing their intentions are

---

* The type of cocreation I am referring to—of presuming equality with God—should not be confused with Allen Arnold's concept of cocreation in his book, *The Story of With*, in which he described a similar process of sub-creating with God.

good. However, it's important to note that modern New Agers and occultists don't usually consider themselves "religious" even if they're practicing spiritual modalities.

Context Is Key

In contrast to the tight association of magic and miracles in the ancient Near East and the first century, today we have come to think of them as entirely separate. It may even be shocking to you that they would be compared at all. It's true that the Bible sometimes uses different words for magic (*mageía* in Greek, *kešep̄* in Hebrew meaning "sorcery") than for miracle (*dýnamis* in Greek, *môp̄ēṯ* in Hebrew). The specific word for magic is used only once in the Bible in Acts 8:11. However, any minor differences in language were meant only to aid us in discerning the source and goal of supernatural power. In fact, the word for *miracle* in Greek, *dýnamis*, translates literally as "power." In 1 Corinthians 12:10, a more direct translation of the spiritual gift listed as "performing of miracles" is "working of powers" (*energēma dynamis*).[34] The strongest distinction made between "magic" and "miracles" is in the story of Simon the magician in Acts 8:11–13 (ESV). The word *magic* (v. 11) is actually put here properly right next to the word *miracles* (v. 13) which could be translated as "power."

> And they paid attention to him because for a long time he had amazed them with his **magic** [*mageía*]. But when they believed Philip as he preached good news about the kingdom of God and the name of Jesus Christ, they were baptized, both men and women. Even Simon himself believed, and after being baptized he continued

> with Philip. And seeing signs and great **miracles** [*dynamis*] performed, he was amazed. (emphasis added)

In the New Testament, the commonly used phrase "signs and wonders" (*sēmeion kai teras*) is used to refer to both good and evil supernatural events.* This is similar to the Hebrew word *môp̄ēṯ*, which we often translate as "miracle" yet literally means "sign" or "wonder." Most of the time, the context of each passage in both the Old and New Testaments distinguishes the source of the power—from God or demons.

Matthew 24:24 says, "For false messiahs and false prophets will arise and perform great signs and wonders to lead astray, if possible, even the elect." The Greek words *sēmeion* (signs) and *teras* (wonders) have a supernatural connotation and don't imply illusion or sleight-of-hand magic. False messiahs and prophets will not only perform supernatural signs but "great signs" (*sēmeion megas*) to deceive many. The indication of whether these events are demonic is the context of the words preceding "great signs and wonders" (false prophets), not the words themselves. Arguably, these signs are a form of demonic power. But Matthew chooses not to distinguish demonic power from divine power with the words *magic* and *miracles*.

Comparatively, Acts 4:29–30 says, "And now, Lord, consider their threats, and grant that your servants may speak your word with all boldness, while you stretch out your hand for healing, and signs and wonders are performed through the name of your holy servant

---

* Matthew 24:24; Mark 13:22; John 4:48; Acts 2:22, 43; 4:30; 5:12; 6:8; 7:36; 14:3; 15:12; Romans 15:19; 2 Corinthians 12:12; 2 Thessalonians 2:9; Hebrews 2:4.

Jesus." Verse 30 is referring to the apostles' performing signs and wonders "through the name of your holy servant Jesus." The Greek phrase for "signs and wonders" in Acts is the same in Matthew 24:24—*sēmeion kai teras*. Context shows that these supernatural signs aren't from demonic powers but from God and through the name of Jesus. In texts like these, we see that the "magic" and "miracle" language dichotomy is not firmly held throughout the Bible.

Translations also sometimes add the word *magic* to certain verses based on the context of the passage so modern audiences understand there are demonic powers involved. Yet this is a more modern use of the word *magic* that helps us understand the sometimes confusing lack of consistent terminology in the Bible. Acts 19:19 says, "While many of those who had practiced magic [*periergos*] collected their books and burned them in front of everyone." The word *periergos* means "curious arts" and can have a pagan or magical connotation and likely does in this passage. An Old Testament example is Ezekiel 13:18 which prohibits "magic bands." The Hebrew doesn't say either "magic" or "sorcery" but only "bands" (*keseṯ*). These translations are based on the context of the passage and knowledge of the surrounding pagan culture. It's added in English because of our modern use of the word, not so much its ancient use.

Other words with a magical connotation include magician (Hebrew: *ḥarṭṭōm*; Greek: *magos, mageuō*), sorcery (Hebrew: *kāšap̄;* Greek: *pharmakeia*), divination (Hebrew: *qāsam*), necromancer (Hebrew: *yiḏʿōnî*), mediums (Hebrew: *ôḇ*), and astrologers (Hebrew: *ʿaššāp̄* or *hāḇar*), which refer to things condemned by God.* The only linguistic exception to this may be the inclusion of Daniel as

* Leviticus 19:31; 20:6, 27; Deuteronomy 4:19; 18:10–12; Galatians 5:19–20; Isaiah 8:18–20; 47:13.

chief of Nebuchadnezzar's magicians (Dan. 5:11). However, this does not imply he was using occultic modalities but simply accomplishing similar supernatural feats by the power of God.

From a first-century perspective, the miracles of Jesus and his disciples weren't seen as different from magicians because the crowds saw them as entirely separate from pagan "magic." The people differentiated them by Jesus's display of a greater degree of power over nature, life, and death that no other spiritual entity ever had and because Jesus chose to heal the weak people of the world to shame the strong (1 Cor. 1:27). It was his great authority and teaching of his upside-down kingdom where the last is first and the first is last (Matt. 20:16; 23:11–12) that provided proof that the God of the Israelites was different—was *holy*—and the source of all power and love in the universe.

Five Fictional Magic Discernment Questions

Just as the language of magic and miracles isn't consistent throughout history or in Scripture, so it isn't consistent in fiction either. Lewis likely didn't intend to collapse categories by using the word magic to refer to the gospel any more than biblical authors through terms like "signs and wonders." Still, we're left to use contextual clues to discern between demonic and divine supernaturalism, or between forces of good and evil in literature and media. We might go so far as to say that Lewis recovered a more theologically correct view of God's supernatural intervention in our lives. This consolidation of terms also created interesting and unique pathways for modern fantasy to expand. Yet from this linguistic ambiguity was born some of the hottest ethical debates the church has witnessed in the past few decades.

The absence of a consistent scriptural label and the presence of mirrored supernatural events in Scripture has had a significant impact on fantastical fiction. The waters are muddy, and even the wisest and most knowledgeable believers are often misdirected and waylaid. But if we dive into God's Word and look where Lewis and Tolkien have further transformed the expectations of the fantasy genre, all the principles we need for discerning fictional magic are already at our fingertips.

The following five questions will help us determine whether fantasy magic resembles demonic or divine supernaturalism in literature, films, and games.

1. **What is the source of the magic?**
   Is it demonic or divine?
2. **What is the goal of the magic user?**
   Does the user desire the glorification of God (as the source) or of themselves? Do they love others or love themselves?
3. **What is the heart posture of the magic user?**
   Is the user humble or proud before God, the source?
4. **What is the setting of the magic?**
   Is the relational setting upside-down or right-side up? Are vulnerable people honored or exploited?
5. **What magical methodology is used?**
   Is the method dependent on or demanding of the source?

Why has there been such a vast misunderstanding of supernaturalism in the church? How far down do we need to dig in order to recover what was once known to first-century Christians? In the next chapter, we'll go back to the basics of the spiritual realm and the source of all magic and miracles.

Chapter 2

Visible and Invisible

As a longtime fantasy reader and writer, I've been in numerous conversations where the issue of fictional magic came up. On a couple of occasions, people have used their own experiential authority to prove fantasy magic is demonic. They regard demonic oppression like germs that can be passed onto them from a mere book simply by reading it or even picking it up. They sometimes go so far as to visit a deliverance ministry—a church or an organization that delivers people from demonic oppression or possession—to rid their life of the demonic influence of a book like Harry Potter. Is it possible to "open doors" to Satan by reading a fantasy book? Is that the true nature of the spiritual battle we're fighting, or is it mere superstition? And if it is only superstition, how does our lack of understanding of such spiritual matters impact how we discern magic in a fantasy setting?

On the opposite extreme—which is even more common among modern Evangelicals—some Christians completely ignore the existence of angels and demons. The idea that reading a book could lead to spiritual atrophy in any way is a ridiculous notion. Yet which of these positions, if either, is more accurate? As we continue to analyze the differences between demonic and divine supernaturalism for the purpose of discerning fantasy magic, we need a better understanding of the spiritual realm and the ancient perspective on the supernatural. This will not only guide us in how to understand the spiritual impact of fantasy in general but also add an important part of the theological foundation we need for discerning fictional magic systems in detail.

Ancient Perspectives

Modern Christians tend to read the Bible in an anti-supernaturalist way, interpreting demonic supernaturalism as an illusion rather than demonic activity. Yet this isn't how ancient people would have understood it. In our materialist and technological age, we often focus on questions such as, *Does God or heaven exist?* These questions are so deeply rooted in our modern psyche that we almost always read them *into* the Bible or history, which alters our understanding of the cultural and historical data. Historical fiction (including historical fantasy) set before the Enlightenment also frequently imposes a materialist or atheistic perspective onto the story world and characters while remaining unaware of the anachronism. The question, *Does God exist?*, is better suited for modern Christian fiction that aims to subvert materialism by sneaking past the "watchful dragons of the mind" through science fiction, urban fantasy, or modern forms of magical realism.[1]

The question of whether God or heaven exists would have been nonsensical during the Greco-Roman and ancient periods. They didn't concern themselves with whether or not miracles, heaven, or spirits existed. They were far more preoccupied with trying to understand how all the entities in the spiritual realm were organized and who was in charge.[2] When the Bible mentions Israel's being faithless or doubting Yahweh, it's not referring to a lack of belief in his existence but in syncretism and worshipping other gods. Being an atheist in the way we understand it today was not an option.* I've heard it taught that the reason the Old Testament doesn't mention demon possession is due to how rare or even nonexistent it was in the ancient world. Yet this is also a materialist perspective. The Old Testament talks about demons less than the New Testament because their existence and interference in the lives of the Hebrews and neighboring nations was already assumed by the original audience and didn't need to be explicitly stated. Leaving out explicit references to demons is like a modern writer excluding proof of the existence of neurons in the brain when writing a book about childhood development. Neurons may occasionally be mentioned, but most of the time, a modern reader will presuppose their existence and operation in a child's brain. So, too, did ancient peoples assume there was a demonic, supernatural reality behind the religious practices of their neighbors.

When reading Old Testament passages where an Israelite discusses Yahweh with a pagan, there is never a doubt that any of their gods (or Israel's God) are real. In Exodus 5:2, Pharaoh doesn't say he can't accept that the Hebrew God is real; he simply says he doesn't know him. At other times, pagans are given visions or dreams from God that don't alter their own religious practices. For example, in

* Socrates was charged with "atheism" due to the fact that he was a free thinker, rejected the gods of Athens, and likely held to monotheism. Yet this is not atheism as we understand it today since he and Plato still believed in a single god. Socrates reasoned that he should always follow the argument wherever it leads, which led him to deny the Greek myths.

Genesis 31:22–30, God speaks to Laban in a dream which Laban later acknowledges openly to Jacob. "I could do you great harm, but last night the God of your father said to me, 'Watch yourself! Don't say anything to Jacob, either good or bad'" (v. 29). Yet this encounter doesn't change Laban's own religious practices, nor is it strange to him. Laban had likely experienced dreams and visions from his own gods, so getting a warning from Jacob's God probably didn't alter anything about his understanding of the spiritual realm.

Materialist Westerners often consider the belief in spirits to be an ancient and prescientific way of thinking—perhaps even barbaric. Yet that's only our "chronological snobbery" talking. Lewis defined this as "the uncritical acceptance of the intellectual climate common to our own age and the assumption that whatever has gone out of date is on that account discredited."[3] Ancient cultures believed in spirits with supernatural power not simply because they had little scientific knowledge but because they were interacting with demons in their pagan religions and, therefore, had more awareness of the spiritual realm. Science and technology are gifts from God. But when they take the place of God in our society, their worship can numb our spiritual senses and desires.

In most Protestant denominations within the modern church, there has been little attention given to the study of angels and demons. I grew up believing they exist and are somewhat active in our world but that there is no real need to try to understand them. I was taught that the Bible is too vague and the only spiritual entity that matters is God. This is a dangerous assertion. It's true that we shouldn't become so preoccupied with angels and demons that we fail to recognize the only object of our worship is God alone. We also should be careful not to add onto Scripture with "pointless" mythology (1 Tim. 4:7) about angels and demons based on obscure passages of Scripture.

Yet in almost entirely neglecting the study of angels and demons, we have abandoned true spiritual warfare and stripped the Bible of the implications of paganism in neighboring nations and idolatry among the Hebrews and early church. Ancient idolatry is not simply about worshipping an inanimate object instead of God; it's replacing him with real spiritual beings who enable such practices as divination. That is the true setting of the Old Testament and the early church. For example, the "super-apostles" Paul mentions in 2 Corinthians 11:5 are directly linked to Satan in 11:3–4, 12–15. Without an understanding of syncretism in the early church and the nature of the *genuine* demonic visions of these false apostles, we strip such passages of their pagan, supernatural roots.

The Unseen Realm

In order for modern Christians to better grasp supernaturalism, we first need to understand where angels and demons reside—in the "heavenly places" (Eph. 3:10 ESV). The fact that we traditionally think of heaven as being upward or in the sky is no accident. The word for *heavens* in both Greek and Hebrew (Greek: *ouranos*; Hebrew: *šāmayim*) can more literally be translated as *sky*. It's used throughout the Bible to mean the atmosphere (Isa. 55:10), outer space (Isa. 13:10), or the spiritual realm (Ps. 33:13; Matt. 6:9; Eph. 6:12). Ancient Near Eastern people viewed the clouds as a source of provision and the stars and "celestial bodies" as outside their earthly reality. Some believed the stars themselves were angels, gods, or even lamps ordered by angels. Context is necessary to determine which realm is being discussed, and there are times when the meaning may be layered.

Matthew 3:16–17 says, "When Jesus was baptized, he went up immediately from the water. The heavens suddenly opened for him, and he saw the Spirit of God descending like a dove and coming down on him. And a voice from heaven said, 'This is my beloved Son, with whom I am well-pleased.'" Here the "heavens" open and the Spirit of God descends. This can be compared to the Old Testament when the sky opens or shuts, which usually refers to rain or drought (Gen. 7:11; 2 Chron. 7:13). But in this context, there's no mention of clouds or rain. Since our immaterial God doesn't dwell in the material sky, we have to assume this is referring to another kind of heavens—an entirely spiritual place where God and the heavenly host reside. It isn't a physical place above us. We could make a case for it to be around, above, below, or parallel to us. Yet even that is too much of a physical description of a spiritual "place." Even the phrase "heavenly *places*" is metaphorical since something that's immaterial can't be placed anywhere at all. The fact that Jesus ascended to heaven in a physical body is even more confusing. As Lord of all creation, Jesus miraculously breaks all rules, and how he is capable of currently dwelling in heaven should be regarded as a mystery.

We as humans struggle to comprehend that the spiritual realm exists when it isn't physically located somewhere. God created us this way, which is why he condescends to us through metaphor. And by condescending, I don't mean he's demeaning. I mean that he's like a loving Father who gets down on the floor to play with his children and teach them. Scripture's use of metaphors is an act of love from our good, patient Father. When physical metaphors are pulled back, biblical descriptions of the unseen realm and the spirits that dwell there are primarily relational in nature. It's possible for humans to have real relationships with demons and the members of the Trinity. We are in a relationship with God whether it's one of adoption and intimacy or of rejecting him as an enemy. Nonbelievers relate to Satan and demons as their master whether they're aware of it or not (2 Cor. 4:4; John 12:31).

The idea that God is omnipresent is a growing revelation throughout Scripture—part of what we call "progressive revelation." Being omnipresent is something unique to Yahweh that no other spirit could mimic. Job 1:6–7 gives a clear example of the limitations placed on where Satan and "the sons of God" can be at one time: "One day the sons of God came to present themselves before the LORD, and Satan also came with them. The LORD asked Satan, 'Where have you come from?' 'From roaming through the earth,' Satan answered him, 'and walking around on it.'" This also seems to imply that God, Satan, and the sons of God are all in the heavenly realms since they had a meeting to discuss Job. We also see this in 1 Kings 22:22 when the "lying spirit" (i.e., a fallen spirit) is sent from God to give Ahab a false prophecy.*

Jeremiah 23:23–24 says, "'Am I a God who is only near'—this is the LORD's declaration—'and not a God who is far away? Can a person hide in secret places where I cannot see him? . . . Do I not fill the heavens and the earth?'" Yet even this concept of omnipresence is semi-metaphorical as it evokes the idea of location. How can God be spirit and yet be described by a physical descriptor such as

---

* Although it's difficult to swallow the idea of a demon among God's divine council, this idea is consistent with many other passages in Scripture where God ordains specific temptations and lies similar to the lying spirit speaking to Ahab's prophets. See Genesis 50:20; Job 1:12; Judges 14:4; Romans 9:17–19; 2 Chronicles 10:15; 18:22; 25:20; 2 Samuel 24:1; 1 Chronicles 21:1.

omni*present*? It's possible it means God can perfectly interact with all creation and have intimate relationships with all people at all times (i.e., being outside of time) without hindrance. Meanwhile, angels and demons who aren't omnipresent can only interact with one thing or person at a time (i.e., inside time).

Although physical, upward language is consistent throughout the Bible, it's clear that New Testament writers like Paul understood the spirituality of the realms. Looking more closely at 2 Corinthians 12:2–4, he explicitly speaks to the spiritual nature of the heavens: "I know a man in Christ who was caught up to the third heaven fourteen years ago. Whether he was in the body or out of the body, I don't know; God knows. I know that this man—whether in the body or out of the body I don't know; God knows—was caught up into paradise and heard inexpressible words, which a human being is not allowed to speak."

Some commentators believe the "third heaven" he's referring to implies a multilevel cosmology common among Jews in the first century.[4] We don't know for sure what kind of cosmology Paul is stating, but his use of the word *paradise* is likely a reference to Eden and the holy of holies.[5] Another way of saying this is that he was "brought into the immediate presence of God."[6]

If Paul is referring to the holy of holies, then what are the other heavenly "places" that aren't the immediate presence of God? Colossians 1:16, 19–20 says, "For everything was created by [Christ], in heaven and on earth, the visible and the invisible, whether thrones or dominions or rulers or authorities—all things have been created through him and for him. . . . For God was pleased to have all his fullness dwell in him, and through him to reconcile everything to himself, whether things on earth or things in heaven, by making peace through his blood, shed on the cross."

We might be tempted to skim over this as a simple restatement of the gospel. But the added phrase "to reconcile everything to himself, whether things on earth or things in heaven" is odd in this context. The average Christian may have an image of God being "up" in heaven seated on his throne and surrounded by a choir of angels. Meanwhile, demons are down on earth causing mischief (Rev. 12:9). Perhaps angels visit from time to time, but surely they dwell primarily "up" in heaven. We already know that the spiritual realm is not a physical place, but there may still be a lingering sense that God and Satan "dwell" in entirely separate places—one up in the sky and one down on earth.

The Bible tells us that Satan was cast *out of heaven* and thrown *down to earth*.* It's unclear precisely what this means since earth is a physical realm and demons are spirits that must reside in a spiritual realm. Paul tells us directly that the powers of darkness dwell in the heavens, and Satan is also able to approach God in Job 1. How can we reconcile these things? Is he cast out of heaven or not? As we often say, we live in the "already-not yet" where Christ has *already* won the battle against sin, death, and the enemy, but we are *not yet* glorified with God in eternity. Satan has *already* been defeated at the cross, but he is *not yet* in hell and separated from us on earth. Fallen spirits are *already* cast out of God's immediate presence in the heavenly holy of holies, but they are *not yet* out of the heavenly places in entirety. Demons must dwell in the heavens in some way because they're spiritual beings.

Since the Bible is vague regarding Satan and the heavens, we must tread carefully speculating about them and not create pointless myths (1 Tim. 4:7). Instead of holding tightly to what we think

---

* Isaiah 14:12–14; Ezekiel 28:12–18; Luke 10:18; Revelation 12:9.

all the heavenly realms are, we should speculate with humility like Paul did in 2 Corinthians 12:2–3 when he speaks of the third heaven: "I don't know; God knows."

If heaven is a kind of parallel, immaterial realm where all spirits dwell, this also calls into question our assumption that heaven refers only to the place where we will spend eternity after our earthly death. We frequently discuss and read entire books about what "heaven" will be like when we finally arrive—whether by death or by the return of Christ. Yet as we've seen, the Bible doesn't use that word with such exclusion. Of course, there will come a time when we will dwell with Christ in the "new heavens and a new earth" (Isa. 65:17; 66:22; 2 Pet. 3:13). In remaking these, Christ has "reconcile[d] everything to himself" (Col. 1:20), both material on earth and immaterial in the spiritual realm. The reconciliation was already accomplished through his blood shed on the cross. The perfection of eternity in the new heavens and earth is still *not yet.* Christ has *already* reconciled all things, but he has *not yet* returned for our final resurrection, to remake the heavens and the earth and cast our spiritual enemies into the lake of fire.

We can speak of the current spiritual realm using more familiar and literary terms such as a "parallel reality" or "another dimension." Any way it's phrased, this place is separate or adjacent to our world yet still "present" enough to have a significant impact on our earthly lives. One of the reasons supernatural events seem to occur out of thin air is that the spiritual realm is invisible. If you've ever seen Peter Jackson's rendition of The Lord of the Rings,[7] you may remember how Frodo (played by Elijah Wood) disappeared into another realm when he put on the ring of power. He was invisible yet present, in another world yet able to affect the objects around him. Although this is an imperfect analogy of the real spiritual realm since Frodo was still physically there and not a true spirit, it's still a helpful visual. Like an unseen force of evil shrouded by the power of the one ring, Satan lurks in the spiritual realm "looking for anyone he can devour" (1 Pet. 5:8). Praise be to God that our Savior, Jesus Christ, is stronger and has already saved us from the power of our invisible enemy.

Sons of God and the Elohim

Modern Christians are familiar with the term "heavenly host," most notably from the Christmas story in Luke 2: "And suddenly there was with the angel a multitude of the heavenly host praising God, and saying, 'Glory to God in the highest, and on earth peace, good will toward men'" (vv. 13–14 KJV). These verses are so familiar, some of you may have read those verses in Linus's voice from *A Charlie Brown Christmas*.[8] This passage is an annual part of our Christmas services, but we are blind to the heavenly host around us on a daily basis. If we could somehow see the spiritual battle being fought for God's glory and our protection, many of our fears would be assuaged. Our faith is not yet sight, but Elisha's servant in 2 Kings 6:15–17 had the unique opportunity to *see* just how many angels were on their side against the Aramean army: "When the servant of the man of God got up early and went out, he discovered an army with horses and chariots surrounding the city. So he asked Elisha, 'Oh, my master, what are we to do?' Elisha said, 'Don't be afraid, for those who are with us outnumber those who are with them.' Then Elisha prayed, 'LORD, please open his eyes and let him see.' So the LORD opened the servant's eyes, and he saw that the mountain was covered with horses and chariots of fire all around Elisha."

In the midst of your greatest fears, how brave would you feel knowing your great God had an army of his own surrounding you? In his commentary on 2 Kings, Adam Clarke says, "Where is heaven? Is it not above, beneath, around us? And were our eyes open as were those of the prophet's servant, we should see the heavenly host in all directions."[9]

Angels and the heavenly host may not be entirely foreign, but the concept of the "divine council" from Psalm 82:1 (ESV) likely is new to many of you. To understand this concept, we first need to establish who the *elohim* are. It's commonly believed that the word *elohim* is one of God's names. This isn't quite true since the Old Testament uses that word a few different ways. There are times when Bible translators replace *elohim* with "God" because they know a specific verse is speaking about Yahweh (YHWH) given the context of the passage. For example, Genesis 1:1 says, "In the beginning, *elohim* created the heavens and the earth." This has to be talking about Yahweh since he is the only *elohim* that has the power and authority to create the heavens and the earth.

Elsewhere *elohim* refers to angels (Ps. 8:5), demons and foreign gods (Exod. 20:3; Deut. 11:16; 32:17), the collective council of God and sons of God (Ps. 82), and when the medium of En-dor sees Samuel's ghost (1 Sam. 28:13).[10] Although some theologians insist *elohim* in Psalm 82 could be translated as human rulers, there is never a time in all Scripture that word is used to refer to a living human. Even the use of it in reference to the deceased Samuel may or may not be prescriptive since it was spoken by a confused, frightened medium. Author Tim Chaffey says of the word *elohim*,[11] "Do all of these *elohim* have something in common? Put another way, how could God, false gods, angels, demons, and the spirit of Samuel all be called *elohim*? Well, they all seem to share a couple of attributes. With the exception of Jesus Christ, none of them possess a permanent physical body. Also, they are all residents of the spiritual realm, or more accurately, the spiritual realm is their primary place of operation."[12]

The concept of the divine council is derived from many texts such as Daniel 7; Revelation 5; and 1 Kings 22.

> As I kept watching, thrones were set in place, and the Ancient of Days took his seat. His clothing was white like snow, and the hair of his head like whitest wool. His throne was flaming fire; its wheels were blazing fire. A river of fire was flowing, coming out from his presence. Thousands upon thousands served him; ten thousand times ten thousand stood before him. The court was convened, and the books were opened. (Dan. 7:9–10)

> Then I looked and heard the voice of many angels around the throne, and also of the living creatures and of the elders. Their number was countless thousands, plus thousands of thousands. They said with a loud voice, "Worthy is the Lamb who was slaughtered to receive power and riches and wisdom and strength and honor and glory and blessing!" (Rev. 5:11–12)

> Then Micaiah said, "Therefore, hear the word of the LORD: I saw the LORD sitting on his throne, and the whole heavenly army was standing by him at his right hand and at his left hand. And the

> Lord said, 'Who will entice Ahab to march up and fall at Ramoth-gilead?' So one was saying this and another was saying that. Then a spirit came forward, stood in the Lord's presence, and said, 'I will entice him.' The Lord asked him, 'How?' He said, 'I will go and become a lying spirit in the mouth of all his prophets.' Then he said, 'You will certainly entice him and prevail. Go and do that.'" (1 Kings 22:19–22)

The varying descriptions of the council in these passages is meant to convey they don't all have the same position or occupation.* This is also why the Bible often uses different titles and language to talk about them—i.e., "spirit[s]" (1 Kings 22:21), "cherub" (2 Sam. 22:11), "sons of God" (Job 38:7), "stars" (Job 38:7), "holy ones" (Job 15:15), and more. We won't always need to speak of them in overly specific terms since we're often just concerned with understanding whether something is from God or Satan, if it's divine or demonic. When I refer to angels and demons in this book, it's in these broad categories and not with specific roles in mind.

We typically think of the idols in Scripture as lifeless statues and nothing more. For these man-made objects to be such a stumbling block to the Israelites and the nations seems frivolous and

* If heaven is not a physical place but a spiritual one, then when God gives these types of visions to his prophets, the images are metaphorical. It's as though God is drawing us a picture book of heaven—something at our cognitive level so we can grasp some measure of understanding of him and his entourage of *elohim*. Angels aren't literally covered in wings and eyes (Rev. 4:8), nor is God sitting on a physical throne. But we do understand that God is so glorious, he's beyond our comprehension and worthy of all praise from all created beings.

barbaric. It feels impossible to comprehend the sins of Aaron and the other Israelites who crafted a golden calf of their own making and declared it had brought them up out of Egypt when it was obviously Yahweh (Exod. 32:1–4). Yet there is so much more going on that our materialist perspective obstructs. Although the idols are statues, they are also demon-gods drawing attention away from the one true God. With their limited supernatural power, they make convincing distractions by participating in supernatural rituals, giving out bits of secret information, or threatening harm to their worshippers.

In 1 Corinthians 10:19–20, Paul says, "What am I saying then? That food sacrificed to idols is anything, or that an idol is anything? No, but I do say that what they sacrifice, they sacrifice to demons and not to God. I do not want you to be participants with demons!" Does this contradict what Paul says two chapters earlier in 1 Corinthians 8:4–6? "About eating food sacrificed to idols, then, we know that 'an idol is nothing in the world,' and that 'there is no God but one.' For even if there are so-called gods, whether in heaven or on earth—as there are many 'gods' and many 'lords'—yet for us there is one God, the Father. All things are from him, and we exist for him. And there is one Lord, Jesus Christ. All things are through him, and we exist through him."

He seems to imply idols are nothing at all, then two chapters later he says they're sacrificing to demons. So, is it an empty statue or a demon? Although we often think it was the literal statue being worshipped, that isn't true at all. In ancient Mesopotamia, when someone crafted an idol statue, they considered it empty until they performed a ritual to invite a "god" (a spirit) to inhabit it. The process of birthing a god included a detailed cleansing of its mouth where the god was meant to enter and animate it. Sometimes they would even cut off the person's hands who crafted the idol and throw their tools into the river. This way they felt safe saying it was divine and had been made by the gods instead of human hands.[13]

Theoretically, demons could choose to participate in the various rituals and attach to the idol to control their worshippers and distract them away from Yahweh. But their "gods" could not be permanently bound by ritual. Satan may have specific limitations on his power, but he has no orderly magic system like those we find in fiction. There will be times when a demon attaches to an object through rituals for the sake of deception, distraction, and control. But in reality, they come and go as it suits them and their own agenda, sometimes leaving the idols as nothing more than "gold and silver, bronze, iron, wood, and stone" (Dan. 5:4).

The following list is a few verses that point to the reality of idols and foreign gods being demons.

> They must no longer offer their sacrifices to the *goat-demons* that they have prostituted themselves with. This will be a permanent statute for them throughout their generations. (Lev. 17:7, emphasis added)*

> They served their *idols*, which became a snare to them. They sacrificed their sons and daughters to *demons*. (Ps. 106:36–37, emphasis added)

---

* The word for "goat-demon" in Leviticus 17:7 is *śāʿîr* in Hebrew which is similar in appearance and sound to the word *satyr*: a faun or woodland demigod. Greek mythology pictured the satyr (or *satyros*) as a man with a horse tail and ears. But Roman sculptors crafted the divine half-goat man (Latin: *satyrus*) we recognize now as a faun. The etymology of *satyros* is unknown.

For he rebuilt the high places that Hezekiah his father had destroyed, and he erected altars for *Baal* and made an Asherah, as Ahab king of Israel had done, and worshiped all the *host of heaven* and served them. (2 Kings 21:3 ESV, emphasis added).

Now the Spirit explicitly says that in later times some will depart from the faith, paying attention to *deceitful spirits and the teachings of demons.* (1 Tim. 4:1, emphasis added)

Ahaziah had fallen through the latticed window of his upstairs room in Samaria and was injured. So he sent messengers, instructing them, "Go inquire of *Baal-zebub, the god of Ekron*, whether I will recover from this injury." (2 Kings 1:2; see Matt. 12:24, emphasis added)

In their case, the *god of this age* has blinded the minds of the unbelievers to keep them from seeing the light of the gospel of the glory of Christ, who is the image of God. (2 Cor. 4:4, emphasis added)

They sacrificed to *demons,* not God, to *gods* they had not known, new *gods* that had just arrived, which your ancestors did not fear. (Deut. 32:17, emphasis added)

> What am I saying then? That food sacrificed to *idols* is anything, or that an *idol* is anything? No, but I do say that what they sacrifice, they sacrifice to *demons* and not to God. I do not want you to be participants with *demons*! (1 Cor. 10:19–20, emphasis added)

There is no pantheon and Christians are not polytheists. The *elohim* are "divine" angels and demons (John 10:33–38) on Yahweh's council. Yet God doesn't need to be told what to do or be given new ideas he hasn't already had. Isaiah 40:13–14 says, "Who has directed the Spirit of the LORD, or who gave him counsel? Who did he consult? Who gave him understanding and taught him the paths of justice? Who taught him knowledge and showed him the way of understanding?"

Why does God need a council of spirits when he can't be taught? In 1 Kings 22:19–23, we see that God is surrounded by his "whole heavenly army," and he asks them who will entice Ahab. Then the spirits begin to discuss the matter, supposedly deciding who will go and what plan to use. The lying spirit comes forward and not only offers to entice Ahab but also gives God his idea for exactly how he's going to do that. God already knew what the spirit would say. He also ordained that this exact scenario would happen in just this way because he is sovereign. But just as he does with human work and intervention, he invites the council into his work. He is like a parent who allows their child to help make dinner. God listens to our ideas and lets us whisk the batter knowing some will splash out of the bowl. He doesn't need our help, but he wants us involved and gives us personal agency. The same is true for the members of the divine council.

Entertaining Angels

After a severe car accident in 2009, my boyfriend—now husband—Tim, lay on a stretcher in the middle of the road unconscious and near death. Days later, I was informed that a woman at our crash site claimed to have seen an angel standing over his body. I was more than a little skeptical. After all, I had met this woman but didn't know her personally. She could have been lying or just insane. There was no way for me to gauge her truthfulness. The presence of an angel seemed possible but unlikely. Yet after spending a few years thinking and praying over that one horrific day, I couldn't ignore the sheer number of details that pointed to God's sovereignty over all of it. He had ordained our crash and miraculously saved Tim's life. The idea that an angel could have been there began to seem less outlandish.

Reflecting on moments like this—because there have been others—it always seems so unique and miraculous that God would choose to help us, to send an angel to protect us. Who were we to warrant something so special and rare? As I've taken the time to learn and meditate on the spiritual realm and the heavenly host, the presence of an angel no longer seems "possible but unlikely." In fact, it is more likely that an angel was present than not. They are God's messengers and helpers in more ways than we know. So often when we say God did something in our lives—an external work not accomplished by the Holy Spirit—it's likely it was accomplished through another spiritual helper. Just as Christ and the Holy Spirit mediate our salvation, sanctification, prayers, and needs to God, so angels often mediate external needs. This doesn't mean we can't say "God saved our lives in the car accident." That is the truth of what happened. It was the will of God to save our lives. Yet just as he uses humans to accomplish things he could have done on his own, so he uses angels to do his will on earth and in heaven.

For most of my life, I believed that the concept of "guardian angels" was mostly fictional. It was merely story fodder for shows like *Touched by an Angel* or Precious Moments figurines. Only someone overly sentimental would believe something like that was real. Yet on a much closer study of the Scriptures, I was once more forced to admit that materialism had spoiled this part of my theological garden.

Matthew 18:10 says, "See to it that you don't despise one of these little ones, because I tell you that in heaven their angels continually view the face of my Father in heaven." In this context, "these little ones" refers to all disciples of Christ (Matt. 10:42).[14] Jesus is giving a warning concerning his followers—that anyone who seeks to harm his disciples would have to contend with a guard of angels. The Psalms echo this idea: "For he will give his angels orders concerning you, to protect you in all your ways" (Ps. 91:11). And in Psalm 34:7, "The angel of the LORD encamps around those who fear him, and rescues them." The author of Hebrews says angels are "ministering spirits sent out to serve those who are going to inherit salvation" (Heb. 1:14). It's unlikely that every believer has one specific angel assigned to him, but it's certainly true that we are protected by God's "servants who do his will" (Ps. 103:21).[15]

It isn't only materialism that has drawn our attention away from focusing too much on angels. It's also the overcorrection of the other extreme of sensationalism, "silly myths" (1 Tim. 4:7), and being more awed by angels than we are by God himself. Yes, all these truths about angels are wonderful and fantastical in the best way. Yet God is so much greater than angels. His lavish love and salvation on us are a thousand times more amazing and miraculous than an angel appearing at a crash site. When we think of the heavenly host surrounding us, of being guarded by angels, the person we should be drawn to worship more is God. The *elohim* that deserves our awe and wonder is *el elyon*—God Most High. He orders the angels and sends them on their way. He is the one who provides protection and mercy in the form of angels. Just as Jesus redirected his followers' attention away from their authority over demons and back toward their own salvation in Luke 10:17–20, so we should primarily rejoice in Christ and the gospel. When our worship is rightly ordered, there is no need to hide what Scripture says about the *elohim*. All Scripture points us back to the wonder and mercy of our ultimate Helper and Protector.

Pointless Myths Versus Materialism

"But have nothing to do with pointless and silly myths. Rather, train yourself in godliness" (1 Tim. 4:7). There is a spectrum between what Paul calls "pointless and silly myths" and the temptation toward anti-supernaturalism. (In this context, Paul is referring to the kind of myth that misleads, not the "true myth" Tolkien spoke of just before Lewis's conversion.)* Oftentimes, these opposing camps are responding to and overcorrecting one another. C. S. Lewis notes this distinction in the preface to *The Screwtape Letters*: "There are two equal and opposite errors into which our race can fall about the devils. One is to disbelieve in their existence. The other is to believe, and to feel an excessive and unhealthy interest in them. They themselves are equally pleased by both errors and hail a materialist or a magician with the same delight."[16]

---

* I'll discuss Tolkien's view of mythology more in chapter 10.

He was primarily speaking about nonbelievers in this context, but this can apply to different denominations as well. Christians don't need to be full-blown materialists to ignore the reality of the spiritual realm. When I speak of "anti-supernaturalist" Christians, I don't mean they don't believe in miracles at all; I mean they tend to be skeptical of the supernatural and would prefer to believe Pharaoh's magicians were merely illusionists. On the other end of the spectrum, Christians don't have to be literal "magicians" to see demons in the pages of every fantasy book or treat God like a miracle vending machine.

When the Bible calls us to focus our attention on eternal, heavenly realities rather than temporal, earthly realities (Phil. 3:12–21), this is primarily a call to "store up" eternal treasure (Matt. 6:20). Secondarily, taking our attention off earthly realities should also make us aware of the heavenly, spiritual realm. What is the anti-supernaturalist tempted to do instead? Consider what Paul says in Philippians 3:19: "Their end is destruction; their god is their stomach; their glory is in their shame; and they are focused on earthly things." This holds true for our generation, but thanks to the materialism creep, it may be said that "their god is their *science*." Only what can be proven through scientific means can be put forward as potentially true. Science is a beautiful thing. But just as good food can easily become a god, so can the material world and scientific method. Meanwhile, superstition and myth about demons have spread like wildfire among some Christians who embrace the spiritual at the expense of the physical.

On one end of the spectrum, Christians may err on the side of attributing all sin to internal temptation and depravity. They may proof text with verses such as James 1:14: "But each person is tempted when he is drawn away and enticed by his own evil desire." It may appear that human depravity is the only source of temptation by reading this verse on its own. However, within the context of the entire New Testament, we see frequent examples of demonic temptation, and Paul even names Satan "the tempter" in 1 Thessalonians 3:5. We should know from age-old debates about faith- versus works-based righteousness that James should always be understood within the wider context of the New Testament and Paul's letters. James is merely saying that when we're tempted, sin follows because of our own desires, and we must take responsibility for our own actions. If he believed temptation was always internal and never came from demons, then he wouldn't say a few chapters later, "Therefore, submit to God. Resist the devil, and he will flee from you" (James 4:7).

Some anti-supernaturalists acknowledge this distinction in James, but it doesn't affect their life in the least. They may know that Satan is real and tempts us since the Bible explicitly states this, but since the results of temptation are fully our responsibility, there is no need to focus too much on demons. If we simply "mortify" our sin and pursue Christ, that's sufficient for fighting off the attacks of the enemy.[17] Their position against demons is often one of passivity in spiritual warfare and an overcorrection of sensationalism and "pointless" myths in the church. They also speak little about the leading of the Holy Spirit in our daily lives out of fear of placing our fallible conscience, words, and emotions in God's mouth.

We're always responsible for our own sin regardless of whether Satan tempts us. And we need to focus more on Christ than on Satan to combat that sin and that our fallible conscience can be wrongly perceived as the Holy Spirit.* But ignoring the guiding presence

---

* What is a fallible conscience? Our belief in right or wrong is trained by our culture and experience. It's possible for it to be more or less restrictive than

of the Spirit and the reality of demons to such an extreme extent places us more in Satan's power. It also disregards Paul's instructions on overt spiritual warfare in Ephesians 6 and Peter's warning to "be alert" in 1 Peter 5:8: "Be sober-minded, be alert. Your adversary the devil is prowling around like a roaring lion, looking for anyone he can devour." Neglecting these parts of Scripture has also left us ill-prepared for the rapid growth of the New Age occult and the inevitable syncretism that accompanies it. The hyperfocus on internal temptation and depravity at the exclusion of external temptation has also aided in producing a dangerous culture of nitpicking sin which has led to forms of authoritarianism, misdiagnosing mental illness as sin alone, and even spiritual abuse in the home and church.

On the other extreme, some err on the side of focusing so much on demonic oppression, temptation, and supernatural experience that they blameshift their own sinfulness onto demons entirely. Some deliverance ministries hold services for casting out the evil

---

Scripture. When our conscience creates a feeling of guilt over potential sin, we need to examine that impulse next to Scripture to see if it's accurate. In *The Adventures of Huckleberry Finn* by Mark Twain, Huck feels guilty for not turning Jim, a runaway slave, into his slave owner. He'd learned in Sunday school that helping a slave run was a sin that would place him in "everlasting fire." He felt convicted to repent of this "sin" of helping Jim run but couldn't bring himself to betray his friend. He eventually says, "All right, then, I'll go to hell." In order to do the right thing, Huck had to fight off a conscience that had been wrongly trained by Southern slave owners. There are times when Christians assume that because they feel a sense of guilt in association with, for example, media intake, this means the Holy Spirit is telling them that particular media is bad or will cause them to sin. However, that isn't always true, as Paul says in Romans 14 when discussing the weaker brother's conscience. To distinguish the difference between our own conscience and the Holy Spirit, we have to spend more time in the Bible and prayer, familiarizing ourselves with who God is and the sound of his voice.

spirit of any sin—the "spirit of anger," the "spirit of lust," and more. The Bible rarely uses such specific language when referring to demons, presumably because fallen spirits don't have such narrow functions as to be identified with one specific sin or affliction. Even in the few verses where a demon is referred to this way (i.e., a spirit of infirmity in Luke 13:11), it's reading into the text to assume that spirit has only one function or that all spirits have only one function. This practice of naming numerous sins and afflictions as demonic spirits also leads people to assume if they're tempted by a certain sin or afflicted in some way, that means they must be oppressed by a demon and are in need of deliverance.

The environment of superstition and sensationalism can be a breeding ground for false teachers and prophets to lure believers away from true repentance through false teaching, supposedly casting out spirits of sin and suffering or guaranteeing healing, as though the Holy Spirit can be commanded. God doesn't promise healing, nor does he grant it based on how much faith someone can muster. This is something commonly taught in the Word of Faith movement, which is a charismatic version of the prosperity gospel and may have originated from New Age syncretism.[18] Some deliverance ministries are genuine, empowered by the Holy Spirit, and call people to repentance as they cast out actual demons.* But some are

* Without repentance and salvation, casting out demons does not deliver anyone long-term. In fact, Jesus teaches in Matthew 12:43–45 that it may place them in more danger of being possessed again with even more demons: "When an unclean spirit comes out of a person, it roams through waterless places looking for rest but doesn't find any. Then it says, 'I'll go back to my house that I came from.' Returning, it finds the house vacant, swept, and put in order. Then it goes and brings with it seven other spirits more evil than itself, and they enter and settle down there. As a result, that person's last condition is worse than the first. That's how it will also be with this evil generation."

false and adhere strongly to sensationalism and "silly myths." These practices form the fastest either from false teachers or from wild speculation about the meaning of obscure passages or Scripture taken out of context. For example, the belief in the existence of "marine spirits" or demonic mermaids is based on extrabiblical stories and Luke 11:24: "When an unclean spirit comes out of a person, it roams through *waterless places* looking for rest" (emphasis added). There are many examples of similar sensational, superstitious, and extrabiblical theology in some charismatic circles that are dangerous and scripturally baseless.

Christians tempted by either anti-supernaturalism or sensationalism have their own unique ways of being tempted by pride of knowledge or—as occultists refer to it—*enlightenment.* As Adam and Eve were tempted in the garden, we are likewise tempted by secret knowledge of good and evil. We like to be in the know and feel as though we have the upper hand on information, just like a pagan trying to become enlightened. As Paul says, "Knowledge puffs up, but love builds up" (1 Cor. 8:1). Some sensationalists may feel pride in their open use of prophecy, speaking in tongues, and hearing messages from the Holy Spirit on a daily basis. Whereas anti-supernaturalists can feel a sense of pride in their emphasis on correct doctrine as though they have the corner market on good theology and can't learn from others who are different. An emphasis on the Holy Spirit is a good thing. Correct doctrine is also a good thing. If our response to either is pride instead of humility, we aren't loving wisdom or others, and we're basking in our own "enlightenment." The more we learn about God, the more humble we should be before him. And the more we should love and learn from people who may be different from us.

These positions clearly have their own strengths and weaknesses. Neither fully reflects how the New Testament writers speak of the work of the Holy Spirit, temptation, or Satan. Anti-supernaturalists should also remember that Paul frequently calls believers to be on their guard against the attack of Satan. As I've mentioned briefly, the most notable is the passage on the armor of God from Ephesians 6: "Put on the full armor of God so that you can stand against the schemes of the devil. For our struggle is not against flesh and blood, but against the rulers, against the authorities, against the cosmic powers of this darkness, against evil, spiritual forces in the heavens. For this reason take up the full armor of God, so that you may be able to resist in the evil day, and having prepared everything, to take your stand" (vv. 11–13).

The language here is active and a real awareness of the devil and his schemes is also heavily implied. We are not in a passive fight against Satan but an active spiritual battle. When we only see our sin and ignore demonic influence, our minds are focused on internal sin and never on external evil which leaves us vulnerable. In 1 Corinthians 12:10, Paul lists certain spiritual gifts, one of which is "distinguishing between spirits." Author Sam Storms defines this well.

> I'm inclined to believe that this is the ability to distinguish between what the Holy Spirit does and what another "spirit" (demonic), or perhaps even the human spirit, does. Not all miracles or supernatural displays are produced by the Holy Spirit. Whereas all Christians are responsible to "test the spirits to see whether they are from God" (1 John 4:1), Paul has in mind here a special ability that is fundamentally intuitive or subjective in

> nature. Given the contextual flow in 1 John, all should test the spirits by evaluating their message; in particular, do they confess that "Jesus Christ has come in the flesh" (4:2)? This requires no special gifting. But the spiritual gift of distinguishing of spirits is probably a supernaturally enabled sense or feeling concerning the nature and source of the "spirit."[19]

As he says, "This requires no special gifting." That means that, at minimum, all Christians should be aware of "spirits" so they can be tested. As with all spiritual gifts, it's something every Christian can do to some degree, although the actual gift is a greater, Spirit-empowered ability. Finding the balance between these two extremes is essential and in line with Paul's view of spiritual warfare.

The charismatic emphasis on the Holy Spirit and spiritual warfare is a strength. Yet if left unrestrained by the guard of Scripture, it can also lead people into superstition. When the primary focus is on warfare at the exclusion of more important aspects of a relationship with Christ, this can breed more fear. Christians may come to fear saying certain words, watching certain movies, or unknowingly owning supposedly cursed objects as though the mere existence of these things will open demonic portals in their lives.

Yes, demons can attack believers and attach to objects temporarily. Christians can also engage in certain behaviors that invite oppression. But it's not the saying of a word, the watching of a movie, or the presence of an object that does this. This type of superstition is part of the reason Paul said it was permissible to eat food sacrificed to idols (i.e., demons) in 1 Corinthians 8:4–13. Since demons attached themselves to idol statues for the sake of deception, it's possible Jews and first-century Christians were fearful pagan sacrifices might be cursed or could open doors to demonic oppression. We misdiagnose the source of oppression when we begin to fear words, media, and objects. We wrongly assume that demonic oppression is automatically transferred to us by objects or media just as the Corinthians may have assumed of food sacrificed to idols. Not only does this superstition of demonic transference wrongly interpret Paul's instruction in that passage, but it's also a kind of "Satanic panic"[20] and fearmongering. We should not assume that curses are that common or you may begin to see them around every corner.

There is a difference between a former pagan moving into a house where a box of occult books is hiding in the basement versus keeping the books stored on purpose because part of the person doesn't want to let go of the past. It would be superstitious to assume the first example of innocent ownership of occult books would automatically draw demonic oppression. Yet harboring part of a sinful past for later perusal is still idolatry and gives Satan a foothold of authority. It isn't the thing itself that opens the door but a heart that's worshipping an idol. As Jesus told the disciples in Luke 9:62, "No one who puts his hand to the plow and looks back is fit for the kingdom of God." He meant we can't do kingdom work and still gaze longingly at our past.

At the Cross

When was the last time you heard a message about Christ's death and resurrection that included an explanation of Satan's role? We know he was defeated when Jesus died and rose again, but why exactly? When we study and teach about such things, we tend to focus solely on the fact that our sins have been wiped clean by the blood of Christ. That is certainly the most glorious truth to be gleaned from that event. Yet there is a spiritual war raging behind the scenes that's hardly mentioned in our churches.

Telling the story of the resurrection without Satan would be like C. S. Lewis writing *The Lion, the Witch and the Wardrobe* without the White Witch. It would hardly be the same story without her. I'll fill in some of the implied theological gaps in the narrative. Edmund stands accused because he sinned against Aslan and his siblings when he valued mere candy over the lives of his own family. Even without the Witch, Edmund would need to stand trial before Aslan. Yet if Aslan is the judge, then who is Edmund's accuser? Who is the prosecuting attorney in the courtroom demanding he face the death penalty for his sins? It is the White Witch who knows just enough of Aslan's Deep Magic to insist that Edmund's blood be spilled for his crimes.

How does she have the authority to accuse him when Aslan is the ultimate authority and his law is the one broken? Edmund's sin was against Aslan first and foremost, and Aslan primarily holds him accountable in the highest court of heaven. Secondarily, by Edmund's act of taking Turkish delight in exchange for his siblings' lives, he naively formed a legally binding relationship with the Witch in the lower courts. Through this, she not only has knowledge of his crime and Aslan's law, but she also has the authority—albeit limited in the lower court—to demand his death.

The name "Satan" comes from the Hebrew word *śāṭān* in 1 Chronicles 21:1 which means "adversary" or "accuser." This was the equivalent to simply giving the title of "the enemy." It wasn't originally meant to be the proper name of *Satan*, yet that's what it became over time. In this title, we find one of his primary roles—to *accuse* guilty sinners before the almighty Judge (Luke 22:31).[21]

The blood of Christ has covered our sins and washed us white. Where Satan thought he had the upper hand, he was instead stripped of any power over God's elect by the resurrection of Jesus. Romans 8:33–34 tells us exactly why Satan as our accuser no longer has jurisdiction over us after we have been made new in Christ: "Who can bring an accusation against God's elect? God is the one who justifies. Who is the one who condemns? Christ Jesus is the one who died, but even more, has been raised; he also is at the right hand of God and intercedes for us." Who can bring an accusation? No one. Who is the one who can condemn? No one.

Paul goes on to say in verses 38–39, "Neither death nor life, nor angels nor rulers, nor things present nor things to come, nor powers, nor height nor depth, nor any other created thing will be able to separate us from the love of God that is in Christ Jesus our Lord." No one can accuse or condemn God's elect because of Christ's sacrificial death and resurrection—no one in heaven or on earth. Christ nailed our sin to the cross, ransoming us from our accuser to God into everlasting life. Satan can and will attack us and injure us. He is like a prowling lion, looking for anyone he can devour (1 Pet. 5:8). But he will never be able to do what he set out to do—to drag us into hell alongside him. At the cross, the power of Satan, sin, and death were all stripped of their sting. Where once we served the kingdom of the accuser with our sin and hatred of God (James 4:4–7), now we have been freed from the authority of it all by the blood of Christ Jesus, our Lord.

Without the ability to think rightly of angels and demons and the spiritual realm, we open ourselves up not only to Satan but to a total lack of understanding about the true nature of supernaturalism.

Chapter 3

Is It All an Illusion?

As a teen enamored with fantasy, it was comforting to know the magic I was reading about was entirely fictional. It had nothing to do with reality. As long as I kept my life separate from my fiction, I was safe. And perhaps compartmentalizing wasn't the most discerning way to view fictional magic, but at least it served to keep me from any interest in the occult. Perhaps for some of you, compartmentalizing doesn't seem necessary because you believe magic doesn't exist in either stories or in the real world. It's all just illusion—sleight of hand and trapdoors. But is that really what the Bible has to say about magic?

Before we dig into Scripture to help us discern fictional magic, we first need to address the most prominent myth surrounding occultic magic—that it isn't real. This is an especially popular idea among Christian fantasy enthusiasts since it reduces the dangers of fictional magic to a nonissue. We live in an age where we're entertained by illusionist magic, where we think fortune tellers are simply skilled liars, and the New Age occult movement is just superstition and harmless yoga stretches. Yet the Bible and the testimonies of those coming out of the occult tell a different and deeper story.

Scripture gives many clear examples of demonic supernaturalism being real and dangerous. Any prohibition of divination, necromancy, and astrology was a law against calling on the power of Satan and his demons to demand power. Anti-supernaturalist and materialist interpretations of Scripture are dangerous as they promote the idea that demons don't have power to affect real change in our world or our lives. This belief distorts the meaning of the passages and leaves Christians and non-Christians alike defenseless in spiritual warfare.

The Medium at En-dor

The story of the medium at En-dor in 1 Samuel 28 is a heavily debated passage. Saul goes against God's law to seek information from a medium—someone who summons and communicates with spirits or the dead, usually for secret information or comfort from deceased loved ones.

In Deuteronomy 18:9–12, we see a list of "detestable" practices God will not tolerate: "When you enter the land the Lord your God is giving you, do not imitate the detestable customs of those nations. No one among you is to sacrifice his son or daughter in the fire, practice divination, tell fortunes, interpret omens, practice sorcery, cast spells, consult a medium or a spiritist, or inquire of the dead. Everyone who does these acts is detestable to the Lord, and the Lord your God is driving out the nations before you because of these detestable acts."

Sorceries of all kinds are listed here along with something as horrific as burning a son or daughter as a sacrifice (v. 10). The fact that these were intentionally placed together should say something profound. First, it's a logical connection since child sacrifice was used in pagan rituals to idols—something demanded of them by their demon gods in a horrific distortion of Christ's sacrificial death. Second, it's as though Moses is saying, "Don't you know there's nothing more evil and abominable than burning your own child as a sacrifice to your idols? That's how much God detests the practice of sorcery." It's one of the worst forms of idolatry that replaces God's authority and Christ's death with demonic authority and power.

In 1 Samuel 28, Saul is gripped with fear by the sight of the Philistine army and doesn't hear from God when Saul calls on him for counsel. He commits a weighty crime in approaching a medium for advice instead (vv. 5–7). His crime is so heavy, God disciplines him by ending his life the very next day in the battle against the Philistines (28:19; 31:1–6). Saul knew of God's commands in the law. We know this because he was the one who had "cut off the mediums and spiritists from the land" (28:9).

Still, Saul went in disguise to the medium and asked her to "divine . . . a spirit" (28:8 ESV) and bring Samuel up from the dead so Saul could consult with him about the approaching battle. A spirit does appear, and the text names him as Samuel. This is the hardest pill to swallow. How can someone literally speak to the dead? Wouldn't it make more sense that she had created an illusion? Or maybe it was a demonic spirit pretending to be Samuel? That's typically what happens when a necromancer or medium attempts to talk to the dead—the demon imitates the dead person being called on since they don't have the authority to speak to the dead. Yet that doesn't fit the description here.

As scary and uncomfortable as this passage is, the most straightforward reading is that Samuel really did come and speak to Saul. But how can we know this for sure? First, it's plainly stated in 28:12–15 that the person speaking is Samuel. No one else is mentioned as an alternative. Second, the medium is terrified by what she sees (vv. 12–13). Some commentators hold that her unexplained fear is because she hadn't meant to bring Samuel forward. It's likely she normally calls on a "familiar spirit" or "spirit guide" (a demon) to impersonate a deceased person, and her description of Samuel as an *elohim* implies she was expecting to see the form of her familiar spirit and saw something different.[1] But even though we can only guess the reason for her shock and fear, it remains a testimony to the unexpectedness and authenticity of Samuel.

Her sudden recognition of Saul brought on more fear since she likely thought she would be caught and killed (v. 12). It's possible that with the surprise arrival of Samuel, she was able to see that only Saul would be visited by a spirit she hadn't intended to call up.[2] Third, Samuel's spirit speaks truth, rebukes Saul for the great evil he's done in turning to magic instead of trusting God, and prophesies Saul's fall the next day (vv. 16–19). No illusion or lying demon would have spoken the truth regarding Saul's sin. Samuel also spoke with significant wisdom and genuine knowledge of future events—two things demons don't have. A demon can make informed guesses about the future in imitation of prophecy, but they can't see the future. Unlike God, angels and demons don't exist outside of time.

Samuel also prophesies Saul's loss of kingship to David, loss of the battle to the Philistines, and the death of Saul and his sons. Each of these comes to fruition in the following chapters, so we can be assured that the prophecy was from God. In fact, it's possible

Samuel didn't appear by the power of demons at all but by the power of God and as an act of judgment. It's also possible God permitted the medium to access more power than she would normally in order to make his power and authority known.

The Egyptian Plagues

In order to understand the Egyptian plagues from an ancient Near Eastern framework, we can't overlook the demonic element. If idols represent demons as Paul says in 1 Corinthians 10:20, then the polytheism in Egypt indicates rampant demonic activity. Even Pharaoh's cobra headdress marks him as being relationally bonded to Satan. A friend of mine once recounted a time she visited a densely populated city in India where Hinduism was predominantly practiced. Simply walking down the street, she felt the dark spiritual presence of demons all around her. Egypt would have been much the same, and Moses knew that better than anyone. Although we moderns can't often detect those implications in his writing, ancient readers understood exactly what was going on since polytheism and the occult surrounded them on every side. The repeated phrases, "You will know that I am the Lord" (Exod. 7:17), and "That you may know there is no one like the Lord our God" (8:10), are also indicative of demonic activity and unseen spiritual warfare. God desires to be known. He desires his people to know he's vastly different from their demon gods. In fact, he's the one who created their gods: "So Moses and Aaron went in to Pharaoh and did just as the Lord had commanded. Aaron threw down his staff before Pharaoh and his officials, and it became a serpent. But then Pharaoh called the wise men and sorcerers—the magicians of Egypt, and they also did the same thing by their occult practices. Each one threw down his staff, and it became a serpent. But Aaron's staff swallowed their staffs" (7:10–12).

Some commentators and theologians argue that Pharaoh's magicians may have created an illusion to make their staffs appear like serpents.[3] Just as scientific explanations of the plagues miss the point of this story, the illusionist interpretation of the staffs turning to serpents would greatly undermine one of the main points of that event.* These things are meant to display God's power as greater and that he has authority over both Pharaoh and the demons that take the form of Egyptian gods. Their "battle pitted Jehovah, the true God, who moved Moses and Israel, against all the false gods of the Egyptian pantheon, backed by a host of fallen angels who had turned from God as part of Lucifer's original rebellion."[4]

God's primary goal of the plagues is that the nations "will know that I am the Lord" (Exod. 7:17; 8:10, 22; 9:14, 29). Through the means of the plagues and overshadowing Pharaoh's magicians—and, therefore, the demons—the nations come to know that "there is no one like [Yahweh] on the whole earth" (Exod. 9:14). Yet theologians have long debated this miracle. Theologians Andrew E. Hill and John H. Walton argue that the Egyptians' magic was performed by the power of demons.

> How did the Egyptian magicians perform counter-miracles against Aaron (7:8–13) and duplicate the effects of the first two plagues (7:14–8:15)? These diviners of Pharaoh's were a powerful and revered priestly class in Egyptian society. They

---

* Anti-supernaturalists teach that the plagues of Egypt can be explained through scientific means. For example, they believe the blood filling the Nile was really red algae, frogs swarmed after a heavy rain, and lice or insects appeared due to the algae and piles of dead frogs.

> were devotees of the moon god, Thoth, who was also the god of magic and divination. According to the teaching of both the Old and New Testaments, these kinds of idolatrous religious systems are energized by demonic powers. (cf. Deut. 32:16–17; Ps. 106:36–37; Acts 16:16–18; 1 Cor. 10:20; 2 Thess. 2:8–12)[5]

On the opposing side of the debate, various commentators note that the Egyptians were adept snake charmers. They had a way of pressing the nape of the snake's neck which made it stiff and immobile. Theoretically, they could have been carrying snakes concealed in their robes and thrown them down instead of staffs. This interpretation is unconvincing since the person they're attempting to impress or deceive would have been Pharaoh, not Moses and Aaron. If this was as common of a practice in Egypt as commentators say, Pharaoh would have known of it, and he wouldn't have been so quickly convinced that the miracles of Moses's God were commonplace. It also doesn't make sense logistically. Once the snakes were thrown down, "juggling or sleight-of-hand had nothing farther to do in the business, as the rods were then out of their hands."[6]

Another theory draws from the Hebrew word, *lahatim*, in Exodus 7:11. It's been translated as "occult practices" (CSB), "secret arts" (ESV), "enchantments" (KJV), or "magic" (NLT). This word, literally translated as "to burn" or "flaming," occurs twice in the Old Testament—once in Exodus 7:11 and once as the root word in Genesis 3:24 referring to the angels' flaming sword outside of Eden. The commentators who hold that the magicians' serpents were mere illusion see *lahatim* in Exodus 7 as having a deceptive implication. We can see this interpretation in *Easton's Bible Dictionary* which gives the word a possible meaning of "something covered."[7] However, if that's the meaning, it's unclear what's covered. Is it sleight-of-hand magic, or is it simply implying they were using real occult—meaning *secret*—power to perform real magic? We are also left to decipher what this has to do with fire. Some say smoke is present to conceal illusion, while others such as Adam Clarke take this to mean there is a ceremonial fire set in order to conjure a demonic spirit to aid in the magic.[8] But we need to use other contextual clues from this passage and what we know about Satan's deceptive nature to help us decipher the meaning of this verse.*[9]

The phrase "became a serpent" (*hāyâ tannîn*) in verse 12 is a direct translation (although the word *tannîn* could be translated as "serpent" or "dragon"). In this passage, the Hebrew word for "became" is *hāyâ*. This word can also be translated as "come to pass" or "to exist." The implication with this verb is that a change took place. What was once a staff *came to exist* (*hāyâ*) as large *serpents* (*tannîn*). The most straightforward reading of verse 12 is that the magician's wooden staffs turned into literal serpents.

When Aaron's staff swallows the magicians', this is a sign of God's ultimate power and authority over the magicians as well as the demons that empowered them. The swallowing of the magicians' staffs also implies that the serpents were real and not an illusion since they couldn't swallow something that wasn't real. More importantly, there would be little glory in God's success here if the snakes had been an illusion or simply charmed into submission.

---

* "'You cannot pass,' he said. The orcs stood still, and a dead silence fell. 'I am a servant of the Secret Fire, wielder of the flame of Anor. You cannot pass.'" I can't help but wonder if *lahatim* was the inspiration for Tolkien's magical "Secret Fire," which, if true, may indicate a more supernatural interpretation from him.

Clarke says this well in his comments on Exodus 7:12: "As Egypt was remarkably addicted to magic, sorcery, etc., it was necessary that God should permit Pharaoh's wise men to act to the utmost of their skill in order to imitate the work of God, that his superiority might be clearly seen, and his powerful working incontestably ascertained; and this was fully done when Aaron's rod swallowed up their rods."[10]

He rightly notes that God permitted the magicians "to act to the utmost of their skill in order to imitate the work of God."[11] This is an incredible observation by Clarke that could be easily overlooked. One of the reasons this particular piece of magic is so difficult to believe is that the magicians created a living thing from a nonliving thing. Since the Bible doesn't always tell us exactly what the limitations of Satan's power are, we can't know for sure if this was something they could do normally. It's possible God permitted it in this situation in order to show his superior power and authority. Either way, it remains true that God does whatever he wants in order to accomplish his goal of making himself known to the nations. As Psalms 135:6 says, "The Lord does whatever he pleases in heaven and on earth, in the seas and all the depths." God does what he pleases. Even in their display of power against him, demons are always subject to God's will.

If the magician's serpents came into being through real magic, what, if any, deception could be implied in verse 11? There are two ways we can answer this question, both of which may be true at the same time. First, it could merely be referring to the occult practices used by Pharaoh's magicians. The CSB favors this interpretation with its translation of *lahatim* into "occult practices." It was likely translated this way because the word *occult* means "hidden or secret." This secret is not one of illusion but of real magic given only to those initiated into a specific occult religion and who seek hidden knowledge.

The second explanation is that the deceptive nature of all occult magic reflects Satan's own nature as a liar. This is clearly stated in John 8:44: "You are of your father the devil, and you want to carry out your father's desires. He was a murderer from the beginning and does not stand in the truth, because there is no truth in him. When he tells a lie, he speaks from his own nature, because he is a liar and the father of lies." Although human magic users seek to serve their own will via demonic power, Satan only ever has one goal—to deceive and distract in order to destroy our faith and drag us into hell alongside him. So long as he can turn our faces away from the glory of God, he has accomplished what he set out to do. Oftentimes this means using the limited power God has allowed him in supernatural ways. The supernatural act itself is not the illusion—Satan's deceptions are. One of the reasons God allows the devil this power is to test the hearts of his children (Deut. 13:3). Kristine McGuire testifies to both the reality of magic and the deceptive tactics of the devil: "Magick is as real as the deceptive beings that empower it. My spells were successful because they validated the ruse these spirits used to convince me I was powerful. The snare tightened with every spell I cast. As a witch I could manifest my own spiritual desires as reality."[12]

Although God's power was vastly superior to that of the magicians who worshipped gods such as Thoth, Pharaoh refused to be impressed with Moses's tricks or relent to his requests. Why? Because God hardened his heart and because he was accustomed to witnessing supernatural phenomena. Pharaoh said he didn't know Moses's God (Exod. 5:2), and we can assume based on his hard heart that he didn't care to know him. As pagans and polytheists, the Egyptians relished in gathering "secret" occult knowledge that is still sought after today. This is a kind of distorted mimicry of the beauty of knowing God. Just as Adam and Eve traded their intimacy with God and knowledge of God in the garden of Eden for the hidden knowledge of good and evil the devil offered, so "Satan's Pharaoh"[13] was content with his demon gods and the lies they served through demonic supernaturalism.

Despite what we may have learned in the past, the Bible teaches that angels and demons are active and have the ability to affect real change on the physical world. The demon-empowered occult existed in ancient Egypt just as it does right now. Perhaps it would be easier for our discussion of fictional magic if we could just say, "Magic isn't real; therefore, fantasy magic isn't dangerous." Yet that wouldn't be intellectually honest, nor would it guide us into a genuine knowledge of how to discern fantasy magic.

The purpose of this discussion is not to completely neutralize or strawman the concern that fictional magic could lead someone into the occult. With what we now know about the spiritual realm and the occult of the ancient world, let's turn our attention to the modern occult and how demons affect change in our world today.

Chapter 4

The Pagan Occult

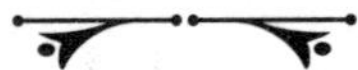

A few years ago, I participated in a pain clinic that required me to go through a set of room rotations during each visit—a group health discussion, massage, chiropractic care, and more. One day, an associate of the acupuncturist called for a group meditation. I went in knowing this particular woman was interested in New Age philosophy and would likely lead a more Eastern-style meditation. At the time, I had no knowledge of the demonic reality behind New Age practices.

We all sat in a circle and were told to close our eyes and completely relax so that the group as a whole could reach a place of deep peace. Although ignorant of the occult, I had a vague understanding that opening my mind up to the "universe" meant inviting demonic influence. So I sat there and decided to relax and meditate in my own way—through private prayer. But I couldn't relax no matter how hard I tried. Internally, I was as restless as a child unable to stop moving during rug time. I hid my discomfort by closing my eyes and remaining completely still. After ten minutes, the woman called off the meditation, declaring it to be the worst she'd ever experienced. Someone had disturbed the energy of the entire room and ruined their session. Then she looked straight at me and glared. I had no category for how to think about this at the time and couldn't understand how she knew it was me. In retrospect, it would seem the presence of the Holy Spirit would not allow a demon to place anyone under a spell of false peace.

What Is the New Age?

Some Christians believe that although real miracles are recorded in the Bible, God and Satan simply don't operate in our lives the same way they once did. Even the believers who are willing to pray for and expect the occasional miracle still can't accept the fact that actual witchcraft could be real and active in modern society. Others believe and teach that demon possession is extremely rare. This is a gross misunderstanding of the supernatural and demonology. Although the occult and New Age are not actually new, this second wave of the New Age accompanies modern technology and the wonder that is YouTube.[1] I've spent many hours reading and listening to two hundred jaw-dropping testimonies of those being saved by Jesus from witchcraft, the pagan occult, and the New Age movement. Based on the many hundreds of YouTube videos that came up when I searched "New Age to Jesus," there are likely far more people being pulled from the clutches of the New Age occult by Christ. If so many people have made their stories known online, how many more are there who have converted but have not gone public? We can only begin to guess.

Some of you may be wondering what the New Age is and what it has to do with witchcraft and the occult. The simple answer is that the New Age has become an umbrella term for any alternative spirituality accompanied by supernatural phenomena. Many of the lighter and more widely accepted modalities are just diet witchcraft—or as former New Ager Zachary Jongejan nicknamed it, "cotton candy Luciferianism."[2] The founder of the Church of Satan and author of *The Satanic Bible*, Anton LaVey, was a practicing occultist around the same time the New Age began in the 1960s.[3] Although he claimed to be an atheist,* LaVey was also a psychic and authored a book on witchcraft. When the New Age spread, LaVey found it offensive that his beliefs were being co-opted and modernized.

> In the scores of books lining the shelves of New Age bookstores, there are instructions for guided meditation, creative visualizations, out-of-body experiences, getting in touch with your spirit guides, fortune telling by cards, crystal balls or the stars. What if Satanists reclaimed these for their own dark purposes and integrated them into rituals dedicated to the Devil, where they rightfully belong? New Agers have freely drawn upon all manner of Satanic material, adapting it to their own hypocritical purposes. . . . But in truth, all "New Age" labeling is, again, trying to play the Devil's game without using His Infernal name.[4]

According to former New Agers Stephen Bancarz and Josh Peck, the New Age movement can be defined as "a spiritual system

* The terms *atheist* and *materialist* may appear to be synonymous. However, people who accept the existence of a spiritual realm are decidedly not materialists and may still reject the existence of Yahweh specifically. Their form of atheism is not anti-spirituality but anti-Christian.

of thought and practice composed of beliefs, values, and traditions from various schools and religions throughout the world."[5] In their book, *The Second Coming of the New Age: The Hidden Dangers of Alternative Spirituality in Contemporary America and Its Churches*, Bancarz and Peck include a list of the most commonly practiced New Age beliefs in the West.*

Buddhism

Hinduism

Mysticism

Transcendentalism

Gnosticism

Paganism

Pantheism

Occultism

Esotericism

Witchcraft

[Eastern] Meditation

Yoga

Psychedelics

Channeling

---

* This list is not exhaustive and doesn't include international practices such as voodoo, African spiritualism, or Santería.

Divination

Sorcery

Mind Science

Reincarnation

Astral projection

Ufology

Spiritual psychology (law of attraction, manifestation, etc.)[6]

Although these practices are wide-ranging, they often come back to the belief that adherents are divine beings seeking secret knowledge and ancient wisdom for the purpose of enlightenment, healing, and control.* That may sound positive on the surface, but at a heart level, it all comes back to pride and power. There is nothing wrong with seeking knowledge or having personal agency rather than living in passivity. But many former New Agers and occultists have testified to struggling with chronic pride and having bought into the lie Satan told Eve in Genesis 3:5: "In fact, God knows that when you eat it your eyes will be opened and you will be like God, knowing good and evil." Bancarz and Peck explain this deception in the New Age well:

> Being God or Godlike is, literally, a Luciferian pursuit that originates from the Garden of Eden where the enemy of God tricks man into desiring

* We'll discuss variations and nuances of some of these religions such as Buddhism and Hinduism in later chapters as the need arises. This core belief is primarily indicative of the occult and the Western New Age movement.

> deification. In the New Age movement, we see echoed the same lie that caused mankind to fall from fellowship with God into the curse of sin. It is being offered to us as the solution to our suffering, yet the Bible attributes it to the actual cause of our suffering. To believe one can be like God or can become God-realized through special knowledge is to believe the first lie Satan ever told mankind.[7]

Everything Satan does or says is a mirrored distortion of something God has already created. Demons can't create anything new. They only produce counterfeit truth and "masquerade as an angel of light" (2 Cor. 11:14 NIV). For example, the law of attraction says you can use the power of positive thinking to manifest good, and negative thinking produces a bad outcome. Good begets good and evil begets evil. Yet that's clearly a twisted version of the retribution principle that says, "For whatever a person sows he will also reap" (Gal. 6:7b). That kind of thinking produces a works-based system in which New Agers try to control their world through their own positive thoughts and behaviors. When things outside their control go wrong, they often blame themselves for not being positive enough or having too many internal "shadows" needing to be purged. Instead of ridding their lives of suffering, they heap more shame on themselves for not being able to control everything. Here are a few other examples of New Age practices that distort biblical truth:

CHRISTIANITY	NEW AGE OCCULT
Speaking in tongues	Light language
Retribution principle (Gal. 6:7)	Law of attraction
Meditation on Scripture/truth	Meditation on emptiness
"Not of the world" (John 17:16)	Star seeds
Resurrection	Reincarnation
Divine council (Ps. 82)	Polytheism
Image of God	Human deification
Knowing God/godly wisdom	Ancient/secret wisdom
Out of body (2 Cor. 12:2)	Astral projection
God-ordained spouse	Twin flames
Prophecy	Divination
Church unity/body of Christ	Oneness
Inspired Scripture	Automatic writing
Christ's sacrificial death	Human blood rituals
Drinking Communion wine	Drinking sacrificial blood

An example of a modern and demonic lie that warps the Genesis 3 narrative is from the occultist H. P. Blavatsky. In her book, *The Secret Doctrine* (1888), she taught that Adam was created as God's automaton to do the will of Jehovah as a slave. In this gnostic-esque story, Lucifer was the true ruler of the world and the liberator of Adam through the gift of knowledge.[8] This deception is exactly what Satan wanted Adam and Eve to believe in the garden. When he said in Genesis 3:4, "No! You will certainly not die," he was planting seeds of doubt about God's trustworthiness and honesty. Satan's tactics are never new or original. He will always seek to make God out as a liar to mask his own deceptions.

The whole of the lie in Genesis 3 was a distortion of truth. Humans are already "like God" in the sense that we're his image and have the potential to imitate his communicable attributes.* Satan presented a different kind of likeness—the potential to not only image God but to be a deity. There is also the lure of "knowing." In the garden of Eden, God dwelt with Adam and Eve. His presence was there in a similar way to his Holy Spirit dwelling in us. Eden presented a chance for great intimacy and for them to know God in a unique, personal way.

Adam and Eve seemed to have some limited understanding of morality since they knew what it meant to disobey God's instructions. Yet what Satan offered was a deeper understanding God had about the nature of good and evil—that which was hidden from them at that point in redemptive history. Knowledge is a good thing, and Christianity is a highly educational religion. Yet God revealed information to his people slowly—a process we call "progressive revelation." So Adam and Eve had less knowledge of good and evil than we did, but they had an intimacy with God that we can only imagine. They traded that intimacy of knowing God himself for hidden knowledge that God possessed, assuming they would be divine "like God" once they had it. As we saw with Pharaoh and the Egyptians, these are the lies of many pagan religions throughout history as well as the New Age movement.

She's Lying or She's Mad

If you listen to these New Age conversion stories for yourself, you may find them as hard to swallow as I did at first. Being Baptist my entire life left little room for a supernatural education. The

---

* God's communicable attributes are those humans can also possess such as love, grace, justice, rationality, mercy, etc. His incommunicable attributes are his alone, including omnipotence, sovereignty, omnipresence, etc.

claims they made about their experiences went far beyond anything I'd ever heard or wanted to hear. Yet the sheer number of people who came online to give their testimonies was simply too many to ignore. Out of hundreds of testimonies from all over the world, every one of them had experienced something supernatural by the power of demons. Not one person claimed the New Age modalities didn't work. Instead, they insisted it did work, but the benefit didn't last, and any worldly gain was not worth the price in the end.

These converts aren't engaging with syncretism and blending their occultic beliefs with Christianity (which is common), nor are they extreme sensationalists boasting of their visions of heaven like the false teachers in Colossians (Col. 2:18). Instead, they're leaving the New Age for the real Jesus and are heartbroken over their sin and deception. As I prayed about what I was hearing, I realized even if some of them didn't always have a theological framework to understand what had happened to them, they weren't crazy. They also weren't saying anything heretical or providing "new" insight which ruled out false prophecy and gnosticism.

Still, I had to use the C. S. Lewis test of truthfulness. Professor Kirke said in *The Lion, the Witch and the Wardrobe*, "There are only three possibilities. Either your sister is telling lies, or she is mad, or she is telling the truth."[9] Although I don't know most of these people personally, there are just too many of them—utterly disconnected from one another across the globe—with strikingly similar experiences with demonic spirits. Even if one or two of them lied about the supernatural things they'd seen, the possibility they were all lying is improbable.

Could they be crazy? New Agers are often told by Christians that they're hallucinating these experiences. Bancarz recounted some of the supernatural events he experienced while immersed in the New Age as a guest on the Cultish podcast. He explained how the anti-supernaturalist evangelistic approach was off-putting to him at that time:

> Whatever the encounter is when it comes to New Age experience and New Age practice, it is a helpful apologetic not to convince these people that they're hallucinating. When Christians in my life tried to do that, it made them seem really unbelievable and really naive. It made me think, "Wow, I know more about the true nature of things and the true nature of the spirit world than these Christians do. They can't possibly have the truth if they're still eating spiritual baby food."[10]

Former witch, Lindsay Smith, recounted her upbringing surrounded by anti-supernaturalist Christians in her testimony video. She was experiencing repeated demonic encounters as a child that she described as "monsters." She sought help from surrounding Christians, yet they all told her she was imagining it. After being told this several times, Smith concluded: "My answer's not in the Christian church."[11] Even as a child, she knew what she was seeing was real and the answers she'd been given were insufficient.

Again, I don't know most of these people personally, so I can't give a firsthand account of their sanity. Yet most of them come across as sane, intelligent, and well-spoken. And just as their numbers and similarity of experience can attest to their truthfulness, so it does to their sanity. With how disconnected they are from one another, we also can't assume this is a mass hallucination. Although I don't doubt their sincerity, there is still room for occasionally reinterpreting their experience based on Scripture. It's also a temptation for some charismatic circles to place experience above Scripture, which can lead to extrabiblical mythology. While experience is important and can shed light on the intended meaning of Scripture, it should never be held as more authoritative than or equal to Scripture.

New Age Testimonies

The stories I've heard vary widely in some ways. Those being saved from the New Age all have a variety of origin stories and supernatural experiences. But the most basic storyline is a background of trauma or mental health problems. As an adult or a child, they're introduced to some kind of New Age practice by a friend, family member, or the Internet. The most common is through an intimate, personal connection. Because of their traumatic background, they're often hurting and in search of healing, spiritual fulfillment, and the ability to control their surroundings.

When they start having supernatural experiences or direct contact with spirits (i.e., demons), they think they're on the right path. They assume that because they've finally discovered that the spiritual realm is real when the surrounding materialist society told them otherwise, they've discovered true healing or are on their way to "enlightenment." Even though some of these spiritual encounters can be frightening or outright demonic, they convince themselves it will be all right and the negative experience is just their own fears and inner shadows being purged on their healing journey. They insist it's still the right path because it's *real.* This also produces pride and a foundation to mock Christianity. Yet since universal truth and critical thinking are discouraged in the New Age, they can't see how relativistic and contradictory their beliefs are.

As time goes on, they get deeper and deeper into the New Age. When their healing journey doesn't go the way they hoped, they try new, darker modalities such as overt witchcraft, astral projection, psychedelic drugs, or even self-harm at the request of a "spirit guide." The demons they interact with often give them the appearance of healing at first, but in the long run, their physical and mental health worsens. The deeper they go and the more Satan makes them run on the New Age hamster wheel, the harder it becomes to convince themselves that everything is really all right or their lifestyle could ever bring permanent healing. Symptoms such as sleep paralysis, depression, anxiety, and relational toxicity become unbearable the more they try to heal with New Age modalities.* The enlightenment, prosperity, or spiritual fulfillment they were after in the beginning didn't last or satisfy for long. Eventually, the demonic element of their lifestyle starts to eat away at their soul.

Then one day, they can't take it anymore. Satan has finally demanded too much of them, and they cry out to Jesus for help, or he reveals himself to them. By the grace of God, they realize they've been wrong all along. Jesus is Lord, and those "spirit guides" they'd been talking to for so long were certainly real, but they were also pure evil. After they're saved, they go through a period of heavier attack as the spirits that had control over their life resist giving them over to Jesus and attempt to steal away their seed of faith.

J. C. Ryle said, "Unbelief about the existence and personality of Satan has often proved the first step to unbelief about God."[12]

---

* From the sample of testimonies I viewed, sleep paralysis was the foremost symptom of demonic oppression. This is so common that the demonic nature and history of sleep paralysis is documented as "hallucinations," "feeling a presence in the room," and "feeling as though something is pushing you down" on common medical websites.

These stories testify that the opposite is also true—that in our materialistic world, belief in the existence of Satan may be the first step in belief about God. If you choose to read or listen to these testimonies yourself, do so prayerfully. Satan doesn't want these stories told, and I can testify to the fact that the weight of darkness can be spiritually and emotionally taxing. These stories may also encourage superstition, Satanic panic, and overcorrection into Phariseeism, which we'll discuss in more depth in chapter 8.

I connected with one former New Ager, Francesca Knapp, after watching her testimony video and discovering she wrote fantasy. Fictional magic had been part of her journey toward the New Age along with other factors. Since many coming from the New Age or occult want absolutely nothing to do with magic—either real or fictional—her journey from the New Age to Jesus to Christian fantasy writer struck me as extraordinary. Yet her story is similar to none other than C. S. Lewis, who was also drawn to paganism in his youth and confessed to having "spiritual lust" for the occult.[13] It's ironic that he left such esoteric religious thought to go on to write of the "Deep Magic" and the gospel as an "incantation" in his fiction. Francesca's story is similarly unique and powerful. The following is an exclusive interview detailing her testimony and convictions.

How did fictional magic (or any supernatural fiction and media) play a role in leading you into the New Age?

Francesca: The answer to this question is really complicated. In a sense, yes. But if I look back and analyze my life, I don't think the fantasy or fictional magic itself led me into the New Age, but instead, the propensity towards escapism. And then, the deep desire to heal myself when I realized I had "so much wrong with me."

If only I had known I was a sinner and needed the Lord.

Was fictional magic the primary reason you became interested in the New Age, or were there other factors?

Francesca: My mother introducing me to New Age was the main reason I got led down a dark path. From a young age my mother taught me many modalities that fall under the New Age umbrella. She also told me things like I was "psychic" and had "abilities." She taught me about astrology and how it can be used to understand others. I also think that being a writer deep down fueled my passion for astrology and any type of "personality system," as I was always trying to understand the story of characters and real people.

I believe coming from a one-parent home led to feelings of neglect and being unloved. So magic, and New Age in itself, offered a way for me to take "ownership" and "responsibility" over my life, emotions, and feelings of powerlessness.

What was your experience in the New Age? What specific beliefs and practices did you engage with?

Francesca: While I had always done some "on-off" practice of astrology and tarot, and maybe some sort of teenage spell book my mother had given me. The main practices I began engaging within the New Age were yoga, meditation, and energy healing.

I was learning a lot about my "depression" and "negative feelings," and I had always been a burden on those around me, such as my family and friends, for feeling this way. So when I discovered the above healing practices, I thought I had an answer!

When doing yoga, I started "intuitively" placing my hands on certain energy channels and would feel energetic movement. From there, I delved into researching what I was feeling. (Remember, I'd always been told by my mum I was special and had magical abilities.) From there, I learned about chakras and became a reiki master. I read the book *You Can Heal Your Life* by Louise Hay and then started doing lots of affirmation work too. I delved into anything I could find and continued down the rabbit hole.

At one point, I thought I was a "Plaedian" and a star child. I studied Chinese medicine at university because I had so many personal experiences with feeling my own, and other people's energy. I was always engaging in manifestation too throughout all these years. The final sort of "belief system" I got into before being saved by Jesus was *Reality Transurfing* by Vadim Zeland.

Throughout the course of most of my twenties, I was also trying to understand what happened to me when I had what seemed to be a "Kundalini Awakening" from my research. And why after that I felt so many dark entities (which I now know to be demons). I also tried to always discover through New Age practices, quests, tarot, psychics, past lives, etc. why I had such terrible sleep paralysis and general feelings that I could speak to beings in other dimensions or realms.

From your personal experience, would you say that supernatural phenomena and witchcraft are real?

Francesca: Absolutely. But even at the time I engaged in these things, I would always question, Where does this power come from? Despite using the techniques myself over and over, I would still warn people and say, "But do we really know exactly what's happening in the spiritual realm?," and I would often go on hiatus from using these techniques and try to completely stop engaging with all belief systems altogether.

Astrology seems to be very true. If not, how could I guess people's star signs over and over? At one point in high school, I went around and guessed everyone's star sign, even the teachers. I think I rarely got it wrong, in a sample of over two hundred people. And even if I got the sign wrong, they ended up being a sign of the same element.

So my answer is yes, there is truth and power in all of this. But once you have Jesus and you've had your eyes open to see that everything God teaches is true and that all of his advice to us is for our own good, you realize the power comes from Lucifer himself. Then you look back on all the turmoil you faced during this dark period of your life and see how you were actually constantly running on a hamster wheel, never getting anywhere. Having bipolar phases of feeling good and powerful, only to be met by depression at the end. You realize that the peace you feel now with Jesus, the way you have to do absolutely "nothing" to get that peace is incomparable, and you can differentiate the good between the evil.

What made you go back to reading and writing fantasy after you left the New Age and converted to Christianity?

Francesca: Prayer. Lots and lots of prayer. As well as talking to two pastors. I finally realized that this is the path that the Lord has paved for me to help other people and share his news. The Lord renewed my passion and vigor for fantasy and storytelling. There is a difference between a "story" and "fiction" and "real life."

What advice would you give to readers and parents who are concerned fictional magic may lead them or their children into the New Age or occult?

Francesca: Teach them about not only the Lord, and make sure you disciple them yourself and show them that you love the Lord. Teach them about the other worldviews and how they lead to darkness. That way, when they read fantasy or fiction, or end up being engaged with other belief systems or practices, they will already be armed with the truth and logic of the Word of God.[14]

The experiences of former New Agers and occultists are clear—supernatural phenomena are real, and Satan will do anything to turn people away from Christ. He will even exploit their desire to help others or find comfort and healing in hidden knowledge. Yet we shouldn't live in constant fear of demons and media because God is both more powerful and sovereign. His will for us always prevails even through the sufferings of demonic attack and spiritual warfare. While we need to accept the fact that demons are active and the pagan occult is a real source of supernatural temptation, Francesca is right that educating ourselves and our children about such things is the primary way we should respond. Censorship of fantasy magic will only further confuse people and muddy the waters around this sensitive topic.

Anti-Supernaturalism and the Occult

Apart from our charismatic denominations, modern evangelicals are more pragmatic than reliant on the Holy Spirit's daily guidance. Catholic occultist Brother A. D. A. states in his book *Ritual Magic for Conservative Christians*: "Differences of almost every stripe exist across the denominational spectrum, ranging from Catholicism and Eastern Orthodoxy which are pretty much pre-packaged magical systems in a state of denial, to the Five-Point Calvinists and Rationalists who intentionally and methodically divorced every shred of spirituality from their religion."[15]

Although this statement is an overcorrection and his book would certainly fall into the category of false teaching and post-modern gnosticism, Brother A. D. A. rightly critiques how much of Evangelicalism has become more rational than spiritual. He wrongly assumes the occult is the remedy for these errors. These extremes present a dangerous dichotomy because "we're not secularists; we're supernaturalists."[16]

Hill and Walton make a similar comparison saying the miracles in Scripture are continually debated by scholars because of "the prominence of anti-supernaturalist assumptions in our post-Enlightenment era."[17] Despite the existence of "Christian" witchcraft and false healers and prophets, it's still the rationalist Christian whom we most often encounter in our Western churches. Another set of extremes is at work here—one that believes God has given us the ability to overpower the laws of nature by our human will alone, and the other remakes God into a being that no longer wills to act in a way that supersedes the laws of nature at all. The naïveté of the latter position leaves us far too vulnerable to the lies of the occult.

Unless more Christians embrace the truth that demons can empower witches and mediums, we won't be equipped to handle the rise of the New Age and paganism such as Wicca.[18] Wiccans have grown from 8,000 in 1990 to 342,000 in 2008 to more than a million in 2014.[19] Yet more than anything, the Covid pandemic had people rushing into the arms of the occult.

> The pandemic proved a boon for the occult. In 2020, social media accounts connected to witchcraft amassed millions of followers and billions of views, the *Financial Times* reported. Today, the TikTok hashtag "#witchTok" has more than 55 billion views. Sales of tarot cards doubled between 2016 and 2021 and tripled during the first year of the pandemic, according to a 2021 *Washington Post* report. Sales of crystals, popularized for their perceived good energy and healing power, were "exploding at the seams," one jewelry designer told *The New York Times* in 2022.[20]

In 2018, Pew Research reported that "roughly six-in-ten American adults accept at least one of these New Age beliefs. Specifically, four-in-ten believe in psychics and that spiritual energy can be found in physical objects, while somewhat smaller shares express belief in reincarnation (33%) and astrology (29%)."[21] They polled Christians with the same four New Age beliefs. It's important to note that four is a limited number within the spectrum of the New Age. "While eight-in-ten Christians say they believe in God as described in the Bible, six-in-ten believe in one or more of the four New Age beliefs analyzed here."[22] These teachings are also becoming more mainstream and packaged as family friendly. In August 2023, Blaze Media featured the headline, "Taxpayer-Subsidized Art Center in Minnesota Holds 'Playful Demon Summoning Session' for Families."[23]

But why is this growth happening? Christians are often tempted to blame fictional magic like Harry Potter for these numbers, but the evidence points in another direction entirely. Out of the two hundred "New Age to Jesus" testimonies I listened to, only eleven of them said fictional magic was part of their journey into the occult, which is 5.5 percent.* That means the vast majority, 94.5 percent of former occultists, were not tempted in that way. By fictional magic, I mean *fantasy* magic specifically, not fictional stories about real magic like the movie *The Craft*—an example of real, demonic supernaturalism in a fictional setting.**[24] Kristine McGuire says, "Would witches and ghosts have interested me if I hadn't heard stories about them in my childhood? The answer is yes, I would have turned to the supernatural anyway. Yes, popular media played its part, but I would have found a way to explore witchcraft eventually."[25]

If not fantasy, then where else might this New Age growth be coming from? If we only look at news articles about the increase, it would appear that people drawn to the New Age and paganism are sometimes extreme feminists looking for ways to increase their power after trauma or against patriarchy[26]—sometimes as a political weapon.[27] In some cases, female empowerment takes on the appearance of a witch. Much like the lie that humans are gods themselves, the "divine feminine" is a major trend on social media. Female New Agers are drawn to the idea that they themselves are reincarnated goddesses.[28]

Yet there are also more common spiritual reasons. First, all humans are spiritual beings created to commune with God and

---

* The fictional magic that was mentioned as a temptation included anime in general, Matilda, Harry Potter, *The Vampire Diaries, Avatar: The Last Airbender, Sabrina the Teenage Witch*, the Wiccan character in Disney's Halloweentown, and talking to animals in *The Wild Thornberrys*.

** *The Craft* is a coming-of-age film where a teenage girl, new to a Catholic prep school, befriends a group of witches who cast spells and curses on their enemies. The depiction of witchcraft in this film is not fantastical in nature and resembles demonic supernaturalism.

others. But our technological and materialistic culture suppresses our spirituality. It's only natural for people to find ways to express this essential part of their nature. Yet in all the testimonies I watched, the primary reason converts gave for entering the New Age occult was trauma or mental health problems: 140 people out of 200 (70%) reported trauma before they became involved. Out of the eleven people who reported being tempted by fictional magic, ten of them also had a history of trauma. In an interview with *WORLD* magazine, Lily Hamilton perfectly describes this dynamic of a young person with trauma encountering fictional magic. Her desire for control after the trauma of her parents' divorce is a common theme for New Agers: "Hamilton's interest in the occult began at age 14, a few years after her parents divorced: 'I was searching for any sense of control in my life.' She devoured the Harry Potter books and came to believe 'magic is real.' Then, she made a friend at school who dressed in all black and described herself as 'Wiccan.' At home, Hamilton turned to the internet to learn more about witchcraft."[29]

Broken people living in a broken world naturally search for answers to address their pain and find healing. Searching isn't bad—it means they're responding by trying to actively address their trauma instead of becoming apathetic or giving up. The danger lies in how desperate people become in their pain, often turning to the wrong person or healing method to find relief. Instead of turning to Christianity, they find the occult instead. The New Age practices promise to heal them and give them a sense of control. For people once made to feel powerless by another person, supernaturalism gives them the opportunity to feel powerful. It also creates the illusion they can heal themselves, which gives a sense of purpose in their pain. Former witch, Jessica Laureano, finds this to be the most common reason people turn to witchcraft:

> Nine times out of ten, witchcraft is a symptom of somebody who's really hurt. So if you're in witchcraft, I understand that you've been hurt, but all of the healing you're looking for, all of the chasing you're doing can come to an end when you look at Jesus and when you trust him. . . . I feel like it's cliché, but God loves you. And I say that with a lot of weight because the one thing I was searching for everywhere that I went was love. And the only place that I found it was in Christ.[30]

In the hit film, *Jesus Revolution*, Jonathan Roumie portrays the hippie evangelist, Lonnie Frisbee, who gives a moving speech on the reasons he has such compassion and heart to reach lost hippies—some of whom were involved in New Age practices—with the gospel: "I know we must seem pretty strange. But if you look a little deeper—if you look with love—you'll see a bunch of kids that are searching for all the right things just in all the wrong places."[31] Those trapped in the New Age are just the same—searching for Jesus and finding Satan.

Worship of the "Will"

Those who practice "right-hand path" magic or more generally seek to bring good into the world through being a "light worker" in the New Age are driven by their own definition of what good is and how they can bring it about by imposing their will.[32] Former witch, Julie Lopez says, "Witchcraft is nothing more and nothing less than control and manipulation. So you're doing things to get your own way. Whether it's white witchcraft, whether it's black witchcraft—it's you taking the control and manifesting what you want."[33]

Thelema[34] is a pagan religion founded in 1907 by occultist Aleister Crowley (1875–1947).[35] The word *thelema* is Greek for "inclination, desire, or divine will." In the Bible, it usually refers to God's will (i.e., "Your kingdom come. Your *will* be done on earth as it is in heaven" [Matt. 6:10, emphasis added]).

While studying at Cambridge, Crowley became interested in mysticism and esoteric religions. He first joined the occult, The Hermetic Order of the Golden Dawn, where he practiced debased ritual spiritualism known as goetia. Eventually, Crowley branched off from the Golden Dawn and founded his own religion. A number of factors contributed to this change, but the one that carries weight for us is his wife's encounter with a spirit or messenger named Aiwass. Crowley later claimed that Aiwass was his guardian angel. Over a three-day period in 1904, this spirit dictated to Crowley's wife, Rose Edith Kelly, while he wrote down everything she said. From this event came the book, *Liber AL vel Legis* or *The Book of the Law*, which became the sacred text for Thelema. It declared the start of the Æon of Horus—or the Age of Horus. Thelemites believe this new spiritually evolved age has one main precept: "Do what thou wilt shall be the whole of the Law." They have many complicated beliefs involving Egyptian-esque gods, but the main goal of this religion is to discover one's own True Will—their ultimate purpose in life. To do this, Thelemites must unite themselves to higher powers or their "guardian angel" (i.e., familiar spirit or demon). They also practice "magick" that Crowley defines as, "Science and Art that provokes Change in conformity with the Will."[36]

Although Crowley said the spirit that contacted him was an angel, he also admitted to speaking to demons. And yet these demons were supposedly just a part of his own mind and psyche. He taught Thelemites to connect with higher powers (angels), but those powers were to be found in themselves as though their own "Will" is divine rather than fallen. In reality, Crowley was likely speaking to real demons that he was led to believe were part of himself. What's confusing about Crowley's language is how deeply conflated his beliefs are.

As former neopagan priestess Sage Romano says, the New Age is a "pick your own adventure kind of spirituality."[37] Either there are no rules, or the rules of each sect are made to be broken since Satan creates chaos and disorder. Some New Agers openly express a desire to be connected with spirits outside themselves, yet it's one's own power, mind, and will that are the objects of worship. The demon, spirit, or "guardian angel" are merely the means to an end of being able to change and control the world around them in alignment with their own "Will."

In this inconsistency we find one of the most dangerous lies that many pagan religions fall prey to—far more dangerous than if Aleister Crowley had just made it all up. They believe they're the ones in control and that these spirits don't have a will of their own. Instead, New Age occultists are naively drawn into an intimate relationship with Satan and his demons. A witch is under the impression they have all the power and agency. They replace God with themselves and create idols in their own image, all while remaining unaware that the will and desire of the demon has control of their fate.

Chapter 5

The Source of Mirrored Magic

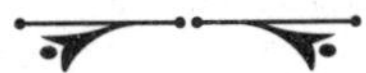

Satan can only copy or twist the truth. He can't make anything new or original. We've seen examples of that in the modern New Age, but the same is true of demonic supernaturalism in Scripture. Yet the ability to copy God isn't unique to demons. Humans do it too. In the cultural mandate from Genesis 1:28, God essentially tells Adam and Eve to reproduce and become authoritative culture makers. We're commanded to take all that God created and mold it into something else. Nothing we as humans make is entirely original. Engineers take natural resources like wood and metal and rearrange them into livable structures. Instruments and voices take existing notes and sounds and rearrange them into music. Fiction borrows from man's nature, history, and experiences and rearranges details into new stories and characters. We can't make something out of nothing, and neither can Satan. Yet where humans can make both good and evil from nature, Satan can only rearrange and *distort* God's creation. When demonic power mirrors goodness, it will be warped—a carnival mirror that bends and distorts the truth of what stands before it.

Divine Source

Question 1: What is the source of the magic? Is it demonic or divine?

In order to explore what the Bible says about the extent and limits of supernaturalism, I'll list categories drawn from Scripture. Some of the following supernatural events can only be caused by God alone. Others have a mirrored event that's accomplished through the power of Satan and demons. There may also be special circumstances where God allows Satan to have more power than usual in order to display God's own glory and strength as far greater and establish himself as the ultimate source of all power.

Second Thessalonians 2:9 says, "The coming of the lawless one is based on Satan's working, with every kind of miracle, both signs and wonders serving the lie." By the power of Satan, the antichrist can perform "every kind of miracle." However, that implies he will have more power than other antichrists or false prophets that came before him and will perform miracles that were previously regarded as impossible by the power of demons. Since this verse implies a shift in the limitations of demonic powers, we should understand the following discussion to apply to what is generally true about demons in Scripture and currently, not what will always be true in the future.

Seeing the future: God gives visions and messages to his people through his chosen prophets or seers in the Old and New Testaments, through Urim and Thummim (Exod. 28:30), and casting lots (Josh. 18:6; Acts 1:26). Foretelling from God (mediated by angels) is inerrant (Acts 7:38, 53; Gal. 3:19; Heb. 2:2). God also occasionally gives visions, instructions, and prophecies to pagans and nonbelievers in order to accomplish his will. For example, he gave dreams, visions, or messages to Balaam (Num. 23–24), Pharaoh (Gen. 41:1–7), Nebuchadnezzar (Dan. 2:1–45; 4:4–18), and Laban (Gen. 31:29). Divine prophecy through both godly and pagan prophets is one example of mirrored supernaturalism that, in this case, emphasizes the source of the power is more important than the prophet. The user may be righteous Daniel or pagan Nebuchadnezzar, godly Joseph or unbelieving Pharaoh. Because of this, all prophecies should be subject to testing by the Holy Spirit, Scripture, and the veracity of their claims (Deut. 18:20–22). God also gives the power to interpret prophetic dreams or messages of others such as Joseph's interpretation of Pharaoh's dream in Genesis 41, Daniel's interpretation of Nebuchadnezzer's dreams in Daniel 2 and 4, and Daniel's interpretation of the writing on the wall in Daniel 5.

Balaam presents an interesting case, since he's a known pagan diviner—someone who practices divination. The word *divination* usually implies a distorted image of divine prophecy. Traditionally, when God gives Balaam a message, we call it "prophecy" instead of "divination" (Num. 22:7). However, the Bible never explicitly refers to Balaam's words as prophecy. We have to use the context of the passage more than the particular words that are used to understand that he's receiving these words from God, not demons. First, Balaam prophesies in Numbers 23:23 that there is "no divination against Israel." Second, Nehemiah 13:2b says, "Instead, they hired Balaam against them to curse them, but our God turned the curse into a blessing." There's a clear shift from a pagan "curse" to a divine "blessing," but both of those words are used by Israelites as well as pagans.

Satan mimics the power of seeing the future through deceit. Since demons are not omniscient or omnipresent, nor do they exist outside of time as God does, they can't see the future. They can direct and move physical objects such as the casting of lots to give a false impression of knowing the future. However, they're intelligent, ancient, and know far more information about human nature and history than we can imagine. This makes them adept at guessing how we'll act or what event may cause certain consequences. They can also tell someone that something will happen in the future and then cause it to happen so it seems as though they were able to see the future.

When a person practices modalities such as divination, mediumship, or astrology, demons are feeding the human diviner a mixture of real and false information. The reason Pharaoh's and Nebuchadnezzar's magicians weren't able to interpret the kings' dreams (Gen. 41; Dan. 2) was twofold—the dreams came from God, and the "familiar spirits" who empowered the magicians likely couldn't read their minds in this situation. Whether demons can read minds is an area of speculation. Total "mind reading" is something only God can do because of his omnipotence and omniscience. The Bible does not speak into this issue directly, but we can assume demons either can't read minds at all or that it's limited. Nebuchadnezzar asked his magi to not only interpret his dream but to tell him what his dream was. He asked them to read his mind, and they couldn't. By contrast, Daniel was given this information from God.

If Pharaoh's and Nebuchadnezzer's dreams had come from a demon rather than God, it may have been possible for the magicians to receive the information from the demon about the given dream and be able to give an interpretation. It's also possible the kings had previously experienced some rare success with their magicians interpreting dreams in the past if the dream had originated with those spirits. The fact that such things are unreliable may be why Nebuchadnezzar tested his magicians by forcing them to tell him what he'd dreamed on threat of death (Dan. 2:5–6). The magicians recognized the impossibility of the task and spoke rightly in 2:11: "What the king is asking is so difficult that no one can make it known to him except the gods, whose dwelling is not with mortals." They believed that only their gods—fallen spirits who had set themselves up as gods—could have potentially given such information, if at all. What they didn't know was that only Daniel's God had the authority to do as the king asked. And only Daniel—counted among Babylon's magicians, mediums, and wise men—could receive the information Nebuchadnezzar demanded.

Speaking to the dead: Commonly called necromancy, Deuteronomy 18:11 explicitly forbids speaking to the dead. Luke 16:19–31 explains why speaking to the dead is not necessary or valuable. In the parable of the rich man and Lazarus, the rich man dies and goes to "Hades" (not "hell" but the "grave" or to "death," meaning the generic realm of the dead). He begs Abraham to send someone back from the dead to warn his brothers of the coming torment so they would repent and be spared. But Abraham insists that "if they don't listen to Moses and the prophets, they will not be persuaded if someone rises from the dead" (Luke 16:31). Not only does speaking to the dead illegally reach into the spiritual realm, but Jesus is saying it's also a pointless pursuit.

There is only one example in Scripture where God empowers this—when Saul seeks the medium at En-dor in 1 Samuel 28. In this story, the Philistines had gathered in preparation for battle with Israel. Saul was afraid, so he sought the Lord's guidance by "dreams or by the Urim or by the prophets" (v. 6). God didn't answer him because the Lord had abandoned Saul to his sin. Desperate, Saul sought help from the deceased prophet Samuel by consulting the medium at En-dor. Both Saul and the medium intended to use the power of demons to speak to Samuel. But God is Lord of both the living and the dead (Rom. 14:8–9). Satan doesn't have the power to speak to the dead. He has the ability to take life (Job 1:12–19), but he can't draw someone back from the dead or the spiritual realm to speak to the living. Anyone who has converted from New Age mediumship can tell you they were receiving information from a "familiar spirit" (a demon) and were deceived into thinking they were speaking to the dead. Yet it was the demon that was only pretending to be the ghost of a dead loved one. It seems neither Saul nor the medium knew of those limitations. The fact that a vision of Samuel actually appears to the medium can only be an act of God or an exception God allowed for that one situation.

Raising someone from the dead: God empowers this on a few occasions. In the Old Testament, the prophet Elijah raises the widow's son in 1 Kings 17:17–24. Elisha raises the Shunammite woman's son in 2 Kings 4:18–37. Then in 2 Kings 13:20–21, a dead man is thrown into Elisha's grave. When the body touched Elisha's bones, he was revived and stood up. In the Gospels, only Jesus is recorded raising people from the dead.* In Matthew 10, Jesus commissions the disciples to "heal the sick, *raise the dead*, cleanse those with leprosy, drive out demons" (v. 8, emphasis added). Yet we aren't given any specific accounts of the disciples raising people from the

* Matthew 27:50–53; Luke 7:11–17; 8:40–56; John 11:38–44.

dead until the book of Acts. That verse is also the only mention of the disciples being authorized to raise the dead in all four Gospels. In Acts, Peter raises Tabitha from the dead (9:36–43), and Paul raises Eutychus (20:7–12). It's also possible that Paul himself was dead and revived by the disciples after being stoned in Lystra in Acts 14:19–20. Yet the text is unclear if he was raised from the dead or simply healed of severe injury. There is no occult equivalent to this power, so it's best to assume Satan does not have the authority to raise the dead. Although debatable, some Christians believe the antichrist (the "lawless one" from 2 Thessalonians 2:9) could have this power.

Healing the sick and injured: There are many accounts of God's healing in the Old and New Testaments, although the majority occur in the Gospels. Most of the healings in the Old Testament come directly from God as a response to prayer and without a human mediator. Besides those, a few healings are recorded at the hands of God's prophets. When God afflicted the Israelites with venomous snakes, Moses made a bronze snake that would heal the bitten Israelites if they looked at it. Elisha healed the Shunammite woman's barrenness (2 Kings 4:11–17) and commanded Naaman to wash seven times in the Jordan River to be healed of leprosy (5:10–14). Isaiah delivered the news that God would heal Hezekiah and then brought him pressed figs to apply to his skin in order to be healed (20:1–7).

In the Gospels, we're only given specific details about a few of the healings Jesus performs such as his healing of lepers, the lame, and the blind. The total number of how many were healed by Jesus during his ministry is so great, only he knows it. The disciples were commissioned to heal, but no details are given of those events in the Gospels. In the book of Acts, there are a number of healings such as Peter healing the lame beggar in 3:1–10 and Paul healing a crippled man in 14:8–10. An account of healing is recorded in Acts 19:11–12 (ESV): "And God was doing extraordinary miracles by the hands of Paul, so that even handkerchiefs or aprons that had touched his skin were carried away to the sick, and their diseases left them and the evil spirits came out of them."

The demonic equivalent of healing is elusive. In Scripture, a true healing at the hand of a demon is either not present or unclear. During the sixth Egyptian plague of boils, all the Egyptian people were afflicted with sores, including the magicians. They were in such pain that they couldn't even stand before Moses (Exod. 9:11). This implies they weren't able to heal themselves or their people from God's affliction. The only potential account of demonic healing might be the pool of Bethesda in John 5:1–9. Many scholars believe this pool had pagan origins since much of Jerusalem and the surrounding area were subjected to Hellenization by the secular Greco-Roman culture, and there is archeological evidence of pagan influence.[1] Others suggest the pool was originally a Jewish *mikvah*—a place of ceremonial cleansing—and became pagan after the first century.[2] John 5:4 is not in the original manuscripts and was added later, presumably by a scribe.[3] This is why many translations jump from verse 3 to verse 5, omitting verse 4 entirely so the pool is not directly linked to Yahweh. That verse says an angel of the Lord stirred up waters so that the first person into the water could be healed. If the pool was originally pagan and healings did take place there, this would be the only account of occult healing in the Bible.

That still leaves the question of Satan's authority to heal somewhat fuzzy since we're told in the New Testament that "false messiahs and false prophets" will do great signs and wonders by the power of demons (Matt. 24:24). Yet the specifics of those signs aren't described. It's possible Pharaoh's magicians couldn't heal for the same reason they couldn't interpret dreams—the demons weren't the ones who inflicted the illness or the vision; God was. Some New Age converts have hypothesized that modern cult healing services are a type of demonic long con. First the demon afflicts a person with an illness or injury similar to the disabled woman in Luke 13:16 ("Satan has bound this woman, a daughter of Abraham, for eighteen years"). Then the demon somehow draws the suffering person to the healing service, ritual, or shaman through trickery. At that point, the demon heals by lifting the illness the demon initially inflicted. If the pool of Bethesda was a pagan place of healing, it may be that a similar method of healing was used there. All of this is speculation, but it's common for New Age occultists to find some measure of temporary relief and healing through demonic supernaturalism regardless of how it's accomplished.

Talking animals: God speaks through one animal in the Bible—Balaam's donkey in Numbers 22:21–39. Although the words the donkey speaks are from the animal's point of view, we know God hasn't actually given animals the power of self-reflective thought or speech since that's part of being God's image. God is speaking through the donkey just as Balaam recognizes God speaks through him: "Look, I have come to you, but can I say anything I want? I must speak only the message God puts in my mouth" (v. 38). Satan also may have spoken through an animal in Genesis 3 when the serpent tempts Eve. This account is much less clear, and scholars are not in agreement on what form Satan actually took since the creation account is filled with both historic and mythic language. Since Satan is a spirit, it's not outside the realm of possibilities that Satan either spoke through a real snake as God spoke through the donkey or that he possessed a snake as the legion of demons possessed the herd of pigs in the Gospels.* It's also possible, even likely, that he didn't physically resemble a snake at all but is referred to this way only metaphorically.[4]

Superstrength: In the book of Judges, Samson is the most notable example of God's empowering someone with supernatural strength (Judg. 13–16). When he uses his gift of superstrength, we're told that "the Spirit of the Lord came powerfully on him" (14:6). There were also David's mighty warriors who each killed hundreds of Philistines (2 Sam. 23:8–39). The passage doesn't explicitly say that the Holy Spirit endowed them with supernatural power as with Samson. Yet that's likely what happened since their conquests don't seem humanly possible.

Demons also have this power, as we see in the account of the demon-possessed man at the tombs (Matt. 8:28–34; Mark 5:1–20; Luke 8:26–39). The man "lived in the tombs, and no one was able to restrain him anymore—not even with a chain—because he often had been bound with shackles and chains, but had torn the chains apart and smashed the shackles. No one was strong enough to subdue him. Night and day among the tombs and on the mountains, he was always crying out and cutting himself with stones" (Mark 5:3–5). Since this is the only account in Scripture of this kind of extreme power from someone demon-possessed, it naturally begs the question of whether the great "legion" of demons he had in him granted him additional strength. I think that's a possibility, but since the passage doesn't say, we can't draw any definitive conclusions.

Teleportation: There are four examples of teleportation—the ability to be instantly transported from one location to another—in the Bible, and most, if not all, are by the power of God. The first is

---

* Matthew 8:28–34; Mark 5:1–20; Luke 8:26–39.

from John 6:19–21, which is somewhat unclear. After Jesus walked on water, he stepped into the boat and "at once the boat was at the shore where they were heading" (v. 21). This may have been teleportation or simply a literary device used to quickly move the story forward. The second is Jesus suddenly appearing and disappearing in the presence of his disciples and followers after the resurrection. John 20:19 says that Jesus suddenly appeared in a locked room. The third account is in Acts 8:39 when "the Spirit of the Lord carried Philip away, and the eunuch did not see him any longer." The implication here is that they were both standing together in the water after Philip baptized the Ethiopian eunuch, and then Philip was suddenly gone.

The fourth teleportation is from Matthew 4 and is also vague. We're told Jesus is "led up by the Spirit into the wilderness to be tempted by the devil" (v. 1). Then a few verses later, "the devil took him to the holy city, had him stand on the pinnacle of the temple" (v. 5). Finally, "the devil took him to a very high mountain and showed him all the kingdoms of the world and their splendor" (v. 8). Verse 1 indicates that the Holy Spirit is the one who drew Jesus to the wilderness to begin with, so he is present and involved. Then the passage twice mentions that "the devil took him." It's possible that Satan transported Jesus. It's also possible that Jesus, along with the power of the Holy Spirit, transported himself as he followed Satan from place to place. The text is not clear, yet we have no other accounts in Scripture of Satan transporting someone from one location to another.

If Satan does not have this power, it's because he isn't omnipresent (everywhere at all times) or omnipotent (all powerful). It seems from Matthew 4 and Job 1:7 ("roaming through the earth . . . and walking around on it") that Satan at least has the power to teleport himself even as a nonphysical entity. Perhaps only the Holy Spirit, who is omnipresent and omnipotent, has the ability to transport someone or something from one physical location to another in an instant. This is additionally mind-bending since the unseen realm is a spiritual and not a physical place. Yet somehow we know that God is everywhere and Satan is not, which implies he somehow relates to physical locations even while being a nonphysical being. This is another aspect of God's nature and Satan's power that's a mystery to us.

Objects with supernatural power: Some examples of objects with supernatural power from God are the ark of the covenant (1 Sam. 5), the manna from heaven (Exod. 16), Moses's and Aaron's staffs (Exod. 7), Urim and Thummim (Exod. 28:30), Elisha's bones (2 Kings 13:20–21), and Paul's handkerchiefs (Acts 19:11–12). This is not an exhaustive list. These objects are endowed with power only as God wills and needs. There are times when they may cause a miracle to occur and times when they don't, depending on the circumstances. None of them are endowed with power permanently. The existence of such objects may seem to give credit to Catholic relics. However, the unpredictability and temporary nature of these objects of power call into question whether a relic could remain endowed with power for centuries.

In the Old Testament, the presence of the ark of the covenant forced the pagan idol of Dagon to fall to the ground and eventually break apart (1 Sam. 5:1–5). Yet when the same ark was brought into battle as a good-luck charm and without God's consent, it did not protect the Israelites in battle (1 Sam. 4:1–11). This is an example of God's doing as he pleases since he cannot be commanded to do as we say. The Israelites may have been led to treat the ark this way because their foreign neighbors treated their own gods and objects of power like good-luck charms. Then in Exodus 16, the manna from heaven would rot and develop maggots if kept overnight except for one day of the week—the Sabbath. This was necessary so that the people could rest and refrain from gathering manna on that day (vv. 17–26). God endows objects with power according to his will, not ours.

There are a couple of times when pagan objects also appear to have supernatural powers. The most notable example is Pharaoh's magicians' staffs that turned into snakes (Exod. 7). There are also references to "magic bands" in Ezekiel 13:18, but we don't know if these bands genuinely functioned in a supernatural capacity because the text doesn't say. Since there are many modern accounts of objects such as crystals and pendants having a supernatural impact on a person's life or body, it's possible Satan empowered these bands in a similarly deceptive way.

Words of power: Scripture gives us three types of "words of power" whose source is God. The first is Jesus's name, the second is prayer, and the third is blessings and curses. In John 14:13–14, Jesus says, "Whatever you ask in my name, I will do it so that the Father may be glorified in the Son. If you ask me anything in my name, I will do it." We don't often think of prayer as supernatural, yet it is. By the power of the Holy Spirit and through Christ as our mediator, we are speaking and communing with God. My husband sometimes says that "prayer is magic." He doesn't mean that if you pray you will get whatever you want or that God is a vending machine. He means that being able to speak to and ask for aid from the Almighty, Creator God and then for him to actually respond to us is nothing short of a miracle. It's also because of Jesus's words in John 14 that we pray in his name. But just as "prayer is magic" is not a statement of receiving whatever a selfish heart desires, neither is Jesus's promise that "whatever you ask in my name, I will do it" (v. 13). Jesus means that whatever we ask for *when we are abiding in him and desire his will*, he will do it. This takes the power and control out of our hands and places it in God's.

When Joshua speaks a prayer that sounds like a command in Joshua 10:12–14, God "listened to a man." "On the day the Lord gave the Amorites over to the Israelites, Joshua spoke to the Lord in the presence of Israel: 'Sun, stand still over Gibeon, and moon, over the Valley of Aijalon.' And the sun stood still and the moon stopped until the nation took vengeance on its enemies. . . . There has been no day like it before or since, when the Lord listened to a man, because the Lord fought for Israel."

Joshua seems to be demanding that the sun and moon stand still, and then it happens. It almost sounds like an incantation rather than a prayer. But we know that God can't be forced to do as we ask. Even though the text doesn't say it directly before the prayer is spoken, we have to assume Joshua was acting within God's will when he spoke those words. Somehow he knew that what he said would happen—not just because he willed it but because God did. Joshua knew that "the Lord fought for Israel." We should be extremely careful using that kind of language ourselves instead of wording our prayers like petitions. It's potentially dangerous to assume you're acting within God's will and demand things from him that he hasn't promised.

Mark 9:29 emphasizes God's ultimate authority as well as the power of prayer. Jesus happens upon his disciples when they are struggling to cast out a demon. Before Jesus casts it out himself, he rebukes the disciples by calling them an "unbelieving generation" (v. 19). When they ask Jesus why they can't do it, he says, "This kind can come out by nothing but prayer" (v. 29). But Matthew 17:20

gives a slightly different answer, and both are simultaneously true: "'Because of your little faith,' he told them. 'For truly I tell you, if you have faith the size of a mustard seed, you will tell this mountain, "Move from here to there," and it will move. Nothing will be impossible for you.'" If this "kind" of demon can only come out through prayer and not by being cast out in Jesus's name, then why does he rebuke them for their lack of faith? How were they supposed to know that information unless he'd told them? The lesson the disciples should learn here is that prayer does have a unique power to cast out demons but only because it shows a unique dependence on God. It seems likely that the disciples had become so overconfident in the authority and call to ministry Jesus gave them that they forgot who was really in charge.[5] Yet through a prayer of genuine faith in the power and authority of Jesus, the demon would have come out.

Jesus's name does have power and authority but only as he wills. It isn't an incantation any more than prayer or Joshua's words were. God is the one who gives authority in the name of Jesus to believers but also nonbelievers at times. In Matthew 7:22–23, Jesus said, "On that day many will say to me, 'Lord, Lord, didn't we prophesy in your name, drive out demons in your name, and do many miracles in your name?' Then I will announce to them, 'I never knew you. Depart from me, you lawbreakers!'" The power is not in the will, heart, or salvation of the person speaking but in Jesus's authority. A powerful modern example of this is from Bancarz and Peck in their book, *The Second Coming of the New Age*:

> Hundreds of people have claimed to be able to stop night terrors, astral attacks, alien abductions, and sleep paralysis immediately by doing nothing

> more than calling out for Jesus.* Beings appear in their room during an astral-projection experience, and those beings retreat when the person uses the name of Jesus. . . . Often, people who call out to Jesus and receive supernatural help with astral attacks don't actually believe in Jesus. Atheists themselves testify to the effectiveness of calling on the Lord when under attack. It's not as though people have faith and bring a certain thought-form into existence in the spirit world using the power of their mind, they lack all faith and cry out in desperation and still receive breakthrough. If true, this seems to imply the spirits fear the name of Jesus regardless of the mind of the person. If you are ever in a scary situation in the spirit, these testimonies are proof that these beings fear and are under the authority of the name of Jesus Christ.[6]

Even with all of this, we can't assume that simply speaking Jesus's name over another person will automatically result in a miracle. If it did, we would be healing one another all the time. However, we do pray and *ask* God to heal in the name of Jesus. This shows submission to God's will in a particular situation as well as faith in his authority and ability to accomplish that miracle.

The third type of "words of power" from God are blessings and curses. These are a kind of prophecy as well as the impetus for its fulfillment. Possibly the most notable blessings in the Old Testament are those given by Isaac to his sons in Genesis 27. These

---

* Former New Agers often refer to alien abductions, yet they view them as a whole-body and mind deception and vision from Satan.

are particularly memorable since Jacob tricked his father into giving him the blessing he'd originally intended for Esau (vv. 5–29)—although we know that God had intended it for Jacob all along (Gen. 25:22–23). Before Jacob goes into his father to trick him, he expresses concern to his mother that Isaac would discover him and speak a curse rather than a blessing. This story can be difficult for us to understand because we don't often grasp the seriousness or the supernatural reality of these blessings and curses. There is a definite implication in the passage that what has been done cannot be undone (27:33–37). Once the firstborn's blessing has been spoken over Jacob, there's no going back. Isaac is forced to give Esau a much harsher blessing that somewhat resembles a curse (27:38–40).

A far more dramatic example of a curse spoken through a man rather than directly from God comes after Israel conquers Jericho in Joshua 6. Joshua spoke the curse: "The man who undertakes the rebuilding of this city, Jericho, is cursed before the Lord. He will lay its foundation at the cost of his firstborn; he will finish its gates at the cost of his youngest" (Josh. 6:26). We also see the fulfillment of this curse in 1 Kings 16:34. Yet the strangest curse recorded in Scripture is in 2 Kings 2:23–24 when Elisha curses a group of boys who are taunting him by calling him "baldy" or "baldhead" (ESV). Then "two female bears came out of the woods and mauled forty-two of the children." This makes little sense to us because we don't understand the true nature of an insult buried under much cultural context. The insult was in response to a miracle Elisha had just performed. Therefore, the taunt was insulting God, jeopardizing Elisha's ministry, and uttering a form of serious blasphemy.[7] We should assume that such a horrific judgment against the boys was actually God's will; otherwise, the curse wouldn't have worked.

Elisha didn't have the authority to direct God's will but only to mediate his power.

Blessings, curses, and speaking in Jesus's name are divine "words of power" since they function only as an extension of his will and strength. When we attempt to use these things for our own selfish desires, the words lose their power. Yet one of the most well-known and controversial demonic distortions of this is the casting of spells (Deut. 18:11). There are no explicit examples of spellcasting in the Bible, but it's possible Pharaoh's magicians could have cast spells when they mimicked the first and second plagues (Exod. 7:22; 8:7). It's also possible that Simon the magician (Acts 8:9–25) and Elymas the sorcerer (Acts 13:4–12) had gained their followers through magic and spellcasting in public. Yet all of this is speculation.

We know only that casting spells was a pagan practice at the time since it was included in the prohibitions in Deuteronomy 18:10–11. The curse that Balak insisted Balaam speak against the Israelites in Numbers 22–24 would have been an example of a demonic curse (arguably a type of spell) had Balaam done as he was asked and intended. In the modern occult, there are many kinds of spells—including blessings and curses—depending on the specific branch or pagan religion being followed. Satan is not picky about which words of power are used so long as he is leading people away from Christ.

Authority over nature: God has total authority over nature, but is there a way in which he allows people to mediate that power? Jesus often displayed his authority over nature, but although he is fully human, he's also fully God. So, how does God allow sinful humans to wield his authority over nature? The Old Testament has many examples of this such as Moses's and Aaron's staffs bringing about seven of the plagues (Exod. 7–12). Moses also did such miracles as splitting the Red Sea (Exod. 14:15–22), bringing water from a rock (Exod. 17:1–7), and more. Other examples of Old Testament nature miracles include Israel's crossing the Jordan River (Josh. 3:9–17), Elijah causing a drought for three and a half years and parting the Jordan River (1 Kings 17:1; 2 Kings 2:8), Elisha healing the water and filling the valley with water (2 Kings 2:21; 3:17), and more. In the New Testament, there are fewer instances of humans mediating God's power of nature since the Gospels only give us details about the miracles of Jesus and not the disciples. In Acts, we're told that Paul and the other apostles did many "signs and wonders" (5:12) without too many specific accounts and details. The one recorded account of Paul exercising authority over nature is when a venomous snake bit him on the Island of Malta in Acts 28:1–6. The island people witnessed the bite and waited for him to swell up or drop dead (v. 6), but he simply shook the snake into the fire and remained unharmed (v. 5).

There are limited accounts of demonic authority over nature, most of which aren't mediated by people. For example, God gives Satan permission to attack Job, which includes fire from heaven (Job 1:16) and a powerful wind (v. 19). Even though this is not an example of magic, this is extremely important in our understanding of Satan's limitations since he clearly has to have God's permission to act. There are few examples of demons using their limited authority over nature through a human mediator. Yet again we come back to Pharaoh's magicians. They are able to mimic three miracles before their power is restrained: turning their staffs to snakes (Exod. 7:11), turning water to blood (7:22), and bringing frogs onto the land (8:7). In light of Job 1, we should understand their magic to succeed through the power of Satan and by the will of God. It's because of their limited success, that God's power is shown to be vastly greater, and God himself to be the ultimate authority over nature.

Supernatural gifting: Special gifting for an individual usually requires spiritual attachment to or possession of the body. Both the Old and New Testaments contain divine supernatural examples of this. Most notably was Samson's selection as a Nazarite who would save the Israelites from the Philistines (Judg. 13:5). His supernatural power wasn't a random occurrence but came when the Holy Spirit rushed upon him. Unlike prophets such as Elijah or Elisha who performed supernatural feats of various kinds and with fewer restrictions, Samson was gifted with only one ability—superstrength. Men like Joseph (Gen. 40–41) and Daniel (Dan. 2; 4; 5) appeared to be especially gifted with an ability to interpret dreams and visions. Most of the Old Testament prophets were only gifted with prophesy with only small deviations such as Isaiah giving Hezekiah a fig paste for healing (2 Kings 20:1–7). In the New Testament, the apostles in Acts were gifted by the indwelling of the Holy Spirit as well as a divine commission from God to spread the gospel and plant churches. Although their power was not as limited as Samson's, they still didn't have the scope of power Elijah and Elisha had. They were usually limited to supernatural feats such as healing, casting out demons, and raising people from the dead (with some exceptions such as Philip's teleportation in Acts 8:39).

Special gifting from demons was possibly limited to types of divining in Scripture. It's possible there were other common occult "occupations" in the ancient world, but the Bible doesn't describe these in detail. Demonic entities more freely give the appearance of power to anyone who asks for it since it feeds Satan's larger goal of distracting away from the truth. The Bible gives repeated warnings against divination, mediums, and spiritists because they were commonly found among their polytheistic neighbors (Deut. 18:9–11; Lev. 19:31; 20:6; Isa. 8:19). We see this with Pharaoh's magicians (Exod. 7), the Babylonian wise men (Dan. 2), and Egypt's mediums and spiritists (Isa. 19:3). These people were likely selected because they showed a particular aptitude for wisdom and divination. In the modern occult, it's commonly believed that certain people are "gifted" to be light workers, psychic mediums, and healers. When they have such seemingly prophetic words of special gifting spoken over them, the label usually becomes part of their identity as does the familiar spirit that attaches to them. Although the demonic supernaturalism they perform and experience isn't an illusion, their perceived identity as a particularly gifted light worker is almost entirely a deception. However, it's possible that natural aptitudes may be exploited by demons for specific purposes and occupations.

Concluding Thoughts

From the distinctions found within the mirrored magic categories, we're often able to discern the potential source of the magic through context. As we begin to understand where God has limited Satan's power, it becomes easier to see his superior power and authority over nature as well as demonic forces.

Chapter 6

Ends and Means

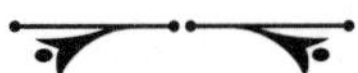

Essential contextual clues in each passage of Scripture not only tell us where the power is coming from but indicate the end goal, the heart posture of the mediator, the relational setting, and the methodology. In this chapter, we'll use questions two through five to help us discern if the scriptural event more closely resembles demonic or divine supernaturalism in these other categories. I placed these in order of clarity and importance, so if there's no clear answer to one of them, simply move on to the next in descending order.

1. **What is the source of the magic?**
   Is it demonic or divine?
2. **What is the goal of the magic user?**
   Does the user desire the glorification of God (as the source) or of themselves? Do they love others or love themselves?
3. **What is the heart posture of the magic user?**
   Is the user humble or proud before God, the source?

4. **What is the setting of the magic?**
   Is the relational setting upside-down or right-side up? Are vulnerable people honored or exploited?
5. **What magical methodology is used?**
   Is the method dependent on or demanding of the source?

A Divine Telos

Question 2: What is the goal of the magic user? Do they desire glorification of God (as the source) or of themselves? Do they love others or love themselves?

The first and most important contextual clue we need in order to determine demonic or divine supernaturalism is the telos or long-term goal of the magic user. A telos is what Aristotle calls the "final cause" or the ultimate goal of someone's life.[1] The Westminster Shorter Catechism says, "Man's chief end is to glorify God and to enjoy him forever."[2] The glory of God and human joy are the telos of all people everywhere. Divine supernaturalism can have nearer goals than this, such as loving others, but when we look closer at Scripture, the telos usually appears as well. With divine supernaturalism, the long-term goal is to glorify God. With demonic supernaturalism, the long-term goal is self-glorification or self-aggrandizement.

There will be times when the short-term goals of both are very similar if not the same. In fact, many occultists testify to wanting to help others and be a "lightworker" or a "white witch" in a dark world. They hope to usher in a new age of enlightenment for all people and end pain and suffering forever.[3] Yet they're blind to their own pride and desire to be more enlightened than those around them. It's also possible for God to work through sinful humans with imperfect goals of their own. It's important to look at the full scope of the narrative and character arc to determine the telos for supernaturalism in fiction. There will also be times when only God's goals are reflective of divine supernaturalism and the mediating character is unaware of or opposed to his goals.

In fiction, the ultimate telos isn't always clear. The particular magic system or world-building involved may make it hard to discern what the ultimate goal is. It's not as clear as identifying whether the author is Christian. Often secular fiction won't explicitly reflect the ultimate telos of glorifying God, but neither are they glorifying the self. When this happens, they're usually prioritizing a secondary goal of loving others. This primary and secondary goal structure is seen in Matthew 22:36–39: "'Teacher, which command in the law is the greatest?' He said to him, 'Love the Lord your God with all your heart, with all your soul, and with all your mind. This is the greatest and most important command. The second is like it: Love your neighbor as yourself.'"

Christ set the standard for what it means to love others when he died on the cross for our sins. By definition, love is *selfless*, not *selfish*. When a secular work of fiction depicts loving self-sacrifice through common grace, that goal can still be considered a reflection of divine supernaturalism even if it fails to recognize our ultimate telos of glorifying God. Likewise, demonic supernaturalism is reflected in sacrificing or exploiting others for the benefit of the individual.

Let's look at two biblical narratives where the telos of God-glorifying supernaturalism is clear. In Exodus 7:5, God makes his goals for the plagues apparent when he tells Moses and Aaron, "The

Egyptians will know that I am the LORD when I stretch out my hand against Egypt and bring out the Israelites from among them." More striking is God's stated reason for hardening Pharaoh's heart after the Israelites had fled Egypt: "I will harden Pharaoh's heart so that he will pursue them. Then I will receive glory by means of Pharaoh and all his army, and the Egyptians will know that I am the LORD" (Exod. 14:4a). Because of this display of power and authority over men and nature, God will be glorified in Egypt and then the world. Moses, as the mediator of God's power, echoes this after the second plague in Exodus 8:10 when speaking to Pharaoh: "As you have said, so that you may know there is no one like the LORD our God." In this account, both God and Moses are aware of the long-term goal from the beginning. This is a beautiful picture of overt glorification of God within divine supernaturalism.

The same passage includes an example of demonic supernaturalism where the long-term goal is self-glorification. Although the magicians are the ones performing magic, the emphasis in the passage is on Pharaoh. We aren't given too much information about the Egyptians' goals during the plagues other than the repeated statement that Pharaoh hardened his heart and refused to let God's people go. Yet after the Israelites had left, they regret losing their slaves so much that they go after them. "When the king of Egypt was told that the people had fled, Pharaoh and his officials changed their minds about the people and said, 'What have we done? We have released Israel from serving us'" (v. 5). Pharaoh is obviously stubborn, prideful, and cruel. But what are his goals? Historically, pharaohs were considered gods—chosen as a divine mediator between their gods and the people. The Egyptians would force their slaves to build cities in honor of Pharaoh (1:11). Their religious occult practices also gave them—and Pharaoh, in particular—a sense of power and identity as an absolute authority. The Satanic element of their faith and Pharaoh's position specifically are clear in the serpentine headdress traditionally worn by Egypt's kings.

In losing the battle between the magicians and Moses, a mere Hebrew shepherd, Pharaoh would have been humiliated. With each subsequent plague and the death of Egypt's firstborns, Pharaoh was continually put to shame by this other more powerful God. His desperate attempt to hold onto his slaves wasn't simply about loss of convenience and labor; it was about his identity as a god to his people. Although Yahweh thwarted the king's plans easily, we can still recognize Pharaoh's telos as self-glorification and a desperate attempt to maintain his deification.

The second example is found in Numbers 22–24 where Moab's king, Balak, attempts to hire Balaam, a pagan diviner, to curse Israel. Instead, Balaam blesses them through a divine prophetic word. The goals of Balak and God are clear from the text. Balak wants Israel cursed because they're more numerous and could pose a threat. His goals are selfish in nature, and he likely wants to be the largest and most powerful nation. God, on the other hand, forces Balaam to bless the Israelites so that everyone will see that Yahweh is more powerful than other gods: "It will now be said about Jacob and Israel, 'What great things God has done!'" (23:23).

Balaam is a confusing figure because it's difficult to tell who's side he's on. In the beginning of the story, Balak sends a message to Balaam saying, "For I know that those you bless are blessed and those you curse are cursed" (22:6). As a pagan diviner, Balaam has a reputation for successfully blessing and cursing, likely for money (v. 7) and by the power of demons since God's power is not for hire (Acts 8:18–23). Yet Balaam also seems to have some knowledge of God since he says, "If Balak were to give me his house full of silver and gold, I could not go against the command of the Lord my God to do anything small or great" (Num. 22:18). This is a strange statement and, at first sight, seems to imply Balaam might worship Yahweh and desire his will. There is a way in which Balaam recognizes the power and authority of Israel's God, but it isn't a wholehearted devotion or outright worship. His split devotion is initially clear when he goes at Balak's summons. Although he's incapable of saying anything other than what God tells him to say, we learn from Numbers 31:16 that it was Balaam who had advised the Moabites and Midianites to prostitute themselves among the Israelites and invite them to offer sacrifices to Baal (25:1–3). This resulted in the deaths of twenty-four thousand Israelites (v. 9). If there's any lingering doubt in Balaam's selfish goals of monetary gain, the New Testament confirms this in Jude 11 and 2 Peter 2: "They have gone astray by abandoning the straight path and have followed the path of Balaam, the son of Bosor, who loved the wages of wickedness" (v. 15). Despite Balaam's sin and the prostitution with Baal of Peor, God's ultimate goal was accomplished. He was glorified among the nations, and Israel was blessed instead of cursed.

Magical Humility

Question 3: What is the heart posture of the magic user? Is the user humble or proud before God, the source?

There's a lot of "heart" talk throughout the Bible. It's a thread we can trace from Genesis to Revelation—from Cain and Abel (Gen. 4:1–16) to Laodicea (Rev. 3:14–20). The most well-known heart passage in the Bible is the Sermon on the Mount in Matthew 5–7. There are only three actual uses of the word *heart* (*kardia*) in this sermon (5:8, 28; 6:21). Yet when we look at the subtext of the passage as a whole, every piece of it is about the heart: those who are humble, meek, and pure in heart will be blessed and comforted (5:3–12); the root of murder is a heart of anger against a brother (vv. 21–26); the root of adultery is a heart full of lust (vv. 27–30); a heartfelt prayer is done in secret and not for the praises of men (6:5–8); and those who eagerly seek the Lord from their heart will find him (7:7–12). Jesus taught the people that their desires, inner thought life, and posture toward God and others determines the presence or absence of virtue (fruit of the Spirit) or vice. The heart is what determines salvation (5:8). In the Old Testament, Samuel goes in search of Israel's next king after God rejects Saul, and he's tempted to assume God will choose David's older, larger brother to be king. "But the LORD said to Samuel, 'Do not look at his appearance or his stature because I have rejected him. Humans do not see what the LORD sees, for humans see what is visible, but the LORD sees the heart'" (1 Sam. 16:7).

In his book *Gentle and Lowly*, Dane Ortlund says of Christ: "But the dominant note left ringing in our ears after reading the Gospels, the most vivid and arresting element of the portrait, is the way the Holy Son of God moves toward, touches, heals, embraces, and forgives those who least deserve it yet truly desire it."[4] It isn't the degree of sin a person has that determines whether God will use them—it's their genuine desire for God and for his forgiveness; it's the heart of repentance to change even when we feel as though we're stuck in a deep, dark pit and can't get out. Men and women with an overabundance of sin and brokenness are frequently chosen by God as his instruments—and often to mediate divine supernaturalism. They are "still sinners" (Rom. 5:8), sometimes committing downright evil acts, but God chooses them in the midst of their sin and forgives them because they desire him and his forgiveness with genuine humility. The heart posture that matters most is not the lack of sin but the presence of faith, love of God, and a humility that produces repentance.

As we've already discussed, those who use the power of demons to control and manifest the world around them desire to "be like God" (Gen. 3:5). They have the heart of idolatrous Israel that surfaces in Judges 21:25 (ESV): "In those days there was no king in Israel. Everyone did what was right in his own eyes." Instead of humbling themselves before God, they prop themselves up as equal to him. The Egyptians and Simon the magician are good examples of this.

> "Now I know that the LORD is greater than all gods, because he did wonders when the Egyptians acted arrogantly against Israel." (Exod. 18:11)

> A man named Simon had previously practiced sorcery in that city and amazed the Samaritan people, while claiming to be somebody great. They all paid attention to him, from the least of them to the greatest, and they said, "This man is called the Great Power of God." (Acts 8:9–10)

Human mediators of demonic supernaturalism not only want control of their own life but also to uncover secret knowledge not meant for them—as Adam and Eve sought to do by eating the fruit in Genesis 3. Steven Bancarz says that in the New Age movement, "God and man are ontologically equivalent."[5] This can be masked initially by New Age beliefs drawn from Buddhism where people attempt to detach from their individual self in order to liberate their ego. From this comes the vice of self-deprecation and dehumanization, which is another distortion of humility. It may even bring a sense of enlightenment above others, which eventually increases the ego. This is also why John the Baptist and Jesus refer to the self-righteous Pharisees as a "brood of vipers" (Matt. 3:7; 12:34). These forms of pride are the heart of demonic supernaturalism and indicate evil forms of magic in literature.

We see this in the Bible when Pharaoh's magicians assume they can replicate God's plagues—that they're equally capable. Yet the power of their demons could only go so far. When the third plague of gnats arrived, they were forced to admit: "This is the finger of God" (Exod. 8:19). The magicians began in a place of pride before God repeatedly humbled them with each new divine supernatural act. Yet this kind of humbling wasn't one that produced genuine repentance in the magicians or Pharaoh (Exod. 8:19; 18:11). Even though the magicians are at least humble enough to admit the miracles are "the finger of God," which implies they understand he's more powerful than their gods, they don't immediately desist in attempting to mimic the plagues and acting on Pharaoh's orders. This demonstrates their lack of repentance.

God's law not only forbids the practice of sorcery but also seeking anyone who practices it (Deut. 18:10–12; Lev. 20:6). When Saul visited the medium at En-dor in 1 Samuel 28, the evil he's committing can't be overstated. He first gives the appearance of humility by seeking the Lord's counsel through dreams, Urim and Thummim, and the prophets. But when God remains silent, Saul demands an answer—secret knowledge of the future—God hid from him by calling on the late Samuel through a medium. In fact, he swears to her that "as surely as [Yahweh] lives, no punishment will come to you from this" (v. 10). Saul first decides he will force God to answer him, and then he makes this oath to the medium on

God's behalf. He does all of this with full knowledge that what he's doing goes against the law of Moses. Saul's pride and lack of repentance came before his fall (Prov. 16:18), since he died in battle the next day. Like Hebrews says of Esau, Saul was also "rejected, even though he sought it with tears, because he didn't find any opportunity for repentance" (Heb. 12:17).

Pride is not only the heart and motive of someone involved in the occult; it also reveals their goals. They elevate themselves before God in order to be "like him" and have the knowledge he has (Gen. 3:5). This is an idolatry that worships the self as god. Idol worship displays a heart of pride by replacing God and his perfect will and provision with ourselves or something of our own creation that we believe will do our bidding and obey our will. John Piper says this well:

> Psalm 96:5: "For all the gods of the peoples are worthless idols, but the LORD made the heavens." In other words, one of the problems with idols is that they contradict the transcendent nature of God as Creator. Any representation of God made with human hands leads to the misunderstanding of God's transcendence. It gives the impression, if not the direct assertion, that God is somehow in our power—we can carve him, or paint him, or put him in our pocket or on our shelf, or carry him on a cart. And so the psalmist says, "No! The Lord made the heavens." In other words, he's absolutely transcendent, and you can't carve him or control him in any way.[6]

We can't be God or demand anything of him. Even when pagans carve idols thinking they can control their gods, the demons give the impression of being within their power or being appeased. When we reject God's transcendent wisdom and authority over our life and put either ourselves or an idol in his place, our heart is full of nothing but hubris. Yet how do we resist Satan's temptation of pride? James 4:6–10 reinforces the need to have genuine, humble repentance: "But he gives greater grace. Therefore he says: God resists the proud but gives grace to the humble. Therefore, submit to God. Resist the devil, and he will flee from you. Draw near to God, and he will draw near to you. Cleanse your hands, sinners, and purify your hearts, you double-minded. Be miserable and mourn and weep. Let your laughter be turned to mourning and your joy to gloom. Humble yourselves before the Lord, and he will exalt you."

If pride dictates the heart of those who seek demonic power, then a heart of humility describes someone empowered by and dependent on the Holy Spirit. Where demons are attempting to draw attention away from God, the humble point to God and glorify his name among the nations (Eph. 1:4–6; Isa. 48:9–11; Rom. 9:17). In alignment with Christ's upside-down kingdom, James 4:10 says, "Humble yourselves before the Lord, and he will exalt you."

Two of the clearest narratives that show the uncommonly humble heart posture of someone given supernatural power and immense political prestige are Joseph in Genesis 37–50 and Daniel (also known as Belteshazzar) in the book of Daniel. Both of them understand they're able to interpret dreams by the power of God alone.

> Pharaoh said to Joseph, "I have had a dream, and no one can interpret it. But I have heard it said about you that you can hear a dream and interpret it." "I am not able to," Joseph answered Pharaoh. "It is God who will give Pharaoh a favorable answer." (Gen. 41:15–16)

> The king said in reply to Daniel, whose name was Belteshazzar, "Are you able to tell me the dream I had and its interpretation?" Daniel answered the king, "No wise man, medium, magician, or diviner is able to make known to the king the mystery he asked about. But there is a God in heaven who reveals mysteries, and he has let King Nebuchadnezzar know what will happen in the last days. (Dan. 2:26–28a)

A far more confusing figure is Samson in Judges 13–16. The Bible is crystal clear that Samson's supernatural strength comes from God since the text says the Spirit of the Lord rushed upon him on three occasions (Judg. 14:6, 19; 15:14). Even though the text doesn't explicitly use that exact phrase every time he uses his strength, the divine source is still implied since Samson loses his power when Delilah cuts his hair in defiance of his Nazarite vows. Although the cutting of his hair is the most infamous part of his story, it's only one of many moments of pride and disobedience. In fact, Samson defied his Nazarite vows on numerous occasions.[7] Most notably was his total disregard for touching the carcasses of unclean animals (Lev. 11:24–28) when he took honey from a lion carcass (Judg. 14:6) and used the fresh jawbone of a donkey to kill one thousand Philistines (15:15). Then after killing the Philistines,

Samson composed a poem that boasts of his own victory and doesn't mention God at all (15:16).

This is one of those moments in which an imperfect human agent of divine supernaturalism is unaware of God's greater goals. Samson is not a hero worth imitating. He's selfish, defiant, prideful, and not very intelligent. He's more of a cautionary tale of someone who was given great power and chose to steward it for personal gain. Yet God uses him despite his sin. When Samson grabbed the jawbone of a donkey—an unclean animal—the Spirit of the Lord rushed upon him anyway. When he declared his own victory instead of God's after killing the Philistines, God didn't leave him. It wasn't until his hair was cut in the ultimate act of defiance against God's commands and his Nazarite vows that his strength left him. When Samson acted out of personal revenge instead of a desire for God's glory, God was still glorified among the nations. Samson's God was still seen as greater and more powerful than the god of the Philistines—Israel's oppressors.

Jon Bloom describes the account of Samson in his book, *Things Not Seen*, as reading "the story of a narcissistic superhero whose pride destroys him in the end."[8] Still, Samson is listed in the hall of faith in Hebrews 11:32. His story has one element of faith and humility. Bloom goes on to say that "[Samson] believed that God would bless his gift of strength when Samson needed it. In that sense, every mighty act [Samson] ever did was by faith. And God used him. . . . The tragedy of [Samson's] life is that he ended up thinking more highly of himself than God."[9]

Although Samson misused his blessing from God to satisfy his own ego, he knew his power came from God and not himself. And that is the single thread of humility in the fabric of his life, which is likely the reason he was included in the hall of faith. He knew this so well that at the end he pleaded with God for his strength to return to him so he might defeat the oppressive Philistines.

> He called out to the LORD, "Lord GOD, please remember me. Strengthen me, God, just once more. With one act of vengeance, let me pay back the Philistines for my two eyes." Samson took hold of the two middle pillars supporting the temple and leaned against them, one on his right hand and the other on his left. Samson said, "Let me die with the Philistines." He pushed with all his might, and the temple fell on the leaders and all the people in it. And those he killed at his death were more than those he had killed in his life. (Judg. 16:28–30)

When he'd previously killed the Philistines, his heart was full of pride, and his goals were personal revenge. In the end, he showed his humility before God in a prayer of petition and the giving of his own life. Yet his goals were still the same—vengeance on his enemies for how they'd blinded him. In his life and death, we see the truth of Proverbs 16:18: "Pride comes before destruction, and an arrogant spirit before a fall." Samson may not be someone to imitate, but his story is still inspiring. It should encourage us when we see God using someone so sinful. When we begin to understand how gracious God is to use us in our weakness, our response shouldn't be like Samson's but, instead, like David's when he gazed upon the beauty of God's creation: "What is man that you are mindful of him, and the son of man that you care for him?" (Ps. 8:4 ESV). In the end, God was glorified. In crushing the idol worshippers in their own temple, God fulfilled his promise to bless those who bless

Israel and curse those who curse them. Before the Philistines and their god, Yahweh declared himself superior.

Upside-Down Magic

Question 4: What is the setting of the magic? Is the relational setting upside-down or right-side up? Are vulnerable people honored or exploited?

The question of relational setting is fourth in line because it's not always evident or overtly present. Jesus states this upside-down structure simply in Matthew 20:16: "So the last will be first, and the first last." While the upside-down kingdom can be traced throughout Scripture, there are times when God also has pity on people in high places as well as low. For example, Elisha healed Namaan of leprosy, a wealthy ruler who attempted to pay for the prophet's services. Even if these themes aren't always present in fiction, keep in mind that a positive portrayal of exploitation of weak or vulnerable people in a story would indicate divine supernaturalism is likely not at work.

In the Sermon on the Mount, Jesus simultaneously establishes the importance of heart motives as well as Christ's upside-down kingdom. This is also a theme easily traced through the entire Bible. In the Beatitudes specifically, Jesus flips the Israelites' worldly perspective on its head when he begins with, "Blessed are the poor in spirit, for the kingdom of heaven is theirs" (Matt. 5:3). The Israelites had misinterpreted verses such as Proverbs 11:18, "The wicked person earns an empty wage, but the one who sows righteousness, a true reward." Paul even repeats this idea in Galatians 6:7: "For whatever a person sows he will also reap." This kind of language was often used by the Jews to prop up a prosperity ethos.

This "retribution principle"—the idea of reaping what you sow—is scattered throughout the Old Testament. It was meant to remind the Israelites that God is just and will teach them that actions have consequences. Yet it was often twisted into something resembling Job's friends who believed his suffering must mean he'd greatly sinned (Job 4:6–8). They assumed if God was just and sovereign over suffering, then any amount of suffering was a direct correlation to one's own sin, whereas wealth or prestige was a sign of God's favor. We see this in the New Testament when the disciples ask Jesus if a man was born blind because of his own sin or that of his parents (John 9:1–3). It may have also been natural for someone like Samson to assume too much about his own righteousness since God chose him as a vessel for such unique power and acts of judgment. The Pharisees certainly would have assumed God favored them based on this misunderstanding, and in turn, likely used their poor theology to fuel their authoritarianism. A modern version of this is the prosperity gospel—a works-based system for gaining worldly wealth, health, and success. So when Jesus presents them with a kingdom where the "last will be first, and the first last" (Matt. 20:16), the concept is groundbreaking. Somehow they overlooked passages such as Psalm 113:5–9a: "Who is like the Lord our God—the one enthroned on high, who stoops down to look on the heavens and the earth? He raises the poor from the dust and lifts the needy from the trash heap in order to seat them with nobles—with the nobles of his people. He gives the childless woman a household, making her the joyful mother of children."

Scripture instructs us on how to behave in this social structure. Operating within the upside-down kingdom requires great humility since we are to do "nothing out of selfish ambition or conceit, but in humility consider others as more important than yourselves"

(Phil. 2:3). And as James 4:10 says, "Humble yourselves before the Lord, and he will exalt you." We aren't meant to put ourselves first because the goal is to serve, not to be served—although this is not meant as a command to permit abuse or being taken advantage of.

In Luke 14:7–11, Jesus tells a parable about a banquet, teaching the gathered Pharisees they shouldn't sit at the head of the table in case someone more distinguished comes and they're forced to take the lowest seat. Instead, they should sit in the lowest place so the person who invited them may come and ask them to move higher. "For everyone who exalts himself will be humbled, and the one who humbles himself will be exalted" (v. 11). This story isn't meant to create a false sense of humility in us. We aren't taking the lowest proverbial seat *so that* we can be asked to move higher. The language of exaltation is there to show that God regards honor as a virtue and desires to honor his children whom he loves. It's genuine humility that's honorable, not false modesty that feels entitled to being honored by God.

Satan works with opposite, although deceptive, tactics. He may have used Scripture to tempt Jesus in Luke 4:1–13, but he twisted it to fit his purposes. Like the ultimate narcissist, Satan is able to convince the weak and vulnerable people of the world that he cares for them and they should attempt to be "good people." He may even "love bomb" them or shower them with material or supernatural blessings for a time. This kind of deception is like a man giving candy to children out of an unmarked van just hoping they'll be swayed to step inside just as the White Witch in Narnia did with Edmund. In the end, this serves Satan's own goals of drawing them away from Christ and building up their pride.

What does all this mean for demonic and divine supernaturalism? The upside-down kingdom is the relational *setting* in which demonic and divine supernatural power operates. Satan will often choose powerful people to work through such as politicians, celebrities, or televangelists. He also targets weak people in order to promise riches and healing and then manipulate or discard them when he sees fit. Meanwhile, God doesn't choose the strongest, smartest, or most righteous people to display his supernatural power and glory.

> Instead, God has chosen what is foolish in the world to shame the wise, and God has chosen what is weak in the world to shame the strong. God has chosen what is insignificant and despised in the world—what is viewed as nothing—to bring to nothing what is viewed as something, so that no one may boast in his presence. It is from him that you are in Christ Jesus, who became wisdom from God for us—our righteousness, sanctification, and redemption—in order that, as it is written: Let the one who boasts, boast in the Lord. (1 Cor. 1:27–31)

Although we often cringe and judge the great sins recorded in Scripture, it's that imperfection that emphasizes the upside-down kingdom. God chose us not because we're righteous but because he is and we are dependent on him (2 Cor. 12:9). And lest we are tempted to think God is a narcissist in the sky, always seeking what's best for him as he seeks his own glory, we must remember how deeply he loves us. So much so that he gave his only Son to die for us while we were still weak and vulnerable sinners (Rom. 5:8). "He protects his flock like a shepherd; he gathers the lambs in his arms and carries them in the fold of his garment. He gently leads those that are nursing. . . . He gives strength to the faint and strengthens the powerless. Youths may become faint and weary, and young men stumble and fall, but those who trust in the LORD will renew their strength; they will soar on wings like eagles; they will run and not become weary, they will walk and not faint" (Isa. 40:11, 29–31).

We see this time and time again in Scripture. When God chose Moses, he was unwilling and declared himself unfit to go to Pharaoh: "But Moses replied to the LORD, 'Please, Lord, I have never been eloquent—either in the past or recently or since you have been speaking to your servant—because my mouth and my tongue are sluggish.' The LORD said to him, 'Who placed a mouth on humans? Who makes a person mute or deaf, seeing or blind? Is it not I, the LORD? Now go! I will help you speak and I will teach you what to say'" (Exod. 4:10–12).

In the Old Testament, God chose humble men like Elisha as he was plowing his fields (1 Kings 19:19) to mediate immense supernatural power—double that of his mentor, Elijah (2 Kings 2:9).* God used Jonah, a reluctant and disobedient prophet, to deliver his message of repentance and salvation to Nineveh. In Daniel 4, King Nebuchadnezzar thought of himself as a god, and the Lord humbled him by making the king like a beast of the field for seven years. In the New Testament, Jesus often healed and cast demons out of the poorest and most vulnerable people in the community. Regardless of social standing or even cleanliness, Jesus fed the five thousand with loaves and fish (Matt. 14:13–21). He loved children and women, who were not highly valued in first-century society (Matt. 19:14; John 11).

Yet for Satan, any appearance of caring for the weak and vulnerable is a ruse and manipulation. The narcissistic-style "love

* Both Elisha and Elijah often ministered to widows and the poor (1 Kings 17:9–24; 2 Kings 4:1–7, 18–37).

bombing" people receive when first entering into a relationship with demons gives a false impression of security. Then after the honeymoon phase, things get very dark. Deuteronomy 18:9–14 gives the Israelites instructions on which foreign occult practices are against his law.

> When you enter the land the Lord your God is giving you, do not imitate the detestable customs of those nations. No one among you is to sacrifice his son or daughter in the fire, practice divination, tell fortunes, interpret omens, practice sorcery, cast spells, consult a medium or a spiritist, or inquire of the dead. Everyone who does these acts is detestable to the Lord, and the Lord your God is driving out the nations before you because of these detestable acts. You must be blameless before the Lord your God. Though these nations you are about to drive out listen to fortune-tellers and diviners, the Lord your God has not permitted you to do this.

We often miss the connection between occult practices like these in Deuteronomy and sacrificing a son or daughter in the fire without a deeper understanding of the occult and demonology. When our materialism sneaks in, we see this as a sign these people were uncivilized and barbaric. Why else would they think up something so evil as sacrificing a child to a god that doesn't exist? But that isn't what's happening here. Their gods are demons who can speak to them directly or through visions and dreams.

To seek payment for more power or material blessings or to appease their anger, the demons would sometimes require human blood sacrifices. This is likely why the prophets of Baal cut themselves when attempting to call down fire from heaven in 1 Kings 18:28. But the greater abomination was the murder of children (Deut. 12:29–32) since they were weak, vulnerable, and defenseless.

Our God sent his only Son to bleed and die for the sins of the world. He is the God who lays down his life for sinners like us so his righteous wrath and judgment against evil might be fully satisfied. Yet these pagan gods demanded exactly the opposite—that children should die to appease them and their unrighteous wrath. This makes the cultural implications of Abraham's near sacrifice of Isaac staggering. God was not only testing his faith but saying, "I am not like the gods of your neighbors. I am holy."

Methods of Magic

Question 5: What magical methodology is used? Is the method dependent or demanding of the source?

We are so often distracted by the method of supernaturalism that we forget the point of it all—the telos of glorifying God. For example, the methods of divine supernaturalism are things such as prayer, healing touch, or casting lots. The methods of demonic supernaturalism are things like casting spells, astrological stargazing, or interpreting omens. The list of occult practices in Deuteronomy 18:10–11 (the Mosaic Law) are some of the methods God forbids, but it isn't meant to be exhaustive. It's a list that implies God's people shouldn't do *any* occult-like things *because they reveal a heart of idolatry*. In this section, we're going to discuss demonic and divine supernatural methodology in general but also focus on how to properly prioritize methods behind the telos.

Often former occultists begin reading the Bible, and God brings them to Deuteronomy 18 where they find their actions are against God's law. They are shocked much like the Israelites when they read the law again after having lost it for many years in 2 Kings 22–23. When the words of the book were read to King Josiah, "he tore his clothes. . . . 'For great is the LORD's wrath that is kindled against us because our ancestors have not obeyed the words of this book in order to do everything written about us'" (2 Kings 22:11, 13). Then the king and his officials removed the idols from God's temple and tore down all the high places where sacrifices were made to foreign gods. It's a shocking thing to learn of your own sin, but how could they have known they were wrong if God hadn't told them in the Torah—the Law? Once they knew, the tearing down of the high places was a symbol of what really mattered—that their desire was for the Lord alone. Once sin is revealed by the law, God gives grace for people to turn their hearts away from idolatry and put their faith in him alone.

It's possible to swap the law and faith in order of priority and importance and mistake works of the law as the end goal rather than the means. We are not justified or made righteous by works of the law but "by grace through faith" (Eph. 2:8). Just as our heads are turned toward obeying God's law as the end (telos) rather than the means (methods) of grace to show our need of grace, so our heads have been turned to focus on the method of supernaturalism (i.e., prophecy, casting lots, etc.) before seeing its goal of faith and the glorification of God.

Methods and works are still important, and we should only use specific, God-ordained means to worship and pray. The methodology just isn't *primary*. A person's desires, intent, and goals are what matter most and what form the core distinctions between demonic and divine supernaturalism. When we focus primarily on outward actions of "the law" as the core of a faith-filled Christian life, we'll be led astray. Just as God's law reveals sin, so does using demonic or divine supernaturalism reveal the heart of the human agent like a "condemning mirror."[10] We may be able to outwardly identify a Christian by what they do—by their fruit and works, but we can't define a Christian's identity without describing how a heart that was once stone has become a heart of flesh through their faith in Christ Jesus as Lord. The same is true for those in the occult or evil forms of literary magic. An occultist is not simply someone who uses crystals and astrological signs. Just as Simon the magician in Acts 8 claimed to be "somebody great" (v. 9) the occultist is an idolater who desires to control the world around them as though they are divine. It's the use of the unlawful methods that reveals a heart of pride and rebellion against God.

For so long, Christians have been defining magic and miracles exclusively by methodology without looking at the heart. Not only does this miss the core distinctives, but it also misleads us into thinking we can understand all that entails demonic supernaturalism simply by making a list of the methods like tarot cards, crystals, Ouija boards, and more. But there's simply no way to find and label every single occult and pagan modality. There are far too many of them. Sometimes occult practices involve rituals that mimic aspects of Old Testament Judaism such as casting lots and Urim and Thummim. Yet that isn't always the case. Satan can use religious rituals and insist that his followers ascribe to a specific set of rules such as speaking specific words used to cast spells or a set of instructions for charging moon water. But that is far from consistent. When we pull back and look at the scope of paganism, the methods used have little to no overarching pattern or set of rules.

The only patterns are in the motives and goals as discussed above. Satan will use *any* means or methods necessary to draw someone away from Christ, both those that have the appearance of morality and immorality.

Just like demonic supernaturalism, divine supernatural events are also unpredictable and widely varied. Jesus healed many people, but every instance is different from the last. He healed with a word (Matt. 8:5–13), rubbed spit and mud on someone's eyes (John 9:1–12), used touch to heal (Mark 3:9–10), and released power through his clothing (Mark 5:25–34). Moses brought water from a rock by striking it with his staff (Exod. 17:6), and later, God told him and Aaron to speak to the rock instead. The brothers were disciplined when Moses struck the second rock (Num. 20:6–13).

In these examples, no set pattern or rule produces specific results. Yet the stories of Moses bringing water from rocks may imply the reason for such variations. God first instructs him to strike the rock and then later tells him to speak to the rock. When Moses disobeys by striking the second rock, God uses strong language to rebuke him: "Because you did not trust me to demonstrate my holiness in the sight of the Israelites, you will not bring this assembly into the land I have given them" (v. 12). Because of this one mistake, Moses and Aaron wouldn't be allowed to see the promised land.

What was the purpose of giving them new instructions rather than the same ones as before? God was testing them. Would they have faith and obey his exact instructions in order to demonstrate God's holiness before the people? Or would they assume they knew better and procure water from the rock their own way? This is another example of pride versus humility in supernaturalism.

Unfortunately, they took the latter path and disobeyed God's instructions. Yet in his great mercy, God permitted the water to come regardless of Moses's and Aaron's sin, presumably because the people needed it. So the power of the act was not in ritual, rules, or Moses's authority but in God's mercy and power.

If methodology is so varied and not the primary distinction, then surely "Christian" tarot cards and Holy Spirit Ouija boards would be okay to use, right? Yet most of us know that there's something deeply wrong with those even if we can't articulate the reasons. People who use those kinds of syncretistic tools to pray, manifest, or attract what they desire are guilty of the same sins as the Colossians when they practiced asceticism and worshipped angels (Col. 2:16–19). They're drinking "the cup of the Lord and the cup of demons" (1 Cor. 10:21). Ignoring God's will and instructions through their methods, they still call themselves Christians with their mouths. They think they're worshipping God when they're actually engaging with demons to satisfy their wills rather than God's.

These methods are *demanding* of God, as though saying, "You *will* give me an answer!" Instead, God desires us to be *dependent* on him, which is why our primary method of obtaining information from him is through reading Scripture, prayer, and discerning the leading of the Holy Spirit. In fact, it's likely due to the gifting of the Holy Spirit that Urim and Thummim—methods of discerning God's will—are no longer necessary. The only casting of lots by believers in the New Testament was in choosing Matthias as an apostle in Acts 1:26. Yet this occurred just before Pentecost and the indwelling of the Holy Spirit in Acts 2. After Pentecost, there are no more records in Scripture of believers casting lots.

C. S. Lewis discusses this distinction between *demanding* and *dependent* forms of supernaturalism in his own terms in a letter to Benedictine monk, Bede Griffiths:

> I think the *essential* difference between Magic and Miracle (leaving out the accidental difference that Magic is usually by means of evil spirits) is that Magic is held to work more or less automatically whereas Miracle is an answer to prayer. Now prayer is a species of request: and the essence of request, whether to God or to a human superior, is that it may or may not be granted, and the essence of faithful and humble Christian prayer is that the petitioner is willing that it [should] not be granted ('Nevertheless not as I will but as Thou wilt'). In Magic, on the other hand, I take it that the Magician expects the ceremonial to produce the result by a sort of necessity. Thus, even if there were a real "white" magic it [would] still be on a lower level than prayer, and not involving a personal relation and the affections but only a skill or technique.[11]

Lewis affirms the distinction that demonic supernaturalism "expects the ceremonial to produce the result by a sort of necessity," and divine supernaturalism is "an answer to prayer" and "a species of request."

Still, we must grapple with the fact that Urim and Thummim and casting lots were used at one time, and it's a method that appears demanding on the surface and greatly resembles pagan divination. Theologian Michael Heiser, author of *The Unseen Realm: Recovering the Supernatural Worldview of the Bible*, went so far as to say that Urim and Thummim are divination—a bold statement given that divination is always condemned in Scripture.[12] While in disguise as an Egyptian, Joseph says to his brothers, "Didn't you know that a man like me could uncover the truth by divination?" (Gen. 44:15). This isn't a depiction of Joseph's actual practices. He was merely pretending to be a pagan occultist to test his brothers. Heiser's point was likely similar to what we discussed in chapter 1 regarding the meaning of terminology being dictated primarily by context, as though "divination" could simply be "prophecy" by another name. Casting lots was another method used by the Israelites (Josh. 18:6–10) as well as pagans (Jonah 1:7). Although we don't know what the items being cast were exactly, in practice, it's equivalent to flipping a coin or rolling dice. An answer *must* appear.

On the surface, this poses another threat to the theory that the difference between magic and miracles is directly linked to methodology—even methods that seem demanding or dependent on the surface. Once again, we're forced to use context to understand what's really going on in Scripture. Although casting lots and Urim and Thummim look almost identical to pagan divination, there is still a difference. That distinction isn't in the objects used but in the heart of the people using them—further proof that the heart posture and goals of the person are primary. When God's people cast lots, they do it under the command of God only (Num. 26:55; 33:54). Urim and Thummim are even more distinct since they can only be used by the high priest in the presence of the Lord (Exod. 28:30). Even then, there is a possibility that no answer will be given. We see this in 1 Samuel 28:6 when Saul inquired of the Lord and received no answer either by dream or Urim. God remained silent, and Saul turned to the medium at En-dor to demand answers.

When we think of methods such as a word of power, incantation, or spellcasting, we tend to think of divine words of power as nonincantations and nonmagic because God draws on his own power. An incantation is a word that initiates the drawing of power from a source outside oneself. Human beings who are drawing on the power of God to do miraculous works use words such as Jesus's name or prayer as *humble supplication* instead of incantations that imply power is being *demanded* from the source. God doesn't require formal words of power outside of the use of Jesus's name because he must be asked rather than ordered. He is not at our command.

Yet how can a mere human demand anything from a demon? Why would those lying spirits comply with our requests? Demons deceive by giving the illusion of being at the command of human will and incantations. There are some branches of the occult that have ritualistic methods and incantations that seem to initiate drawing on the power of a demon, and in the simplest way that's true. The spell may produce the intended results. But this distinction between demonic and divine words of power is superficial because the demon doesn't actually submit to human commands the way occultists think they do. The appearance of being ordered around is a deception and a distraction away from truth. A demon will distract and deceive through any means, whether a word of power or otherwise.

People initiating through spells could change their mind and drop one occult system for another that doesn't use incantations yet still produces supernatural results. Even without a spell, the demon would still allow their power to be used so long as it distracts away from Christ. The entire ritual is an illusion, including the incantation itself. So much occult methodology is created like a remote control that accesses the power of a television. Yet demons are sentient, not inanimate pieces of wires and metal. They have a will of their own, giving the illusion of power to humans who, in reality, have none.

Demonic supernaturalism deceives with promises to give hurting, powerless people agency and control. In reality, we have more agency under God's authority than apart from it. Dependence on God is not a position of passivity but of activity. God hasn't called us to be ignorant, passive observers of life. In the parable of the talents in Matthew 25, the servants who invested and multiplied their master's money are honored and given more responsibility. But the servant who hid his talent in the ground and returned it without interest is condemned. The master even calls him an "evil, lazy servant" (v. 26). God gives the supplies of our work and charts the path, yet we must take an active part in walking that path. Just because we're dependent on God doesn't mean we're called to live a life of apathy or laziness.

Prayer is our most powerful and active method of supernaturalism. As I said in chapter 5, "Prayer is magic." I don't mean God is a vending machine. We can't tell him what to do, and we should expect our requests to be denied or delayed sometimes. But through active, frequent prayers of supplication, supernatural acts still occur today. James 4:2b–3: "You do not have because you do not ask. You ask and don't receive because you ask with wrong motives, so that you may spend it on your pleasures."

God may be sovereign, but his will is to *work through our work*. Just as we are created to be active culture makers, so we must also be active in prayer. We don't need to feel powerful by using tarot cards, crystals, Ouija boards, or the law of attraction because we have prayer instead. Do not be discouraged or become prayerless because God hasn't answered your prayers to end your suffering. Sometimes the answer is no in the hardest of life's moments. But keep praying—using the most active, change-inducing methodology God has gifted us.

The Condescension of God

We've looked at five discernment questions about supernaturalism. Yet there's one more characteristic of God that will help inform those questions and add some necessary nuance. What does it mean for God to meet people where they are in their occult practices and draw them to himself? In the story of the magi following the Christmas star, we see God condescending to their level to bring them out of their paganism and to the feet of Jesus.

> After Jesus was born in Bethlehem of Judea in the days of King Herod, wise men from the east arrived in Jerusalem, saying, "Where is he who has been born king of the Jews? For we saw his star at its rising and have come to worship him." . . . After hearing the king, they went on their way. And there it was—the star they had seen at its rising. It led them until it came and stopped above the place where the child was. When they saw the star, they were overwhelmed with joy. Entering the house, they saw the child with Mary his mother, and falling to their knees, they worshiped him. Then they opened their treasures and presented him with gifts: gold, frankincense, and myrrh. And being warned in a dream not to go

> back to Herod, they returned to their own country by another route. (Matt. 2:1–2, 9–12)

In Matthew 2, the "wise men from the east" or "magi" were similar to the wise men and magicians of Babylon discussed in Daniel 2.* They were pagans and presumably astrologers since they followed God's star.** Since they're referred to as *magos* in the Greek, meaning "magician" or "sorcerer," it's possible they had other occultic skills beyond astrology, but the text doesn't say. From what we know of Persian wise men, they were likely trained in many disciplines—languages, government, philosophy, and various forms of sorcery and divination. When we think back on how much God abhors demonic supernaturalism, this becomes a difficult passage to understand. Why would God lead magi to Jesus using their own pagan methodology? Wouldn't that send the wrong message about the holiness of God among the nations and enforce the wise men's occult practices?

Isaiah 47:13–14 speaks strongly against astrology: "You are worn out with your many consultations. So let the astrologers stand and save you—those who observe the stars, those who predict monthly what will happen to you. Look, they are like stubble; fire burns them. They cannot rescue themselves from the power of the flame. This is not a coal for warming themselves, or a fire to sit beside!" Astrology is no light matter before the Lord. But before we

---

* "So the king gave orders to summon the magicians, mediums, sorcerers, and Chaldeans to tell the king his dreams" (Dan. 2:2a).

** Scholars debate on how long the magi followed the star—either all the way from Persia or just from Jerusalem to Bethlehem. Either way, it's clear they placed enough significance on astrological signs to warrant traveling hundreds of miles to find Christ.

can answer the questions above, we need to understand something about the way God often chooses to interact with us.

We briefly touched on the idea that God condescends to us as his children. This is commonly referred to as "the condescension of God." Usually, the word *condescension* has a negative connotation. If someone is being condescending, we usually think they're belittling us as though we're overly juvenile or unintelligent. That isn't what's meant by the condescension of God—it's his humbling of himself. When theologians speak on this topic, they focus on the pinnacle of his condescension—the life and death of Jesus Christ. He came to earth as a human, humbling himself to the point of infancy, condescending to meet us in our flawed, broken state (Phil. 2:5–8). When he laid his life down on the cross and took on the sins of the world, he who knew no sin became sin on our behalf (2 Cor. 5:21). There is no greater act of humility and condescension that ever has or ever will take place.

Although Christ's humanity and sacrifice is the most important way God condescends, it isn't the only way. Our all-powerful, incomprehensible God communicates with us through means that we as imperfect humans can comprehend. This often involves meeting us where we are in our sin, cultural bias, limited experience, and even our false beliefs about himself and his Word. God bears "the weaknesses of those without strength," as we are likewise called to do in Romans 15:1. Yet when he speaks to us according to our experience and flawed understanding of himself, he doesn't condone our imperfections. He also doesn't change his own nature and laws to suit our preferences. Instead, he's like a father who crawls around on the floor with his children building forts, solving disagreements, and speaking with simplicity and gentleness in order to love and instruct them well.

In our pride, we often assume that God's nearness and assistance in our lives or ministries implies everything we do, everything we believe about the Bible, everything we think about Christianity is wholly true and sanctioned by him. Both theologically conservative as well as liberal believers fall into this trap of egoism and fail to acknowledge that *we are all wrong about something* for "now we see in a mirror dimly" (1 Cor. 13:12 ESV). We will all reach heaven one day and discover which aspects of our beliefs were incorrect. Here on earth, we're far more like Samson than we know. We strut around our churches or on social media assuming that because God has not withheld his Spirit and power from our lives, we are in the *only* right denomination or theological community. While Christ desires us to be a unified body, it's Satan's task to turn us against one another. For this reason, it has become commonplace to call other believers heretics and false teachers online based on tertiary disagreements. As Relient K sang in 2001, "The enemy is much ignored when we fight this Christian civil war."[13]

Yes, it's possible to be more or less right about doctrine. Yes, we should challenge one another in love and humility. And no, we shouldn't hold our convictions too loosely in an overcorrection of pride. We should still attempt to understand Scripture perfectly despite the fact that we never will. However, we need to acknowledge the condescension of God at work in the vast fabric of Christendom. God meets us all where we are, not to condone our flaws, not to change his own nature to be more like us, but to draw us to himself exactly *as he is in his Word.* Just like a patient father playing on the floor with his child, he isn't in a hurry for the child to grow or change at the snap of a finger. If only we as believers had such love and patience for one another. If only we were more ready to admit we could be wrong.

In order to fully grasp the idea of God using a star to lead astrologers to Jesus, we first have to understand that it doesn't offend God's conscience to draw a pagan to himself using something similar to the pagan's own methods. Paul echoes this mindset of humility for his own evangelism in 1 Corinthians 9:22: "To the weak I became weak, in order to win the weak. I have become all things to all people, so that I may by every possible means save some." If the calling for the magi by a star had happened recently and been reported through social media, modern Christians would be deeply offended and claim God would never give the appearance of using occult practices to save a pagan. Yet God is sovereign and charts the path of the lives of all people. He knows what will and will not cause them to stumble in their faith. God's primary goal is that these men come and worship Jesus. We don't know the end of their story, but it's safe to assume based on their genuine faith that the wise men likely did not return to idolatry or embrace syncretism.

Even though God is primarily concerned with the magi's worship of his Son, there is still something different about this star than traditional astrological star charts. It's unique and supernatural—moving in the sky as no other star or planet can. It can't be charted or explained scientifically because God is directing its path in unpredictable ways.[14] Matthew 2:9 says the star "led them until it came and stopped above the place where the child was." Astronomer Danny Faulkner noted that if you were to see a star over the top of a house then walk to a different location, the star would no longer appear over the same house.[15] If the magi were trained astrologers, as they likely were, they would have known that stars don't appear over one location when you're moving. In the case of Christ's star, it would have to move in relation to the movement of the magi as they traveled to Bethlehem, which indicated a unique, supernatural phenomena.

This event was certainly similar to pagan methodology, but the magi would have been able to detect the supernatural distinctions and the incredible authority Yahweh had over the heavens in order to bring this about. Even in this act of condescension to pagans, God was still making himself known as the Lord of lords and God above all other gods. When he meets us where we are, he's not condoning or encouraging sin or wrong beliefs any more than he's encouraging the magi in their astrology. He's simply not as surprised by sin as we are. Dane Ortlund says, "The cumulative testimony of the four Gospels is that when Jesus Christ sees the fallenness of the world all about him, his deepest impulse, his most natural instinct, is to move toward that sin and suffering, not away from it."[16] In the same way, God is not repelled by the pagan wise men and their divination. It's also not our place to dictate how God chooses to reveal himself to us. "Our God is in heaven and does whatever he pleases" (Ps. 115:3).

Just as God gets down on our level to communicate truth through the narrative language of Scripture and the parables of Jesus, so, too, do we use stories to give and receive truth. So, how do we take these principles gleaned from Scripture and apply them to books, films, and games? Not every story's message reflects biblical truth, so, what else do we need to know before we can start using these discernment questions while engaging with media?

PART TWO

DISCERNING FICTIONAL MAGIC THROUGH SCRIPTURE

Chapter 7

Why Does the Church Need Fantasy?

Why does a genre as trivial and fringe as fantasy matter to the church and the Christian life? Why should you care about fantasy and magic? Some of you picked up this book with someone else in mind. Perhaps you're a parent with a voracious reader. Maybe you're a teacher wondering how to guide your students through classics like *The Lion, the Witch and the Wardrobe* and *The Hobbit.* Before we get to those specifics, I want you to know I didn't just write this book for your kids or the fantasy lover in your life. I wrote it for *you.* Because you're the image of God, and fantasy and imagination are an important part of that identity. So before we continue to build our house of magic and miracles, let's first pour the foundation of the fantastical properties of *imago Dei.*

The Image of God

While many modern books and sermons on the image of God choose to focus on how we should reflect God's character, church history concerned itself more with the specific ways humans ontologically image God. Thomas Aquinas quoted Augustine saying, "Man's excellence consists in the fact that God made him to His own image by giving him an intellectual soul, which raises him above the beasts of the field." Aquinas adds: "Therefore things without intellect are not made to God's image."[1] While animals can seemingly mimic reasoning skills by acting on instinct, emotion, and memory, they don't have genuine, reflective intellect. Only humans can make truly rational choices and think about thinking. Aquinas is specifically referring to human *potential* for rationality, meaning a fetus or someone who has lost brain function still images God in this way. Though heavily debated, this interpretation has been the consensus throughout church history. Aquinas even argued that the eternality of the soul is under the umbrella of the intellectual soul and not a separate aspect altogether. But where do theologians find this reflected in Scripture?

On the sixth day of creation, God makes "the wildlife of the earth" (Gen. 1:24–25) before man and woman: "Then God said, 'Let us make man in our image, according to our likeness. They will rule the fish of the sea, the birds of the sky, the livestock, the whole earth, and the creatures that crawl on the earth.' So God created man in his own image; he created him in the image of God; he created them male and female" (vv. 26–27).

We begin to see the contrast between animals and humans on the sixth day, and that distinction is highlighted all the more in the next chapter. While Genesis 1 gives the order of creation, Genesis 2 zooms in on the creation of mankind. Instead of making man and woman at the same time, God declares he will make a helper corresponding to Adam (Gen. 2:18). Before God makes Eve, he takes Adam through an interesting exercise of naming the animals (v. 19). Through this, Adam recognizes that the creatures parading in front of him are different from him. "The man gave names to all the livestock, to the birds of the sky, and to every wild animal; but for the man no helper was found corresponding to him" (v. 20).

God could have made Eve immediately after Adam and had them name the animals together. Yet he orchestrated a situation where Adam could observe the animals and use his intellect to *create* names for each one. He then synthesized his observations and drew his conclusion—none of these creatures would make a good companion. Only another creature made in God's image would do. This is not only a picture of how important the distinction between humans and animals is but *what* it is that makes them unique. Adam uses the power of reason to determine that he is different. What an incredible way to learn of his and Eve's humanity—their *imago Dei*.

Reason—or as Augustine calls it, an "intellectual soul"—is a power with many properties. The mind or intellect is not just a thing we use in school. It's the root of our justice, morality, politics, humor, friendship, culture-making, and most important for our purposes—creativity. This is also the first attribute of God we see in Genesis 1:1: "In the beginning God created the heavens and the earth."

Imagination, creativity, and artistic expression. Our society tends to see reason as a power separate from these, as though reason belongs only in the left hemisphere of your brain, creativity in the right, with the two rarely crossing paths. Despite those who argue otherwise, creativity and imagination aren't separate gifts that only some people possess. Just as Adam used both his intellect and his imagination in the process of naming the animals, so we often do the same without realizing how creative and intelligent we really are. These are essential human functions and symptoms of reason. What makes us unique individuals is how we each manifest and invest in our creative function. We flourish as the images of God when we synthesize informational input such as experience, visuals, sound, or taste to create various forms of art and work. We are acting as rational, reasonable beings and fulfilling the covenant to "fill the earth, and subdue it" from Genesis 1:28.

The Cultural Mandate versus Pragmatism

After God created Adam and Eve on the sixth day, he gave them a set of instructions in Genesis 1:28 known as *the cultural mandate*: "God blessed them, and God said to them, 'Be fruitful, multiply, fill the earth, and subdue it. Rule the fish of the sea, the birds of the sky, and every creature that crawls on the earth.'" This mandate is given to Adam and Eve before the fall, since they are the representatives of the human race.

Author and apologist Nancy Pearcey explains the cultural mandate this way:

> If you go back to Genesis 1, God has created the universe, he's created the earth, he created the animals, he creates the first couple. And then he tells them what they're there for. "Why did you create me?" "What's our purpose?" And he says, "Be fruitful and multiply and subdue the earth. And in the very streamlined language of Genesis, we have

> to unpack that. "Be fruitful and multiply" doesn't just mean have kids. . . . What it really means is develop the social institutions. "Subdue the earth" means harness the natural resources. . . . As civilizations develop, it's building bridges, buildings, designing computers, and composing music.[2]

The cultural mandate isn't just a command to procreate. It's a command to all people, not just all Christians, to fill the earth, create culture, gather its resources, and use them to their full potential for a myriad of purposes. Genesis 1:28 is not just a command; it's a prefall covenant. "God blessed them" is covenantal language. When this is paired with the instructions to fill the earth and rule over it, we find our occupation and purpose.

What are we ruling over? *Everything*. David said in Psalm 8, "You made him ruler over the works of your hands; you put everything under his feet" (v. 6). Under God's authority, we have dominion over the earth and its resources. We're a social community of creative culture-makers and procreators. Living out that purpose is at the heart of human flourishing and the application of our intellectual soul. As a central property of reason and being the image of God, imagination and creation are primary functions within this prefall covenantal framework. First, we must imagine what we can make with our resources and then use our hands to create it. Our creativity also reflects God's first displayed attribute of Creator as seen in Genesis 1:1, and it is an indispensable part of how we reflect him as his images in the cultural mandate of Genesis 1:28. Suffice it to say, creativity is a rather important part of what it means to be human. Anyone who asserts, "I am not a creative person," may as well say they aren't a person at all.

Unfortunately, we often replace creativity with pragmatism. It has become a stronghold as we focus far too much on the practical value of media for evangelism and education and neglect our identity as creative culture-makers. This is something handed down to us by our Protestant ancestors, the Reformers and Puritans. After becoming disenchanted with the Catholic Church, the Reformers overcorrected and discarded the high value placed on beauty, art, and wonder right along with Catholic theology. Puritans furthered this divide with their extreme pragmatic legalism. The effects of such a drastic misstep have been felt by Evangelicals for generations. Some Christians even have a completely negative view of art and media and see it as a distraction to the boots-on-the-ground work of evangelism. This kind of mindset reflects little of a biblical view of God and the church.

Leland Ryken says, "Christians have often perpetuated the utilitarian outlook to the disparagement of literature."[3] I think it's safe to broaden this idea from just literature to all forms of art, including popular-level media. Evangelicals have taken our strength of adherence to the Great Commission and made it our weakness. God never called us to preach the gospel to the nations *at the expense* of the cultural mandate—nor the reverse. He called us to preach to the nations while remaining within the culture-making framework—each set of instructions supporting the other and bringing glory to God. In part, the command to evangelize and expand God's kingdom spiritually fulfills the cultural mandate's command to be fruitful and multiply. But since we have been culture-makers from before the fall, we will continue to do just that for eternity and long after evangelism is obsolete. The presence of the Great Commission shouldn't make culture-making impractical or of lesser importance.

When Christians set out to tell stories, our love for Christ and the gospel bubbles up from within us and presents itself within our art often without plan or effort. C. S. Lewis addressed this in his essay "Sometimes Fairy Stories May Say Best What's to Be Said." When asked how he first thought of the concepts behind *The Lion, the Witch and the Wardrobe*, he denied the assumption that he set out to write a story to teach the gospel to children. "Everything began with images; a faun carrying an umbrella, a queen on a sledge, a magnificent lion. At first there wasn't even anything Christian about them; that element pushed itself in of its own accord."[4]

In this fantastical medium, Lewis found that these images and stories could slip past a person's materialist inhibitions and plant themselves in the mind unawares. "But supposing that by casting all these things into an imaginary world, stripping them of their stained-glass and Sunday school associations, one could make them for the first time appear in their real potency? Could one not thus steal past those watchful dragons? I thought one could."[5]

Lewis set out to tell a story about a faun standing by a lamppost and a little girl named Lucy. But Aslan and the stone table bubbled up from the very heart of who he was—a follower of Christ and a lover of the truth. Through this story, the gospel has been preached to millions.

Without a strong bond between faith and imagination, the church suffers. Even evangelism—the goal of much of our pragmatism—suffers from lack of imagination. For years we've prioritized only those things that have practical value and more closely resemble a tool than a work of art. When we do create, we draw strict boundaries so all art has a more practical function. From this was born the unfortunate trend of "bad Christian art"—the cheaply made movies, cheesy gospel tracts, poorly written Christian fiction, and more. Those negative associations with cheesy Christian art don't reflect historical Christianity. When Lewis was still an atheist but considering the concept of God, he reflected on how his favorite authors were all Christians and that their books seemed to have far more substance than the secular authors he'd read.

> All the books were beginning to turn against me. Indeed, I must have been as blind as a bat not to have seen, long before, the ludicrous contradiction between my theory of life and my actual experiences as a reader. George MacDonald had done more to me than any other writer; of course it was a pity he had that bee in his bonnet about Christianity. He was good in spite of it. Chesterton had more sense than all the other moderns put together; bating, of course, his Christianity. . . . On the other hand, those writers who did not suffer from religion and with whom in theory my sympathy ought to have been complete—Shaw and Wells and Mill and Gibbon and Voltaire—all seemed a little thin; what as boys we called "tinny." It wasn't that I didn't like them. They were all (especially Gibbon) entertaining; but hardly more. There seemed to be no depth in them. They were too simple. The roughness and density of life did not appear in their books.[6]

So, what's the cure for our habit of producing "tinny" Christian art and fiction? It's remembering our prefall purpose statement of multiplying and culture-making, or as Tolkien calls it in his essay "On Fairy-Stories"—sub-creating.

We must also be careful not to overcorrect to the right or the left (Prov. 4:27). It's certainly not wrong to use art to preach the gospel. That method of evangelism can be extremely effective. We also shouldn't focus so much on art that we neglect preaching the gospel. In fact, Jesus often used stories (parables) to teach and communicate truth. Fantasy author J. J. Fischer sees her calling as a Christian fiction writer like a diamond:

> I've often thought that the gospel is like a multi-faceted diamond. Shine a beam of light, and you'll illuminate one facet of the gem—one powerful truth that will pattern and colour your life, should you allow it. Turn the gem a little to the side, and you catch another sparkling surface—another startling, life-altering truth. You can live a hundred years in this world and still be surprised by a beam of light shining on that gem, illuminating something you never noticed before. The words of God are truly living and active (Hebrews 4:12). Christian fiction, very simply, aims to touch our hearts with stories that illuminate particular truths; which have the power to permeate and pattern every aspect of our life. With such potential, was it any wonder that Jesus himself often spoke in the language of stories?[7]

It's the communication of truth that should be at the core of both our culture-making and our ministries. All sub-creations, even those not intended to be a tool or used directly in ministry, should communicate truth.

Faith-Filled Imagination

We've established that creativity is an important aspect of being the image of God and that we are to implement it as a community of imaginative culture-makers. But what does all that have to do with the fantasy genre specifically? Imagination can be used in endless ways, not just the creation of fantasy stories and art. A businessperson uses their imagination to come up with new solutions to financial or marketing issues. An architect designs new, energy- and space-efficient buildings. A teacher imagines a new curriculum that meets the needs of the specific students and their learning styles. So, what, if anything, is special about fantasy for the Christian mind? Let's define some terms, and hopefully the answer to that question will begin to take shape on its own.

> *The Merriam-Webster Dictionary* defines *imagination* as "the act or power of forming a mental image of something not present to the senses or never before wholly perceived in reality."[8]

> Tolkien defines *fantasy* as "images of things that are not only 'not actually present,' but which are indeed not to be found in our primary world at all."[9]

> The Bible defines *faith* as "the reality of what is hoped for, the proof of what is not seen" (Heb. 11:1).

Did you see a pattern? The through line that connects imagination, fantasy, and faith is *seeing what cannot be seen*—imagining what exists and does not exist in our perceived reality. That connecting thread involves conceiving that another world or spiritual realm is alive and active where we cannot see it. It involves believing that a spiritual God, an all-powerful, invisible being, exists and loves us. It's knowing the same God provides such grace and blessings in this broken world and beyond that we can't even begin to comprehend. It's guarding ourselves against our invisible enemy in the spiritual realm.

The definitions of *imagination*, *fantasy*, and *faith* may be similar, but how do we see this connection reflected in Scripture? Leland Ryken said in his book, *How to Read the Bible as Literature*,

> In the strange and frequently surrealistic world of visionary literature, virtually any aspect of creation can become a participant in the ongoing drama of God's judgments and redemption. It is a world where a river can overflow a nation (Isa. 8:5–8), where a branch can build a temple (Zech. 6:12) and a ram's horn can grow to the sky and knock stars to the ground (Dan. 8:9–10). Sea, clouds, earthquake, storm, whirlwind, and assorted animals are constant actors in visionary literature. This is obviously a type of fantasy literature, not because the events symbolically portrayed are unreal or untrue, but because the form in which they are pictured as happening is purely imaginary. The visionary strangeness of such writing leads to a related rule for reading it: visionary literature is a form of fantasy literature in which

> readers must be willing to exercise their imaginations in picturing unfamiliar scenes and agents. It requires what the poet Coleridge called "the willing suspension of disbelief." We know that people do not fly through the air on wings, but when reading such visions we suspend our disbelief and enter the realm of make-believe in order to appropriate the truth it conveys about reality. The best introduction to such visionary literature in the Bible is other fantasy literature, such as the Narnia stories of C. S. Lewis.[10]

"Visionary" literature, such as the prophets and Revelation, are the most prominent places the Bible uses fantastical images to convey truth. There are also more subtle images in Scripture that are often portrayed in fantasy literature and not other genres. For example, the existence of separate or invisible realms that influence our daily lives, supernatural events, superhuman feats, miraculous blessings and curses, an army of resurrected corpses, a talking donkey, people walking through fire, and much more. Without imagination, we too quickly dismiss what Paul says in Ephesians 6:12: "For our struggle is not against flesh and blood, but against the rulers, against the authorities, against the cosmic powers of this darkness, against evil, spiritual forces in the heavens." Any fictional story using this same language of invisible "heavens" would be categorized as nothing other than fantasy.

In fact, the climax of all Scripture and history is a fantastical, supernatural act—the resurrection of Jesus Christ from the dead. Denying the power and importance of supernatural stories, especially those that seek to shed light on the truth of the gospel, undermines the single event on which the veracity of Christianity depends.

Giving parts of the Bible the label of "fantasy" is controversial due to the genre's poor reputation, associations with magic, and overall strangeness. Yet we're referring to the broadest definition when we discuss fantasy. It includes, but isn't limited to, dragons and fairies. It's simply anything we can imagine that doesn't normally appear in our visible, "primary world."[11] From that definition, books like Revelation fit easily within this genre.

Fantasy is not faith. But when we exercise the muscle of imagining what we can't see, we're also strengthening the part of our mind that can perceive God exists and that he can do extraordinary, miraculous things. Fantastical imagination and faith are like two separate muscles in the same limb that must be exercised in order to grow. When we imagine strange, impossible things, we have a unique opportunity to increase our capacity to trust in God's ability to do the impossible while pragmatism and materialism work against this. Modern science has given us a name for this kind of mind exercise—neuroplasticity. *Neuro* refers to the nervous system and *plasticity* to the ability to be molded like plastic. It means that the wiring of our brains is not permanent but can be changed or grown through habitual thought and action.

The more we invest in seeing the unseen, the more we can conceive of the greatness of God and all he can accomplish. Without the pursuit of strange, otherworldly imaginations, faith remains one-dimensional. With our materialist dispositions, we rob faith of much of its power. It takes small faith to believe there's an apple tree outside even if you haven't seen it versus believing there's a giant, fire-breathing horse outside. The smaller we make God, the less faith we need to believe in him. The smaller our faith in God is, the smaller our awe and joy are in him. We live in a fantasy land of invisible realms, millions of angels and demons, and supernatural phenomena. What better way to tell of the reality of the hope that is in us than an entire literary genre dedicated to seeing the unseen? Spurning fantastical fiction is not a spiritually mature response. As Lewis famously said, "But some day you will be old enough to start reading fairy tales again."[12] Once we grow enough to release our tight hold on what we insist maturity must look like, we will be able to see clearly what it actually is.

But doesn't fantasy appeal to certain people who just happen to like that genre? That is like saying people who dislike sports don't need to exercise. Of course, it's your decision if you want to exercise or not, and you can survive without doing it regularly. Yet we know that people who choose to exercise will reap greater health benefits than those who do not. People who don't like the machines at the gym but want to enjoy exercising usually find something that uniquely suits them such as hiking, Rollerblading, or even taking dance lessons. There's something for everyone even if you would never use an elliptical or lift weights. Fantasy is much the same. If the broadest definition of *fantasy* is "images not found in our primary world," that's a large genre umbrella. Not everyone needs to like The Lord of the Rings or The Chronicles of Narnia to engage their imagination in seeing beyond material reality through speculative fiction.

In his essay, "On Fairy-Stories," Tolkien explains why Christians often reject fantasy. Although he was referring to the literary genre, this will give us insight into why it's also rejected as a biblical genre. "Fantasy, of course, starts out with an advantage: arresting strangeness. But that advantage has been turned against it, and has contributed to its disrepute. Many people dislike being 'arrested.'

They dislike any meddling with the Primary World, or such small glimpses of it as are familiar to them. They, therefore, stupidly and even maliciously confound Fantasy with Dreaming, in which there is no Art; and with mental disorders, in which there is not even control: with delusion and hallucination."[13]

"Arresting strangeness" can be shocking and even anxiety inducing to a mind anchored in only what it can see of reality. Yet what can be seen of the world is not all that truly exists, nor does the Bible shy away from excessively strange imagery. In his book, *Understanding Spiritual Warfare*, Sam Storms says, "Whether through arrogant presumption or outright neglect or even a fear of being laughed at by others, people ignore the spiritual realm. They live as if it didn't exist, or if it does, it has little to no bearing on their daily routines."[14] This modern perspective impacts scriptural interpretation. Without a robust understanding of ancient perspectives on the supernatural and demonology, we often fail to grasp what's really happening in passages like Saul's meeting the medium at En-dor (1 Sam. 28) or the magi(cians) following the Christmas star (Matt. 2:1–12).

In order to comprehend the invisible realm and demonology, we must "walk by faith, not by sight" (2 Cor. 5:7). This can and often does include using the unreality of fantasy to shed light on concealed reality. When we're confronted with the strangeness of fantastical images in Scripture, we shouldn't just walk away shaking our heads in confusion. We should press into it to understand why God would choose to communicate with his people in such outlandish ways. In so doing, we grow our understanding of the otherness of God and increase our faith in his power and character. Sub-creation—the act of creating a fantasy world in imitation of God's creativity—has the same effect on our minds as those who take part in created fantasy worlds. It allows us to fully immerse ourselves in a place and time that we can't see. More specifically, Christian fantasy presupposes a gospel framework that further rewires our minds and hearts around the otherness of Christ and his upside-down kingdom (Matt. 20:16; 23:11–12).

Fantasy is so closely tied to the supernatural, it's exactly the thing our society needs. Why should the New Age be the gateway from materialism to spirituality when Christian fantasy has the ability to shed such a bright light through supernaturalism and unreality? As our imaginations expand to include those things, we lessen the impact of materialism on our hearts and minds and open ourselves up to the reality of God and Satan. Secular and atheistic fantasy writers unknowingly use an artistic medium that contradicts the materialistic perspective they espouse. They do this by marketing their creation as "entertainment" or "escapism"—ugly and inefficient words for anything that increases our imagination and, thereby, our capacity for a deeper faith in God.

So Great a Cloud of Witnesses

Hebrews 11—nicknamed the "hall of faith"—provides a lengthy list of Old Testament figures who had great faith. "Now faith is the reality of what is hoped for, the proof of what is not seen. For by this our ancestors were approved. By faith we understand that the universe was created by the word of God, so that what is seen was made from things that are not visible" (vv. 1–3).

There are a total of fourteen faithful individuals named in Hebrews 11 along with two groups—the Israelites and the prophets. Out of those sixteen mentioned in this chapter, eleven of them had faith that God would not only prepare a way for them in the future, they had faith he would do something supernatural. Noah believed the earth would flood even though he had never seen rain. Sarah had faith God would give her a child even though she was well past the age of childbearing. The Israelites had faith that God would part the Red Sea and tear down the walls of Jericho. The reality they hoped for and couldn't see wasn't simply material provision. They expected something that took a great amount of imagination to believe could come into existence. Yet the passage also tells us they did not receive what they were ultimately promised—a homeland (vv. 13–16).

Those who reached the promised land of Israel and saw God's miraculous power in their life still didn't witness the culmination of God's promises to them. We should have faith in momentary provision and miracles as God wills. Yet he has promised us something far greater that we cannot see and can hardly comprehend—a perfect home on a new earth with Christ as our king (11:32–35, 39–40).

The author of Hebrews takes us through the narrative of the Bible, showing us both the temporary and eternal things hoped for. It was in these smaller moments of faith that God's people looked forward to something even greater, something eternal and distinctly *other*. This new and perfect place is so far outside of our current perception of reality that it takes a great amount of imagination to comprehend its existence. When we—all saints throughout history—finally see the fulfillment of this homeland, we will no longer have faith in what is not yet seen because it will be fully realized (1 Cor. 13:12). The hymn "It Is Well with My Soul" says in the last verse, "And Lord, haste the day when my faith shall be sight. . . . Even so, it is well with my soul." What a beautiful summation of the heart of the believer who has faith that God will answer their prayers only to die before the fullness of their hopes becomes sight.

Beyond seeing the unseen, what does this have to do with fantastical fiction? The author of Hebrews doesn't end this section at the bottom of Hebrews 11. The very next verse in 12:1–2 is the application of the hall of faith. "Therefore, since we also have such a large cloud of witnesses surrounding us, let us lay aside every hindrance and the sin that so easily ensnares us. Let us run with endurance the race that lies before us, keeping our eyes on Jesus, the pioneer and perfecter of our faith. For the joy that lay before him, he endured the cross, despising the shame, and sat down at the right hand of the throne of God."

The "large cloud of witnesses" here isn't referring to us being watched as some believe but to the biblical figures of the Old Testament witnessing *to* us. Their faith-filled lives testify to future generations so that we can "lay aside every hindrance" and "run with endurance the race that lies before us, keeping our eyes on Jesus" (vv. 1–2).

When we face trials and our faith is as small as a mustard seed, we rely on stories to tell us what's true about God—about his power and faithfulness to fulfill his promises. Characters in stories—a large cloud of witnesses—testify to the reality of the visible and the invisible. We have living, breathing witnesses from the whole of Scripture as well as great Christian heroes from history that bolster and build our faith. They prove that these things are very *real.* Yet fiction and fantasy shape our minds in a similar way, which is why Jesus chose to tell fictional parables—some of which were fantastical, such as the rich man and Lazarus (Luke 16:19–31). When we walk in another person's shoes, seeing the strange otherness of our world and our God, we grow as the character grows. Our empathy, virtue, and faith expand beyond what our own life experience can afford us. As we read, the cloud of witnesses who testify to us grows, and so does our faith.

What Will We Lose without Fantasy?

Although every generation has its own unique cultural blind spots, we have never been more steeped in materialism. Technology and the idolatry of modern science obscure such unseen realities as the spiritual realm and the hope of eternity on the new earth. Worship of the self and placing creation over the Creator blinds us to the existence of the kingdom of Christ. This is one of the largest contributors to pragmatism for the church even while we deny materialism with our mouths. Even more than materialism, many of us have become anti-supernaturalists, denying the existence of divine supernaturalism either in this generation or altogether. This is not a scriptural position even for the strictest cessationists (those who do not believe miraculous spiritual gifts still exist). Within this anti-supernatural framework, both God and our prayers grow smaller and smaller as we unconsciously regard him and his power as limited.

A few years ago, a friend told her four-year-old daughter that magic wasn't real. A little time went by, and the girl came back and asked how she could know if God was real when magic wasn't. In her mind, magic was anything supernatural. And if the supernatural didn't exist, then neither did a being that had the power to create the entire universe with a single word. How perceptive and challenging children can be!

Author Tony Reinke said of fantastical fiction,

> To view imaginative literature as a genre fit only for the amusement of children is an act of spiritual negligence. . . . Once I began developing an appreciation for fantasy and imaginative literature like Homer's *The Iliad* and *The Odyssey*, C. S. Lewis's series *The Chronicles of Narnia*, and of course J. R. R. Tolkien's *The Lord of the Rings*, I discovered that my appreciation for Revelation has grown and the weight of its images have pressed heavier on my soul. As I have read imaginative literature, my imagination has developed. As my imagination has developed, I have found myself reading Revelation more patiently, allowing the images to emerge in my mind until I feel the full spiritual shock of their intended voltage. The lesson I have learned is that a failure to cultivate the imagination leads to an unintended neglect of the imaginative literature of Scripture, and this in turn leads to some degree of spiritual atrophy. For Christians, the stories of Revelation are not optional reading. Nor are they child's play. Imaginative literature—the kind of literature that invites us to see in our imaginations what we cannot see with our eyes—is an important part of the Christian's literary diet. It challenges our idols. It challenges what is false and trivial in our lives.[15]

When we see faith-filled imagination as childish or optional, we tend to focus more on those passages in Scripture that have the most practical value. At the same time, we avoid more fantastical language and images from the prophets and Revelation that are too strange for our modern minds to digest in a Sunday sermon or daily devotional. We become skeptical of the stories we hear from overseas missionaries who report converts having dreams of Jesus or being demon-possessed. We pray small, lack courage in evangelism, and forget that our suffering is part of a much larger, future plan. In short, without imagination, creativity, and Christian fantasy, the Christian mind is unable to develop a robust faith and, instead, applies only the softest of expectations to an all-powerful God. If we want to see God as the promise keeper that he is and to love him for all of his otherness, we must embrace the unseen realms of reality and the fantastical art that sheds so much light on it.

How do we go about embracing fantasy when so much of it contains magic and potentially demonic supernaturalism? Where do we draw the line with fictional magic—between Narnia and Hogwarts? Shouldn't we just play it safe and keep books like Harry Potter out of our homes just in case they're demonic? In the next chapter, we'll discuss license, legalism, and how to think rightly about making laws regarding fantastical media.

Chapter 8

The Dangers of Overcorrection

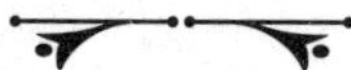

We were listening to a sermon on the sovereignty of God as we drove through the open, Arizona desert. It was supposed to be our first year at a seminary in Illinois. I took a turn sitting shotgun while my boyfriend, Tim, drove and his dad sat in the back seat.

My eyes drooped. It was an overwhelming exhaustion—as though a spell had been cast over the Jeep. I immediately paused the sermon and closed my eyes.

I wasn't sure how long I'd been asleep before I heard my boyfriend's father shout, "Tim!"

When I forced my heavy eyelids open, I saw the car drifting off the side of the highway. I hadn't been the only one placed under that sleeping spell.

Startled awake, my boyfriend wrenched the steering wheel to the right. The cruise control was set to 75 mph, and we were going too fast. He overcorrected then wrenched the car back to the left, overcorrecting a second time. A last jerk of the wheel forced the Jeep perpendicular on the road. Laden with boxes and luggage on top, we flipped down the desert highway like clothes in a dryer. Every window shattered along with my boyfriend's skull as it hit the steering wheel.

A woman stopped to help us and called 911. A helicopter and ambulance delivered us to a hospital in Flagstaff, where my boyfriend had emergency brain surgery. His father and I lay strapped down in the ER, wondering if he was still alive. If he was, would his brain be okay? Would he still be able to become a philosophy professor like he'd always wanted?

He lived to earn two degrees in theology and two more in philosophy, become a professor, marry me, and have three rambunctious kids. Since then, Tim has had two more hospital stays and surgeries to patch a hole in his skull. All three of us in that car suffer from chronic pain and headaches. I've sometimes wondered why God felt we needed this particular trial in our life. Was it meant to strengthen our faith? (If so, it was working.) Was it so we could comfort and share in the sufferings of others with chronic pain? No doubt it includes that and more. Yet, as time has gone by and God has laid certain things on our hearts and important message has emerged—overcorrection is extremely common and potentially fatal.

Legalism or License?

While teaching at a Southern Baptist seminary in the early and mid-2000s, Russell Moore guest-hosted a Christian talk radio program and occasionally engaged in the Harry Potter debate: "I learned a lot from the experience. One thing I discovered is that two issues, more than any others, would prompt rage from the listeners calling in. One of those subjects was any critique of Christian romance novels. And the other was any positive assessment of Harry Potter. I said to a friend at the time, 'I'm never talking about Harry Potter again.'"[1]

Aside from politics, few things spark a controversy at the level of Harry Potter. With the growth of the occult, the discussion of fictional magic is making its way back into the limelight. Debates surrounding fantasy have become a hotbed of overcorrection on both ends of the spectrum—of both legalism and license. This hasn't significantly improved over the years because there is widespread misunderstanding of what legalism and license really are and how to avoid them. We assume we understand this issue because the Pharisees seem so ludicrous and vicious in the Gospels. But the truth is, we are far more like them than we realize. Most people fall into some form of legalism and license at one time or another—what I refer to as *accidental legalism*. The Old Testament occasionally repeats the phrase, "Don't turn to the right or to the left" (Prov. 4:27). In order to face the task ahead without overcorrecting—turning to the right or the left—into either extreme regarding fictional magic, we first need to define our categories.

> **License (or licentiousness):** A minimization of laws, rules, or morality. Indulgence in immoral behavior or trying to get away with as much as possible. Exemplified by the "sinners" or the "tax collectors and prostitutes" in the New Testament.

> **Legalism:** Separating the law from its original context, works-based righteousness, and living by extrabiblical commands with rigidity and at

> the expense of grace.[2] Emphasizes methodology and works over principles and heart. Exemplified by the Pharisees and Sadducees in the New Testament.

Legalism is far more complicated and nuanced than most people realize and can be just as insidious as license. It, too, creeps into our lives and practices without our knowledge, since many people fall into defining legalism based on issues such as schooling preferences or media regulations rather than based on principle. Those specific examples could be valid uses of the label "legalism," but focusing on individual issues is often a distraction. When we make laws about skirt length or health food options, we demonstrate a poor understanding of the root cause of legalism. While license and legalism are equally dangerous, Jesus saved his harshest words for the legalistic Pharisees and Sadducees. They were supposed to be God's representatives to the people. Jesus said in Matthew 23:23, "Woe to you, scribes and Pharisees, hypocrites! You pay a tenth of mint, dill, and cumin, and yet you have neglected the more important matters of the law—justice, mercy, and faithfulness. These things should have been done without neglecting the others."

Sproul's Legalism Trifecta

In his article, "3 Types of Legalism," R. C. Sproul says, "[Legalism] is often bandied about in the Christian subculture incorrectly. . . . The term legalism does not refer to narrow-mindedness. In reality, legalism manifests itself in many subtle ways."[3]

Sproul's first type of legalism is treating the law (either the Mosaic Law or New Testament commands) as the ends rather than the means. It separates God's commands from the larger narrative of Scripture and the gospel of grace. Instead of rules being used as a means of grace to love God and others, they become the goal of the Christian life. This often dispenses entirely with grace, and the Bible becomes only a list of dos and don'ts. A biblical example of this is in Luke 14:1–6 and Matthew 12:9–14 when Jesus tests the Pharisees by healing on the Sabbath. He knew their interpretation of the fourth commandment to not labor on the Sabbath was stretched beyond its intended use. The Pharisees only cared about keeping lists of rules and not the purpose of the rules—a means of grace. If they had cared about their greater purpose, they would have rejoiced in people being healed on the Sabbath since that was an act of grace.

In *The Lion, the Witch and the Wardrobe*, the White Witch is guilty of the first form of legalism. She attempts to exploit the letter of the law—the Deep Magic—to her advantage by threatening Edmund's life so she might eventually take Aslan's instead. She knew that the penalty for sin was death and that she had the right to kill Edmund for what he'd done under the law of Deep Magic. After Aslan resurrects from the dead, he explains what the Witch didn't understand about the law.

"'It means,' said Aslan, 'that though the Witch knew the Deep Magic, there is a magic deeper still which she did not know: Her knowledge goes back only to the dawn of time. But if she could have looked a little further back, into the stillness and the darkness before Time dawned, she would have read there a different incantation. She would have known that when a willing victim who had committed no treachery was killed in a traitor's stead, the Table would crack and Death itself would start working backwards."[4]

What is this "incantation" and "deeper magic" that causes death to work backwards? It's the gospel of grace which is the end and goal of the law and the Deep Magic. Not only did the Witch neglect to look back before the dawn of time, but she also couldn't comprehend a love like Aslan's for Edmund. There was no way for the Witch-as-Satan to anticipate such a sacrificial act because demons are incapable of empathizing with such humility.

The second type of legalism divorces the letter of the law—the outward method—from the spirit of it—the heart and goal. This kind of legalist obeys the letter of the law but violates the spirit which sometimes looks the same as the first type of legalism externally. A biblical example is found in Matthew 12:1–8. The Pharisees criticized the disciples for picking and eating heads of grain on the Sabbath. Jesus answered them by saying David was guiltless when he ate the Bread of the Presence in 1 Samuel 21. David broke the letter of the law but kept the spirit of it. Sproul gives an example of a man who always drives the exact speed limit—never over or under—even during hazardous weather conditions where driving the speed limit puts lives in danger. Usually civic laws about road safety boil down to valuing safety and human life. Without that understanding of why we do the things we do, it can be difficult if not impossible to make wise choices while driving or even crossing the street. The same is true with the Bible. If we don't understand why God requires certain outward actions or methods, we may unknowingly slip into this second type of legalism.

The third type of legalism is the creation of extrabiblical commands that are treated as equal to God's law, which Sproul believes is the most common and deadly kind. Christians sometimes refer to this as "making law." The Pharisees often did this by taking their own Jewish traditions and creating new laws around them. It's important to remember that just because our culture is not as centered on tradition, we are still capable of creating new laws—even unorthodox or non-Christian law as seen in cancel culture and cultural and progressive fundamentalism. In Scripture, unorthodox legalism is most similar to the Sadducees since they rejected core Old Testament beliefs such as the resurrection of the dead and the existence of an afterlife while still overtly condemning others. A biblical example of the third type of legalism is found in Mark 7:1–23, where the Pharisees criticize Jesus's disciples for not washing their hands. In verses 8–9, Jesus says, "'Abandoning the command of God, you hold on to human tradition.' He also said to them, 'You have a fine way of invalidating God's command in order to set up your tradition!'"

We manufacture rules for ourselves about anything and everything. We have extrabiblical rules about homemaking and parenting, about the volume of music and the use of fog machines in a worship service, or about how many minutes per day to read the Bible. We will never run out of opportunities to create and enforce our own laws as though they are God's. Sometimes these are merely preferences or "wisdom issues." Yet when we begin to strictly regulate ourselves and others based on those preferences, we are doing just as the Pharisees did by abandoning the command of God and holding onto human tradition.

Former New Age teacher Lorna Vaughn describes how the temptation toward works-based Christianity is also present in the New Age occult. "We would rather be in a ratio-istic, legalistic exchange system with God, where if we do *this* we get *this*. . . . New Age really wants God to be like a super-computer. I put *this* in and get *this* out."[5] It's not only the occult that has this mindset; it's a temptation for all of us. We are so focused on sin, on rebellion against God since the flesh doesn't desire to do good (Rom. 7:18; John 3:20), that we often forget it's also part of human nature to long for the ease of the law and desire that life would be as simple as following a rule to automatically get what we want.

Legalism is *demanding* of God rather than *dependent* on him. We are tempted by the idea of putting something into an equation and getting exactly what we want out, as though God is just a math problem to be solved. God is logical in that he is unchanging and doesn't contradict himself, but he is not formulaic. Nor is Scripture a morality machine where we can put in one or two details of a complicated situation and get a definitive moral solution. Attempting to do so treats obedience like an incantation—say the right words, do the right action, and the desired outcome will occur. Satan will exploit this tendency of ours in many ways if we are not guarding against his machinations.

Instead, God desires us to strive for holiness and grace-filled lives. We should live each day focused on him and growing in virtue and Christlikeness rather than building up extrabiblical laws. "But the fruit of the Spirit is love, joy, peace, patience, kindness, goodness, faithfulness, gentleness, and self-control. *The law is not against such things*" (Gal. 5:22–23, emphasis added). When we think that living with precision will merit a specific intended result, we miss the heart of the gospel of grace. We slip into the same lie as New Age occultists by putting ourselves in the place of God, saying, "I demand this law will produce good fruit and righteousness." We use rules to control outcomes and the behavior of others. In doing so, we can slip unawares into works-based living, authoritarianism, and even spiritual abuse. People who are legalistic often find their self-righteousness in being unlike a "sinner"—the licentious or progressive community—Christian or secular. Yet the heart of both groups is the same. The progressive says, "I am my own ruler and make my own laws or lack thereof. I can do whatever

I please"—spoken in the name of Christian freedom or as a total rejection of God's authority. The legalist says, "I keep my law better than those sinners, and in this way I am righteous" (see Luke 18:9–14). It's in the heart of all humankind to desire what Satan tempted Eve with in the garden—to be like God, not in reflecting his character but in being divine and making our own rules.

Subcategories of Legalism

The following subcategories of legalism are not exhaustive. Humans are creative, and we can come up with many ways of destroying the gospel and the law. The following two categories are both prominent and have bearing on our conversation about fictional magic.

The first subcategory is what I call "minority rules legalism" which is a kind of the second type of legalism. This universalizes the temptations of the minority—or the weaker brother from Romans 14. It usually involves keeping a long list of overextended scriptural commands that should only be held by those with either a weak conscience or with a specific history of temptation. For example, the Bible says getting drunk is sinful. Yet those who believe no Christian should drink alcohol under any circumstances often insist that getting drunk could become a real temptation for all believers. They then prohibit all use of alcohol for all people based on this assumption. We can have grace for this position and assume they may fall under the umbrella of the weaker brother (Rom. 14). People who struggle particularly with alcohol or have been alcoholic in the past should certainly not partake in order to avoid temptation. Yet the need to avoid alcohol completely is far from universal or a temptation for the majority of people. Paul instructs those who value their freedom in Christ to have peace with the weaker brother and not to try to convince them to go against their conscience (Rom. 14:19–23). A real problem only arises when a legalist with a weaker conscience becomes judgmental and tries to convince others to abstain as they do.

This book should not be understood as an attempt to convince people who are strongly opposed to fictional magic to read controversial fantasy books. My intentions are to give guidance only to those who seek it and have a desire to learn. I pray you don't walk away from this discussion with an agenda to change the weaker brother's mind but to create more peace and respect for others surrounding this topic.

On the opposite extreme, people who value Christian freedom can become entitled to do as they please. It becomes a point of pride as Paul notes in 1 Corinthians 5:1–2, 6: "It is actually reported that there is sexual immorality among you, and the kind of sexual immorality that is not even tolerated among the Gentiles—a man is sleeping with his father's wife. And you are arrogant! Shouldn't you be filled with grief and remove from your congregation the one who did this? . . . Your boasting is not good. Don't you know that a little leaven leavens the whole batch of dough?"

The Corinthians were so assured of their "freedom," they were actually arrogant about sexual immorality. Paul is warning them that such a disregard for morality can spread throughout their entire church body. This is not a mature response as we grow in our Christian freedom and unshackled conscience. When we begin to shed legalism, it's tempting to see ourselves as apologists against previously held dogma. Our response should be humble submission to God and a desire to love others well. Sometimes that may include loving conversations with people who disagree but not always. In this conversation about fictional magic, discussing the theology of the supernatural and appreciation for fantasy is valuable but not at the expense of either disregarding actual immorality in fiction or harming the weaker conscience of another person. If after reading this book you face the temptation of pride or weaponizing theology against another person, you have missed the entire point of this discussion.

"Minority rules legalism" is frequently applied to fictional magic. A person or child becoming interested in the occult because of Harry Potter is not impossible, but it is rare. Let's go over the statistics for the occult once more. From my research into the testimonies of former New Agers, 5.5 percent (eleven out of two hundred) mentioned fantasy magic as part of their journey, and only 1.5 percent mentioned Harry Potter specifically.* Out of those eleven people (5.5%), the primary reason people were drawn to the New Age was either trauma or mental health problems. Only one person out of the eleven didn't mention a history of trauma, although there were other factors leading to occult involvement. Out of the entire sample size of two hundred, 70 percent mentioned a history of abuse, a traumatic event, or mental health problems. The two out of the eleven that I spoke with personally insisted fictional magic was not the primary or even secondary reason they got involved. Not only are New Age occultists a minority group in larger society, but within that minority, those tempted by fictional magic are a small subminority group. Although such statistics are not widely known, it is still accidental legalism to universalize this minority temptation to the majority.

---

* This number doesn't include fictional stories of real occult supernaturalism such as *The Craft*.

It's possible for license to slip in as an overcorrection to minority rules legalism. When Christians observe this kind of legalism, they may be tempted to do the exact opposite in the name of Christian freedom or to simply avoid legalism. Instead of universalizing minority temptations, they make light of majority temptations as though it's not as pervasive as it really is. This usually involves minimizing scriptural teachings on morality. For example, lust is a temptation most people and both genders face with varying degrees of frequency and severity. Despite those variations, it should still be regarded as a majority issue and something the Bible speaks about with strong language. However, due to the dogmatism and legalism of the Purity Culture era of the 1990s, Christians are sometimes tempted to overcorrect those errors into license regarding lust, sexuality, and sensuality.

That overcorrection has had a weighty impact on Christian-made art. The modern immersive writing styles—not bad in and of themselves—often propagate even more sexual content in adult and young adult novels (books intended for teenagers) that go far beyond the sexual metaphors of Song of Solomon. Christian writers and readers sometimes use the Song of Solomon as a way to legitimize sex and sensuality in media. That drastically flattens the nuances of the issue and disregards how much more explicit films and literature have become. Christians who advocate for sex- and sensuality-free fiction are seen as legalists, lawmakers, and purity culture warriors. However, that's not a fair or nuanced assessment since the New Testament outright commands us not to have sensual minds or engage with sexual immorality regardless of any misapplication in the past.* Ironically, the belief that most women are

* Mark 7:22; Romans 13:13; 2 Corinthians 12:21; Galatians 5:19; Ephesians 4:19; 1 Peter 4:3; 2 Peter 2:18.

not tempted to lust by reading sensuality in fiction presupposes the purity culture rhetoric that women are less sexual than men.

I'm not advocating for excluding real, human temptations and darkness in media. The Bible doesn't do that, and we shouldn't either. It isn't a matter of whether we speak about darkness or sexuality at all but about *how* we speak about them. Most general market fiction and even some Christian fiction in the adult and young adult genres is overtly sexual and pornographic. Even the less blatantly erotic books can act as a gateway drug into pornography for women and girls.

The last subcategory is what I call "just in case legalism" or "logical extreme legalism" which is a combination of Sproul's second and third types of legalism. This is when we take a biblical command and stretch its logic too far past the point it was intended to go *just in case* we might err. A biblical example is the Pharisees creating additional laws surrounding the Sabbath as we discussed above. They took God's command to rest on the Sabbath to a logical extreme, creating additional laws that restricted Jesus's ability to serve people through healing (Luke 14:1–6; Matt. 12:9–14). A modern example is some of the extreme restrictions put on women in the home and church. The command for women not to teach or exercise authority over men is often taken to logical extremes *just in case*. In some churches, this means women can't pray in front of men, teach older children in Sunday school, or even speak into a microphone unless singing backup.

Adding onto the existing command fails to understand the historical context and purpose of it. When we are concerned with living holy lives, we naturally want to avoid the posture of Christian license that says, "How much can I get away with?" Yes, that heart posture is dangerous and doesn't reflect a genuine desire to live a holy life before God and others. Yet it's possible to go to the extreme in the other direction and add rules onto an existing command "just in case" or take a biblical command to a "logical extreme" when God may have intended it for more specific, limited situations. The Bible often presupposes much more nuanced application of the wisdom it teaches. In applying such things, we have to consider cultural context, the particular temptations and people present, and more. Wisdom necessitates asking about particulars. Legalism attempts to stretch Scripture into a one-size-fits-all umbrella, leaving no room for individual, nuanced circumstances.

This also applies to fictional magic. Although the Bible puts clear restrictions on practicing real witchcraft, creating the same laws around reading and writing fictional forms of supernaturalism is an overextension of that command and misses the point and nuance of the fantasy genre. Of course, sometimes we will need to censor certain types of fictional magic. But to censor all of it without nuance *just in case* is taking the Bible's commands regarding demonic supernaturalism to a place they were never intended to go.

Excess and Deficiency

Aristotle's golden mean defines virtue as the "mean" (the midpoint) between two extreme vices—the excess vice and the deficient vice.[6] Yes, Aristotle is an imperfect, secular philosopher. Yet, despite this, his teachings have been highly respected throughout church history, and his concept of the golden mean is extremely helpful. It gives a more thorough system to the repeated biblical command, "Don't turn to the right or to the left" (Prov. 4:27).

In Aristotle's ethical system, there's an alternative way to define license and legalism in how we as Christians engage with secular culture specifically: *indulgence and abstinence.* Let's take a look at how indulgence—the excess vice—can affect the church in regards to media intake. The community of Christians who read and write speculative fiction (science fiction and fantasy) varies widely. Some make great efforts to think critically about how far they should go with their reading and writing and how closely it should resemble that of the secular market. Then there are others who, after observing the problems with legalism and abstaining from much of popular culture, delve headlong into secular media without restraint. Some of their fiction may include sex, sensuality, or the unapologetic use of "black" magic by protagonists, which is a glorification of evil. They see themselves as critical thinkers because they dodged the bullet of "legalism." In their supposed freedom, they display a lack of restraint against indulgence, seeing it as good or the lesser of two evils. Yet cultural indulgence is prone to either deleting parts of Scripture or twisting the meaning to fit perceived needs.

Where the indulgent delete or twist Scripture, the culturally abstinent tend to add to it or stretch it until it's no longer recognizable. When engaging in popular culture and media, the baby is often thrown out with the bathwater. More times than I can count, I've witnessed Christian parents join social media groups and request book recommendations with zero violence, magic, fantasy characters, rule-breaking, or romance. They aren't looking to avoid books that specifically glorify those things; they're looking to avoid them altogether. Although there may be times when those need to be restricted depending on the circumstances and age of the child, avoiding all of these all the time removes the need for critical thinking, developing discernment, and the discipling of a child through the real world. Holding opinions about "wisdom issues" is good and helpful. However, it isn't biblical or Christlike to use those opinions as a way to make law, neglect discipleship, shelter children overmuch, or look down on others who've made different choices about their media intake.

We're called to live holy lives before God and others, not indulge in worldly passions. In such cases, the warning of James 4:4 rings true: "You adulterous people! Don't you know that friendship with the world is hostility toward God? So whoever wants to be the friend of the world becomes the enemy of God." There's a delicate balance to seek here—a narrow road that doesn't turn to the right or the left. Nor should those who walk on it do so in pride but in meekness, humbling themselves before the Lord.

If we're not careful to avoid overcorrection, we can fall into reactionary thought patterns—forming our opinions as a response to what someone else believes rather than what is objectively true. Look no further than American politics to find examples of overcorrection, reactionary thinking, and relativism. This tendency is rampant in many parts of church culture, not just in politics. With the growth of the Internet which grants widespread access to far too much information and opinions, extremism and cancel culture have become the new gold standard for online communication. Not to mention the fact that higher education—Christian and secular alike—often dispenses with essential classes like basic reasoning and logic, which would have helped curb some of these tendencies. The exclusion of basic philosophy in education is also a telltale sign of Satan's cultural influence since discouraging critical thinking is a primary marker of groups such as cults, the New Age, and pagan religions. And now it is a distinctive trait of modernity.

Out of the Pan and into the Fire

As I researched the New Age and started following former occultists and New Agers on social media, a pattern emerged. As we've seen, it's in our nature to overcorrect after trauma or perceived threats. New Age converts often overcorrect from their extreme, pagan lifestyle (license) into legalism. They escaped Satan in the occult and ran headlong into another Satanic temptation in the form of Phariseeism. When I say that former New Agers are tempted by Phariseeism, I don't mean they are unsaved like the Pharisees. I mean Satan tempts Christians with legalism to shipwreck their faith.

It certainly is not an overstatement to call the Pharisees Satanic. As early as Matthew 3:7, John the Baptist refers to the Pharisees and Sadducees as a "brood of vipers." He goes on to say that they are like trees that don't produce good fruit and are thrown into the fire (of hell). References to serpents in Scripture are metaphors for Satan and evil, which the Pharisees knew well. They would have understood John's statement as a severe insult and accusation. Jesus repeats John's words in Matthew 12:34, "Brood of vipers! How can you speak good things when you are evil? For the mouth speaks from the overflow of the heart." Going along with John's imagery of good and bad fruit, Jesus takes the accusation a step further by calling the Pharisees "evil."

Most blatant of all, Jesus says to the Pharisees in John 8:44, "You are of your father the devil, and you want to carry out your father's desires. He was a murderer from the beginning and does not stand in the truth, because there is no truth in him. When he tells a lie, he speaks from his own nature, because he is a liar and the father of lies." He delivers these harsh words as proof of why the Pharisees don't believe him since he only speaks truth and not lies.

In Colossians 2, we see another connection between Satan and legalism. The Colossian heresy references extrabiblical laws based on "human tradition" (v. 8) such as ascetic practices, the worship of angels, and accessing a "visionary realm" (v. 18). "If with Christ you died to the elemental spirits of the world, why, as if you were still alive in the world, do you submit to regulations—'Do not handle, Do not taste, Do not touch' (referring to things that all perish as they are used)—according to human precepts and teachings? These have indeed an appearance of wisdom in promoting self-made religion and asceticism and severity to the body, but they are of no value in stopping the indulgence of the flesh" (vv. 20–23 ESV).

What exactly these things mean is debated among scholars. It's at least clear that worship of demons who pretend to be angels and seeing into the spiritual realm through demonic visions were, and still are, common pagan practices. What I think we're seeing in this letter is gnostic syncretism similar to "Christian witchcraft." But instead of Satan tempting the Colossians with licentiousness, he's drawing them into legalism through ascetic practices. Paul says these "regulations" are worldly and from the "elemental spirits of the world" (v. 20 ESV).

James also uses strong language when speaking of the heart condition of self-righteous believers. In James 3:13–15, he connects the kind of pride exemplified by those tempted with Phariseeism to demons: "Who among you is wise and understanding? By his good conduct he should show that his works are done in the gentleness that comes from wisdom. But if you have bitter envy and selfish ambition in your heart, don't boast and deny the truth. Such wisdom does not come down from above but is earthly, unspiritual, demonic."

Satan doesn't exclusively use paganism or licentiousness to deceive us and draw us away from Christ. He will use any means necessary to shipwreck our faith—including the trap of legalism and materialism. After all, he "disguises himself as an angel of light" (2 Cor. 11:14) because he wants his message to sound good and moral. This is just one more reason we must test every spirit and message against the Word of God (1 John 4:1).

This kind of overcorrection isn't limited to people who have been in the New Age themselves, but also Christians who are aware of their stories and the dangers of the growing occult. With witchcraft and New Age practices becoming mainstream, we are entering a new phase of Satanic panic similar to the 1980s and 1990s. At that time, Christians began to react to the fruit of the first wave of New Age beliefs and Satanic cults that began in the 1960s and gained prominence in the 1970s. Christians engaged in panicked censorship such as frequent boycotting of companies or holidays, burning supposedly demonic products such as Cabbage Patch dolls,[7] and censoring rock 'n' roll music due to the belief that its rhythm was intrinsically evil.[8] Harry Potter entered the Satanic panic scene at the tail end in 1997. But it wasn't too late for Harry and J.K. Rowling to be thrown into the mess of fear and hatred.

Some Christians have a tendency to create pointless myths (see 1 Tim. 1:4) and superstitions surrounding demons and spiritual warfare. They may speak of demonic oppression as though merely saying a word, touching or owning an object, or watching a movie will automatically transfer some kind of demonic oppression to you like germs. This is not at all biblical and should send up a red flag of warning when you hear it. Just as Paul instructs the Corinthians that food sacrificed to idols (demons) is safe to eat (1 Cor. 8), so is secular media so long as you are not sinning or worshipping when partaking in it. If the Corinthians had been worshipping the idol the food was sacrificed to, it wouldn't be safe to eat. Paul assumes they weren't involved in the actual sacrifice of the animal but only buying the meat in the market after the fact. It isn't the external temptations or worldly things that determine whether or not you're "opening doors" to demonic oppression, but a person's heart. Is worship involved? Is this secular book, film, or song an idol or a source of temptation? Is it shepherding your heart and mind toward unrighteousness? These are the questions people need to ask themselves because it's the condition of the heart that gives Satan a foothold in your life.

Individual people and families are free to make their own choices of whether they want to read a certain book, listen to rock 'n' roll, or buy specific products. If they feel something is dangerous, or they just don't want their children exposed to those choices at an early age, that's a perfectly acceptable way to exercise Christian freedom. The problems arise when those preferences are made into laws for all Christians or when people become overwhelmed by fear of the devil as though he was not defeated at the cross. "For God has not given us a spirit of fear, but one of power, love, and sound judgment" (2 Tim. 1:7).

God is sovereign and he is good. Satan can do nothing without God's permission. Yes, spiritual warfare is real, and we should be educating ourselves about it more than we do. But being afraid and overcorrecting are not symptoms of wisdom and "sound judgment." Satan has already been defeated, and Christ is King *right now*. He has given us everything we need in his words to fight back against the schemes of the devil.

Chapter 9

Your Parenting Superpower

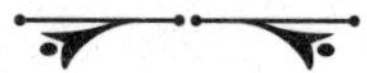

A few years ago, a friend's middle-school son made his own Ouija board with a neighborhood friend. The boys used it and witnessed a brief apparition. Terrified by what they'd seen, they quickly confessed to their parents and gave up the board. My friends responded by guiding their son through an in-depth study of what the Bible said on the topic of demonic supernaturalism. They didn't remove any of his fantasy games, books, or toys from the home but chose to teach him rather than censor him. He has since grown in wisdom and shunned anything resembling the occult.

Meanwhile, their son's friend was met with a very different response. His parents immediately removed everything in their home having to do with fantasy magic. I don't know what happened to that boy, but I do know his parents' actions likely didn't send the message they intended. Is it possible the boy was struggling with spiritual lust and couldn't handle the temptation of fictional magic? Yes, it's possible. And since I wasn't there, speaking of this is only theoretical. But it's also possible the parents responded in fear and didn't take the time to help him work through the issue with wisdom, nuance, and proper application of Scripture.

When to Restrict Media

This isn't a parenting book, but many of you reading right now are parents wondering if you should let your child read fantasy. When is it appropriate to restrict content, and when should you allow them to read and trust them to be discerning about a story? Restricting media, even for adults, is necessary at times, especially when something directly disobeys God's commands or causes chronic temptation. In fact, restriction of certain things is not only necessary but imperative. Yet it shouldn't be our first and primary response—especially not to minority temptations like fantasy. Your parenting superpower is not censorship but discipleship and education. Our children will come in contact with secular ideas whether we like it or not. By the time they reach middle school and high school, our primary job is no longer protecting them from the world but teaching them how to think and navigate society with prudence and godliness.

Before we discuss how and why we should teach our children discernment, let's first nail down the benefits of restriction for younger children. When they're little, the purpose of restricting media is not to control or manipulate them into becoming mature Christians. Parents are not their children's Holy Spirit. The purpose is to carry the burden of something too heavy for them. It's an act of humble service to a child who doesn't have the emotional or psychological capacity to bear the full weight of the world on their heart and mind. We wouldn't let small children use a stove, not because we don't want them to learn but because it's dangerous until they're mature enough to fully understand fire safety.

When parents share far too much popular culture with their young children, they may hope to avoid their teenagers rebelling against censorship. There is a trend in parenting that says children are more capable of handling the difficult things of life than we give them credit for, which often leads to parental oversharing. When *Doctor Strange in the Multiverse of Madness*[1] came out, I was working part-time at a movie theater. I scanned tickets for the morning shift the Saturday of opening weekend, watching as family after family came through with small children. The youngest child taken to see the film that day looked around eighteen months old. Every time these families came through, I politely said, "Just so you know, this film is very dark and has horror-level violence and gore." Sometimes the moms would look annoyed and say their husbands looked it up and said it would be okay. But during a five-hour shift, only one lone father with three small boys turned around and switched his tickets. I went home that day on the verge of tears but thanking God for that one man who cared for his children so well.

Of course we want to be honest with our children about the world. But consider that honesty can be expressed to small children in other ways—through telling them their parents are carrying a heavy burden so the child doesn't have to. They can just be a kid for a little while. That way, instead of attempting to build trust through oversharing before they're ready, it's built through honest communication about the parent's heart to serve and love their child. Then, little by little, as the child matures, they can carry heavier burdens and more knowledge of evil in the world. By the time they leave the house for college or a career, there should be no more secrets remaining. Of course, they'll need a lot more life experience and maturity to handle new things that come their way. But ideally—allowing that our messy lives are not usually ideal—they'll have the training they need to understand that evil exists, people sin, and the world doesn't have the same moral standards they or their parents do.

There may be times when parents need to wait until children mature before giving them certain fantasy books, movies, or games. Personally, I think letting children under the age of ten read the entire Harry Potter series is not age appropriate. The older the students, the darker their battle against evil becomes. They also need to be mature enough to understand how to discern fictional magic since Harry Potter is not a perfect example of divine supernaturalism. I'll discuss why we've chosen to let our kids read Harry Potter later. For now, I'll just say that it's okay, even healthy, for children to wait between books in a series. We managed it as children in the 1990s and early 2000s while waiting for the whole series to release. Of course they will beg to read the next book since they want to know what's going to happen, but learning to wait and trust their parents' discernment on timing is good for them.

Warfare Training Ground

Although media restriction is necessary at times, our superpower as parents is still primarily discipleship. We can't force our children into loving Jesus or being wise. Only the Holy Spirit has the authority to soften hearts. Yet we can educate them, prepare them, and be used by the Spirit to guide them toward truth. When exposing children to fantasy, they need an age-appropriate understanding of demonic and divine supernaturalism so they can begin to discern the context of fictional magic on their own or with parental guidance. That means teaching them about spiritual warfare and even the occult in developmentally appropriate ways. It's usually best to start with Scripture and walk through passages like 1 Samuel 28 where Saul visits the medium of En-dor. This passage demonstrates both the superior power of God as well as what mediums attempt to do apart from him.

As I've studied the New Age occult and its growing numbers, I've also shared a little of that information with my children. I don't want to overburden or scare them, but I do want to prepare them for media discernment as well as the growth of the New Age. At the time of writing this, they're twelve, ten, and seven years old. I can't tell my twelve- and ten-year-olds about the darkest parts of witchcraft, but I can teach them about demons and a little about lighter occult and New Age practices. My seven-year-old gets even less information about the occult, but I do tell him that angels and demons exist. He knows that if he is ever afraid at night, he can pray to Jesus for help. When he was six, he insisted our soft-closing toilet seat snapped back open on its own after he'd closed it. Since I hadn't seen it myself, I wasn't sure what really happened. I neither confirmed nor denied what he'd witnessed was supernatural. I didn't want to cast doubt on his word or make him feel as though something like that wasn't possible. So I just hugged him, prayed, and we sang "God Is Bigger [than the Boogie Man]" from VeggieTales.[2] It still took him some time to feel completely safe. But he eventually grasped in his childlike way that Jesus was stronger, and my son can call on him if he's afraid.

My husband and I also chose to teach them about spiritual warfare and the occult because it became increasingly obvious to me that they might come into contact with another child whose family was involved in the New Age, and that's exactly what happened. A girl in the fourth-grade class at our private Christian school informed my ten- and twelve-year-old daughters that she was a "mailbox for spirits." She recounted a story of visiting the house of a medium where she and her mother communicated with the spirits of deceased warriors. The girl insisted that she was now speaking to spirits who used her to send messages to other people. My daughters were able to immediately recognize what was really going on and informed her that she was speaking with demons. Although their friend rejected this information, they continued to befriend and pray for her.

Much of this kind of confusion is avoidable if we as parents and churches were better at educating ourselves and children about spiritual warfare and the growing occult. Out of the two hundred "New Age to Jesus" testimonies I listened to, 72 percent had a history with wider Christianity growing up. Their Christian upbringing included everything from nominal belief with limited church attendance to fully devoted regular Protestant or Catholic church attendance. Many of these people expressed regret that they never knew much about the Bible or Satan as a child or teenager. They knew vaguely who Jesus was and maybe even the basics of the gospel, but that was all. They had never been taught that God prohibited divination or that spirits could speak to them, move objects, or deceive them. They never learned they should "not believe every spirit, but test the spirits to see if they are from God, because many false prophets have gone out into the world" (1 John 4:1). They regretted that they hadn't read or been taught biblical warnings regarding spiritual warfare, demonic supernaturalism, or the armor of God (Eph. 6:11). They also expressed regret they hadn't known about the dangers of the New Age occult sooner. After converting, they still gave glory to God in all he'd taught them through their journey away and back to him. A thorough education of Scripture alone will never save someone. But without it, we're sending our children into battle against the enemy devoid of the armor of God.

Andrea Huertas was introduced to the occult by a warlock in middle school.[3] She'd grown up in a strong Christian family where "Jesus was everything" in their household. When her warlock friend talked to her about witchcraft, she didn't know anything about it or that it was wrong. She became curious and started borrowing the boy's occult books including *The Satanic Bible*. "For some reason, I started to connect with these books. It's like the books wanted me to read [them]." She grew increasingly curious and was influenced by overt depictions of witchcraft in films like *The Craft*. After playing with her friend's homemade Ouija board, the boy told her she could find the real board at Toys"R"Us. She asked her parents for a new board game, and they took her to the store and bought it. Her parents didn't know what the board was, nor was there any teaching at church that would have prepared them for such a moment. Andrea was addicted until the day the demons controlling the planchette (the indicator) told her to kill her family. She immediately broke the board in half and put it in the trash outside. After school the next day, she found it sitting on her bed in one piece. She tried to tell her parents, but they didn't believe her. On her own, she burned the Ouija board and the borrowed books. This began her journey through many painful years of rebellion and trauma until Jesus eventually snatched her from the clutches of the enemy.

Without previous knowledge of spiritual warfare and occult modalities, someone could be taken in by these deceptions. Demons can oppress anyone, regardless of age (Mark 9:17–18; Acts 16:16). Out of the two hundred testimonies, 32 percent experienced some form of demonic supernaturalism during childhood. This included everything from an early introduction to the occult to overt demonic attacks. Although we need to restrict the darkest parts of demonology for their mental and emotional well-being, most children above the age of seven or eight can understand the basics of the unseen realm and how to pray in Jesus's name when they're afraid.

Teaching children about spiritual warfare may seem too scary and heavy to explain to those who haven't experienced overt demonic attacks, but it isn't dissimilar from "stranger danger." We tell them of the dangers of talking to strangers before something bad happens so they're prepared. Educating them about spiritual warfare is not unlike telling them that their bodies shouldn't be touched inappropriately and to inform us right away if that ever happens. Lessons like that are a weighty but necessary thing for a child. Instructing them about the dangers and deception of invisible enemies is no less important. Yet we should also be aware of each child's sensitivities and take into account whether or not they have the maturity to understand that God is greater than the devil. I often tell my children they're safe under the shadow of his wings (Ps. 91:4) and pray that verse over them before bed.

Your Discipleship Superpower

Armed with knowledge of the invisible enemy, how much more are children able to understand and discern supernaturalism in fiction? In addition to the benefits of fantasy we discussed earlier, engaging with fictional magic and asking the five discernment questions can help children practice wisdom regarding real spiritual warfare issues. When we first began discipling our children through supernaturalism, we would ask them what they thought of magic or witchcraft in media. We welcomed their questions that led to fruitful conversations about theology, the nuances of the magic systems, story worlds, and characters. Since they already had a surface-level understanding of demonology and the occult, their ability to discern between divine and demonic supernaturalism in fiction came much faster. They have much to learn as they grow older, but they've already begun to show their own discernment with children's fiction, television, and board games.

When we're reading a book or watching a movie, we often filter the content automatically, running it through whatever mental sieve each of us has in place. Regardless of personal preferences, what should catch our attention more than anything is whether worldly content is being glorified or encouraged in the wider narrative of the story. Are evil actions and character traits presented as good or bad in the story? Are compassion, humility, mercy, and forgiveness presented in an attractive way? Is the villain "cooler" than the good guy? Are we being emotionally manipulated into desiring evil so the protagonists can succeed in their goals? Is the book or film displaying real occult magic in a fictional setting?

Just because there is evil present in the story doesn't mean it's being glorified or recommended. This often confuses Christian parents when they're looking for stories with no evil or sin present at all. Doing so will only further mislead children as they grow and begin to grapple with the world around them. It's far more important that children, teens, and even adults engage with stories that show the world as it is, within reason, and the negative consequences of complying with evil. Stories appeal primarily to our emotions and secondarily to our minds. The message the narrative is trying to convey has the power to change someone's mind *through* their heart and emotions. A good story will shepherd a reader's emotions through suffering and into the light of truth. A bad story will manipulate the reader's emotions and sympathies into adopting untruths.

In the award-winning film, *Inception*, Cobb (played by Leonardo DiCaprio) steals corporate secrets through dream technology.[4] For a particularly difficult job, Cobb and his elite team are forced to delve into the deepest parts of Robert Fischer's (played by Cillian Murphey) mind and plant a new, manufactured memory—one that is deeply personal. Once Fischer's heart has been pierced by such a strong emotional connection to his deceased father, he quickly decides to do exactly what Cobb was aiming for—breaking up his father's company.

The brilliance of this movie is that director Christopher Nolan intended it to be a commentary on moviemaking.[5] Through emotional connection, the mind is changed. This is exactly what happens to us when we engage with stories and characters. The irony of *Inception* is that it's an inception itself. The viewers are so deeply involved in Cobb's life and work that they can only focus on desiring him to succeed. Yet Cobb is a criminal invading Fischer's mind in a gross invasion of his privacy for the purpose of helping a rival company. Despite this, we're easily persuaded to desire that Cobb succeed because of the emotional connection formed by skillful storytelling and his traumatic backstory.

Once someone makes a strong emotional connection to a story or character, it often becomes extremely difficult to discuss the possibility there could be flaws in the narrative. When people relate to or deeply sympathize with a character and the character's journey, they no longer desire to tear the story apart and acknowledge the pros and cons. On an emotional level, holding negativity in the back of their mind could ruin the experience and love of the story. This refusal to acknowledge imperfections is just one more area of growth for both adults and children. The more we accept that there is no perfect story apart from God's story, the more comfortable we become being entertained by imperfect stories, within reason, and appreciating something for what it is rather than what we want it to be. As we continue to discuss stories in the following chapters, remember that analyzing something isn't meant to ruin it. In fact, I hope that in the long run you can enjoy these stories even more the deeper you understand the realms and their people. No human is capable of sub-creating perfection—not you nor anyone else. The more comfortable we become with our own inadequacies, the more we understand our dependence on God, and the better we're able to rest in the perfection of his narrative about our imperfect world.

The following questions are discussed at length in the book *The Pop Culture Parent: Helping Kids Engage Their World for Christ*[6] and have been adapted from Ted Turnau's book *Popologetics*.[7] These five questions will help children and adults alike think through the story in a simple, straightforward way. They're intended to help you and your child first understand the plot, the structure of the story world, the goodness and common grace found there, the false messages, and how Jesus and the gospel are the ultimate fulfillment of the story's hopes. "As parents, we need to *understand* popular culture and parenting according to God's Word. Only *then* can we avoid both (1) fearing popular culture and (2) embracing it with little discernment. And only then can we apply this truth to our parenting and to the entertainments our children love. That way, we can best glorify God as we fulfill our incredible and biblical calling as parents."[8]

Five Simple Questions to Ask about Popular Culture

1. What is the story?
2. What is the moral and imaginary world?
3. What is good, true, and beautiful in this world (common grace)?
4. What is false and idolatrous in this world?
5. How is Jesus the true answer to this story's hopes?[9]

Individual people and families will draw the line between restricting content or discipling through it in different places. Not only is this an exercise in Christian freedom, but it's also a good thing. God didn't intend us to be carbon copies of one another. We all have different life experiences, traumatic events, temptations, dispositions, and personalities—as do our children. We won't always understand why others make the choices they do. But we can respect one another by speaking to and thinking of each other with grace and knowing that we may not have all the information about someone else's circumstances. This extension of grace is not only needed for more restrictive families to show to less restrictive. Misplaced judgment of other believers can go both ways. There may be times when we might consider cautioning someone against a choice they've made, but this should be done with prayer and gentleness.

What are the best ways to guide our families through a fantasy story if we aren't experts in literature? Thankfully, you don't have to be an expert to understand the basics of story structure, metaphors, and how to apply those to fictional magic.

Chapter 10

Literary Considerations

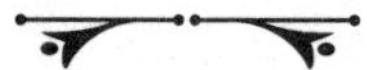

Evangelicals sometimes read stories the way we read the Bible—without an understanding of literary devices and genres. Reading this way can skew our understanding of the author's intent and make it appear as though evil is being glorified or encouraged when it isn't. In order to properly answer the five fictional magic discernment questions, we need to define some literary terms. Without that information, you might miss the nuances of the story structure and character arcs. Christian film reviews don't always take these categories into consideration and end up giving a distorted or overly critical perspective of the filmmaker's intent or miss the purpose of the movie. Sometimes we think because we're learned in theology and culture, this makes us capable of analyzing art and stories. Yet that's rarely the case. This is also misleading for parents who are dependent on online reviews to help them choose a good film for family movie night. Christian book review sites can also be misleading at times, although they are much harder to find. (See the appendix for a list of resources for Christian media reviews.)

There are many things to consider when analyzing a story. The first considerations are how an understanding of story structure and character arcs change how we interpret narrative themes. Story structure is how the narrative is organized. A character arc is the inner transformation each character undergoes during the course of the story. The arcs, plot structure, and themes of the story often go hand in hand and enhance one another. There's more than one structure used by writers, but the most common is the "three-act structure" you'd see in a full-length play. "Discovery writers"—people who choose not to follow a specific structure while writing—will often edit in such a way that intrinsically creates unintended structure or natural story beats. Author K. M. Weiland provides an example of each character arc and the three-act plot points in her books, *Structuring Your Novel: Essential Keys for Writing an Outstanding Story*[1] and *Creating Character Arcs: The Masterful Author's Guide to Uniting Story Structure, Plot, and Character Development*.[2] The following is a summary of only the main plot and character arc points from Weiland and are intended as general guidelines rather than story laws. See her books and website for a more detailed list.

- **The First Act** spans from the 1-percent mark to the 25-percent mark and presents the foundational period of setup for the story to follow.[3] It introduces all characters who will be important catalysts within the conflict, as many prominent settings as possible, the protagonist's personal dilemma and goal, the main conflict and the antagonistic force driving it, and the stakes if the protagonist fails within the conflict.[4]

- **The First Half of the Second Act** spans from the 25-percent mark to the 50-percent mark. This notes a period of reaction for the protagonist, in which he tries to cope with the events of the first plot point.[5] The character ventures (or is thrust) into uncharted territory and gets lost. He may not see it that way himself, but this is where he begins to discover that the old rules (the lie he believes) no longer apply.[6]
- **The Midpoint** occurs at the 50-percent mark and is a moment of revelation for the protagonist as he comes into a clearer understanding of the true nature of the conflict.[7] The midpoint's emphasis is always placed on the protagonist's shift from a reactive role (not in control of the conflict) to an active role (taking control of the conflict).[8]
- **The Second Half of the Second Act** spans from the 50-percent to the 75-percent marks. This is a period of action for the protagonist. Armed with his new understanding, found at the midpoint, he can now take the action right to the antagonistic force.[9]
- **The Third Act** is the final quarter of the book, spanning from the 75-percent mark to the end, in which the conflict is finally resolved, one way or another.[10] The third act is all about his figuring out if he really wants to serve the Truth after all. Is it worth the

price he's just paid at the third plot point? If he's ever going to return to his life of "safety" in the lie, this is going to be his last chance.[11]

- **The Climax** starts halfway through the third act, around the 88-percent mark, and is heralded by a final turning point that pits the protagonist against the antagonistic force in the final battle.[12] The conflict has revved to the point where a confrontation must happen between the protagonist and the antagonistic force. If the protagonist is to have any chance of winning that conflict, he must prove he is able to stick with the Truth for the long haul.[13]

Case Studies

Two notable examples of film reviews gone wrong are the widespread misconceptions of the Disney films *The Little Mermaid* (1989) and *Frozen* (2013). For years, Christian sentiment regarding *The Little Mermaid* has focused primarily on the fact that Ariel is a rebellious teenager. Parents often censored this film, believing it would promote rebellion in their home. In the film, King Triton is initially an authoritarian figure who responds to Ariel's adventurous spirit too harshly. This pushes Ariel even farther away in the second act, and she responds by doing something she knows is wrong—selling her voice to the sea witch, Ursula, in exchange for legs. She's attempting to take charge of her own future and resist Triton's plans for her. This familial dynamic seems to place the father in the role of the villain and Ariel as the victim of his overbearing authority.

If we stop analyzing the story right there, it certainly doesn't look good. That's the thing about stories—you often have to see how they end and the full scope of the character arcs to understand the protagonist's poor decisions in the second act. For this story to "encourage teenage rebellion," Ariel's defiance and actions would need to produce good results, but they don't. Yes, she gets Eric to fall in love with her. But the plan she concocts with Ursula at the story's midpoint—the point at which the protagonist switches from reacting to acting—fails miserably. The price she paid to have legs and be with Eric was far too high. Instead of her rebellion paying off, Ariel doesn't meet the contract requirements, and Ursula curses her to live forever in her creepy garden of shriveled merpeople. This is the story's third act and climactic moment when all hope seems lost. Ariel's actions have now cost her everything—her life, family, friends, and the man she loves. If this is meant to encourage teens to rebel against their parents, this moment misses the mark entirely.

But suddenly the "villainous" father, King Triton, appears to save the day. What had originally seemed to be an ugly portrayal of a parent, we now see was just overprotective, misplaced affection. In trying to keep her safe, King Triton had made mistakes of his own. Thankfully, he's not the villain of our story but the savior. When he realizes his daughter has signed a contract with the sea witch, he takes her place, signing his own name on the document in Ariel's stead. While she's free to go, the king himself shrivels into almost nothing. This isn't a story that demonizes parents but celebrates a father and a king laying down his life for a rebellious child. It's a reflection of the gospel.

After Ursula is killed, her spells are broken and Triton returns. But Ariel still can't leave the sea to be with Eric. Nothing she's done has panned out, and she's powerless to reach her goal. Again, Triton appears in her hour of need and shows more mercy than Ariel deserves because of his great love for his daughter. He gifts her with legs and blesses her marriage to Eric in the end. Every happiness she has is because of the grace her father showed despite her rebellion, not because of it.

Not only does *The Little Mermaid* unintentionally paint a common grace picture of the gospel, but it also has a clear and realistic depiction of the occult and the lure of demonic supernaturalism in Ursula and her contract. Former New Age occultists often speak of their relationship with demons in legal terms. They feel as though they opened the door for demons to enter their life, unknowingly binding them in a contractual relationship that eventually gains more power over their life as time goes by. Likewise, Ariel comes to realize she didn't fully understand what she was signing up for. Nor was Ursula's contract worth losing her or Triton's life. In the end, attempting to pull away from that contract proves more difficult than she could have ever known. For an occultist, leaving their familiar spirits behind is impossible without Christ. Even then, spiritual warfare only increases after conversion as the enemy punishes them and attempts to steal away their seed of faith. This film, full of so much magic and rebellion, should not be seen as a story that will draw children into the occult but push them farther from it.

The second case study is the beloved Disney film *Frozen*. It's equally as misunderstood as *The Little Mermaid* but presents a slightly more complex situation structurally. The biggest critique of this film by Christian parents and reviewers lies primarily in the lyrics of "Let It Go" where Elsa says, "No right, no wrong, no rules for me. I'm free!"[14] This is seen as an expression of relativism and a rejection of absolute truth. In the early phases of production, Elsa was the antagonist in alignment with Hans Christian Andersen's fairy tale, "The Snow Queen."[15] As composers Kristen Anderson-Lopez and Robert Lopez began to write "Let It Go"—what would have normally been her villain song—they empathized with her affliction and depth of feeling. Anderson-Lopez recounts their thought process in an interview: "Once you have a character who sings with this amount of emotion, she couldn't be the villain anymore. And we put ourselves in the mindset of someone who would leave everything behind and be stuck out on a mountain and how cold and scared she would be at that moment. . . . Once we found that song, we had building blocks for the rest of the movie."[16]

The beginning of the second act is usually where Disney places the villain's song (with some exceptions such as *The Little Mermaid*'s villain song being at the midpoint). And the beginning of the second act is exactly where Elsa sings "Let It Go." It's a somewhat confusing moment structurally since this is where the antagonist should be flexing their muscles. With the switch from an antagonistic *character* to an antagonistic *force*, Elsa and "Let It Go" must play dual roles.

We see the expansion of Elsa's ice as a beautiful expression of her freedom apart from the fear she'd grown up with. Her demeanor and change of clothing from modest to sexy is a release of the confines her parents had mistakenly placed on her out of their fear of her ice. This is clearly a moment where the writers want the audience to celebrate with Elsa as she embraces who she was born to be and sheds the fear and guilt she's felt all her life. But from a structural standpoint, this should be one of her low points. Not only does Elsa still have a lot of growth left in her character arc, but the freedom she's embracing isn't real. When Anna finally locates the ice castle and Elsa discovers she isn't really free, she's devastated, and the fear comes rushing back in worse than before.

The relativistic lyrics in "Let It Go" actually fit where Elsa should be in her character arc—newly aware that she'd grown up believing a lie but under a false understanding of how to fix it. She feels temporary freedom because she doesn't have all the facts and is replacing the first lie—fear of herself and her ice—with a second and more deadly one—she doesn't have to be afraid because there is no right, no wrong, no rules. She's also making the selfish decision to run away from her family and responsibilities as queen. In *Frozen II*, Elsa sees a memory of herself singing "Let It Go," and she groans and turns away from the vision as though embarrassed. In the end of the first movie, the antagonistic force isn't Elsa's ice but fear itself. There's a beautiful moment where her sister, Anna, sacrifices her own life for Elsa in an act of true love. In that moment, it finally clicks that Elsa can control her powers as well as her fear through love. This not only defrosts Anna and their frozen kingdom but stands in direct contrast to Elsa's isolated moment on the mountain where she somewhat selfishly sang "Let It Go." It's also reminiscent of 1 John 4:18 which says, "Perfect love casts out fear" (ESV).

The lyrics of "Let It Go" wouldn't seemingly glorify evil or present an issue for Christians if it was obvious to the audience this was a low moment in Elsa's arc. The problem is that it's not obvious. Changing a character's role from antagonist to protagonist mid-production created a confusing moment at the beginning of the second act. The progressive lyrics, extremely catchy tune, beautiful ice castle, and clothing swap only added to our disorientation since it seemed like a moment of celebration rather than the low point that it really was. Small children won't be able to understand the complexity of this moment for Elsa, but more mature children and teens should be able to grasp the nuances if parents take the time to discuss the confusion of her arc.

Literary Typology

The second consideration that's sometimes misunderstood by reviewers and parents is a type of metaphor similar to allegory. If you ask a true Narnian fan whether Aslan is Jesus, they will deny it instantly. In a private letter, C. S. Lewis explained how Narnia is not an allegory. "If Aslan represented the immaterial Deity in the same way in which Giant Despair represents Despair, he would be an allegorical figure. In reality however he is an invention giving an imaginary answer to the question, 'What might Christ become like, if there really were a world like Narnia and He chose to be incarnate and die and rise again in that world as He actually has done in ours?' This is not allegory at all."[17]

This slight distinction of Aslan not fully representing Jesus has always seemed picky to me, but it has still had a significant impact on the way Christian writers view the use of allegory. Instead of the term *allegory*, Lewis preferred *supposal*, meaning that The Chronicles of Narnia was like supposing how Jesus and redemptive history would have happened in another world. Allegories such as *Pilgrim's Progress* have more direct symbolism or a one-to-one correlation.

Much like Tolkien and Lewis's dislike of allegory, modern fantasy authors tend to steer clear of it and other overt literary metaphors in favor of more covert gospel messages, supposals, and even typologies.*[18] Allegory does still have a place in litera-

---

* Tolkien wrote in the introduction of *The Fellowship of the Ring*, "But I cordially dislike allegory in all its manifestations, and always have done so since I

ture. Still, many Christian writers see it as having a rather Sunday school tone that often fails to sneak past the watchful dragons of the mind. As modern writing styles change and adapt to reader and market demands, fictional magic is couched in far more subtle, in-world modalities. Even Lewis's Deep Magic, brilliant and groundbreaking as it was, is far more direct as a literary supposal than The Lord of the Rings or more modern fantasy magic systems. Even then, metaphors are often still present, buried under layers of plot and character arcs.

More often than not, we find something more akin to typology used more than allegory in fiction. Typology is normally something the Bible uses to describe early figures or scenes in Scripture that are *types* of later New Testament figures and scenes. Romans 5:14 says, "Nevertheless, death reigned from Adam to Moses, even over those who did not sin in the likeness of Adam's transgression. He is a type of the Coming One." Paul is saying that Adam is a *type* of Christ. Typology is a kind of literary foreshadowing of Jesus and the gospel, yet the correlations aren't perfect or direct. For example, biblical figures such as Adam, Moses, and Joseph are Christ types who foreshadow Jesus's life. They aren't allegorical since they're imperfect humans foreshadowing the coming of a perfect Savior. Because of Aslan's perfection and identity as the son of the "Emperor-beyond-the-Sea," he more directly reflects Jesus.

Type figures can have far fewer distinguishable similarities. Israel as a whole nation is also a Christ type when they flee from

---

grew old and wary enough to detect its presence. I much prefer history, true or feigned, with its varied applicability to the thought and experience of readers. I think that many confuse 'applicability' with 'allegory'; but the one resides in the freedom of the reader, and the other in the purposed domination of the author."

Egypt. Hosea 11:1 says, "When Israel was a child, I loved him, and out of Egypt I called my son." This foreshadows Jesus leaving Egypt as a child to live in Nazareth (Matt. 2:15). An example of a type scene in the Bible is men meeting potential brides at wells where someone draws water for the other. This happens with Abraham's servant and Rebekah (Gen. 24:12–54), Jacob and Rachel (Gen. 29:1–12), then Moses and Zipporah (Exod. 2:16–22). This pattern foreshadows Jesus, the Bridegroom of the church, meeting the Samaritan woman at the well and offering her living water (John 4:1–42).

In fiction, a typological pattern can emerge within the story itself from scenes and characters that prefigure something to come after the midpoint. We usually refer to this as merely foreshadowing. When characters and scenes in fiction mimic biblical figures, this is more akin to typology. This doesn't necessarily have a repeated pattern within the narrative itself but is usually Christological threads that appear in stories whether on purpose, accidentally, through special revelation, or common grace. Humankind can't seem to stop telling stories about someone sacrificing themselves for others despite disagreements on the definition of love. Whether we're aware of it or not, humans have a deep, immovable understanding that love is self-sacrificial, which is perfected and completed in the death and resurrection of Jesus Christ. Even moments in secular stories create unintended Christ types such as King Triton taking on the weight of Ariel's broken contract with Ursula and giving his life up for hers. In Christian fantasy, typology is even more commonly used to convey the gospel while still keeping the book in the general market as Lewis and Tolkien did. When discipling children through secular stories, teach them to find any gospel-like moments in the narrative. Even if it's imperfect, this is a healthy way to celebrate that general revelation cries out in worship of Christ and his death on the cross.

(The following contains spoilers for Harry Potter.)

Harry Potter is another example of an author intentionally creating an imperfect Christ type. In the end of the seventh book, Harry willingly faces Voldemort—arguably a Satan type—and gives his life for all people still threatened by their formidable enemy. The killing curse intended only for Harry rebounds onto Voldemort and sends them both into spiritual limbo. Harry's protection of supernatural love, gifted by his deceased mother, protects him from death once more. In the spirit realm, the mentor character, Dumbledore, tells Harry he isn't dead because Harry was a willing sacrifice—someone who lays down his life for his friends (John 15:13). In contrast, the Dark Lord's goals were a distortion of the truth found in 1 Corinthians 15:26 (KJV): "The last enemy that shall be destroyed is death"—the words Harry finds on his parents' grave. Rowling admitted that she had the gospel-like ending of the series planned from the beginning yet never disclosed the scriptural influence to avoid spoilers.[19]

The Supernatural as Natural

The next consideration for proper literary discernment is something I call *the supernatural as natural*. It's extremely common and can be confusing for all ages if not categorized properly. Only the *elohim*—beings residing in the spiritual realm—have the power to bend the laws of nature. When humans participate in those actions, it is only by the *elohim*'s power, while demons and angels are under God's authority. There is no human, animal, or object that has permanent supernatural abilities. Yet *the supernatural as natural*—having innate supernatural abilities—is one of the most common fictional magic tropes in all of fantasy literature.

Fictional magic is not often used as a way to express genuine occult involvement or the glorification of evil—although that is slowly growing as the New Age occult increases. Using contextual clues when discerning fantasy fiction is becoming more and more important as the New Age progressively becomes more mainstream. Movies and shows like *The Craft, Practical Magic*, "Chilling Adventures of Sabrina," and some horror films are not examples of *fantasy* magic but of real, demonic supernaturalism in a fictional setting. For Christian-made fantasy or nonoccult-affirming novels, magic is usually the method our subconsciousness uses to express the dual reality of *spirituality* on a *material* earth. The joining of the spiritual with the physical is often exhibited through the supernatural joining with material and scientific realities in uniquely fictional ways. For example, Superman has supernatural abilities, but it's a result of his Kryptonian heritage coming into contact with Earth's yellow sun. The explanation sounds scientific, but it's actually paper-thin on closer examination. Audiences must suspend disbelief in order to enjoy the story instead of being annoyed by the fact that his powers are scientifically impossible.

Metaphors and real-life correlations form without effort when the supernatural is portrayed as a permanent, inseparable part of a character. This innate aspect of them forces the character to grapple with real questions such as, "How can I use my powers for good and not evil?" This is the equivalent of asking, "How can I use my talents, gifts, and personal strengths for good rather than evil?" Suddenly what felt otherworldly and out of reach is now relatable to our everyday lives. Real supernaturalism that doesn't have much of a discernable "system" is now bound by specific laws and limitations within fiction. When we apply our discernment questions to stories where magic is innately present in material reality, the source is often the same as any naturally occurring talent.

One of the clearest examples of this is the *X-Men* who are portrayed as humans with a gene mutation which gives them supernatural abilities such as telepathy. Similar to Superman, nature and science are used to explain something we all know can only be supernatural. When evaluating these systems, innate magic shouldn't automatically be categorized as deification if a person initially appears to be the source of their own power. Instead, we should see it through the lens of literary metaphor and an extension of natural gifting. In that way, the source of all nature is not the self but God. The question then becomes whether or not the author (or character) acknowledges God's presence and ultimate supernatural authority within the story world and narrative. There may be times where innate magic is a sign of deification, but that's not very common.

A positive example of innate magic is The Ravenwood Saga* by Christian author Morgan L. Busse.[20] In a world where the Great Houses protect their lands with innate supernatural abilities, Selene Ravenwood was born a dreamwalker. In this series, God is known as "the Light," and the demon-like entity is "the Dark Lady." Although the Light gave all seven Great Houses supernatural powers that are passed through their bloodlines, the Dark Lady gains control over House Ravenwood and distorts it for sinister purposes. Although much of this magic system doesn't mimic real supernaturalism, the correlation of the demonic and divine is clearly defined

* This series is best for older teens and adults. It contains some violence, demonic powers, and mild sensuality between a husband and wife. There is an implication of sex, but nothing is shown.

and well represented. The power is innate, yet the characters openly acknowledge their dependence on the Light as the true source of their strength. Selene may have a kind of magic within her body, but she is still powerless against the Dark Lady without calling on the name of the Light to help her overcome the darkness.

A poor use of innate magic is the change we see in Elsa's character in *Frozen II*. (The following contains spoilers.) In the first movie, Elsa's innate magic was never said to be sourced from God since it was a secular film. It's still possible to categorize innate magic as divine supernaturalism since it's part of God's creation. Yet that possibility is ruined by the additional information we're given about Elsa's powers and the spirit world in the sequel. In the beginning of *Frozen II*, Elsa responds to a siren's song and accidentally wakes the elemental spirits of an enchanted forest. When the spirits invade Arendelle, she and her family embark on a journey to find the siren with the help of an indigenous people that practice a form of animism.*

Elsa finally reaches the source of the song and finds the memory of her deceased mother was the siren calling her. In the song "Show Yourself," Elsa's mother sings that Elsa is the one Elsa has been searching for. The bridge between humans and the magic of nature, the mysterious fifth elemental spirit, is *herself*. Although the magical river, Ahtohallan, is said to be the source of Elsa's power, positioning Elsa as the mysterious fifth spirit is a kind of deification and self-aggrandizement. If Ahtohallan is a more powerful deity, then Elsa is a kind of demigod. When talking through a story with

---

* Animism is the belief that all of nature—animals, objects, and locations—contain spirits or a spiritual essence. In this way, all of nature is seen as sentient. Various forms of animism are practiced by indigenous people groups around the world.

these kinds of pagan ideas with children, the magic could be recategorized as pagan mythology such as Hercules or Thor. The first *Frozen* film, taken by itself, doesn't fit as pagan mythology but as *the supernatural as natural.*

Pagan Mythology

The last consideration is mythology. This can be a confusing thing for Christians to understand or teach their children since the stories are often pagan and potentially demonic in origin (although not always). *The Merriam-Webster Dictionary* defines *myth* as a "traditional story of ostensibly historical events that serves to unfold part of the world view of a people or explain a practice, belief, or natural phenomenon."[21] In the Western world, we tend to think of myths as synonymous with fiction. However, the people who first created these stories didn't always think they were just stories. Mythology is deeply religious and was intended to make sense of the natural world, a people's origin, and their gods. That's why some of them are still incorporated into pagan practices today. Tolkien recognized this distinction and insisted mythology was an invention about truth. It was this belief that eventually led Lewis to recognize the gospel as a true myth and profess faith in Christ. Below is an excerpt from Humphrey Carpenter's *J. R. R. Tolkien: A Biography.*

> After dinner, Lewis, Tolkien, and [Hugo] Dyson went out for air. It was a blustery night, but they strolled along Addison's Walk discussing the purpose of myth. Lewis, though now a believer in God, could not yet understand the function of Christ in Christianity, could not perceive the meaning of the Crucifixion and Resurrection. He

declared that he had to understand the purpose of these events—as he later expressed it in a letter to a friend, "how the life and death of Someone Else (whoever he was) two thousand years ago could help us here and now—except in so far as his *example* could help us."

As the night wore on, Tolkien and Dyson showed him that he was here making a totally unnecessary demand. When he encountered the idea of sacrifice in the mythology of a pagan religion he admired it and was moved by it; indeed the idea of the dying and reviving deity had always touched his imagination since he had read the story of the Norse god Balder. But from the Gospels (they said) he was requiring something more, a clear meaning beyond the myth. Could he not transfer his comparatively unquestioning appreciation of sacrifice from the myth to the true story?

But, said Lewis, *myths are lies, even though lies breathed through silver.*

No, said Tolkien, *they are not.*

And, indicating the great trees of Magdalen Grove as their branches bent in the wind, he struck out a different line of argument.

You call a tree a tree, he said, and you think nothing more of the word. But it was not a "tree" until someone gave it that name. You call a star a star, and say it is just a ball of matter moving on a mathematical course. But that is merely how you see it. By so naming things and describing them you are only inventing your own terms about them. And just as speech is invention about objects and ideas, so myth is invention about truth.

We have come from God (continued Tolkien), and inevitably the myths woven by us, though they contain error, will also reflect a splintered fragment of the true light, the eternal truth that is with God. Indeed only by myth-making, only by becoming a "sub-creator" and inventing stories, can Man aspire to the state of perfection that he knew before the Fall. Our myths may be misguided, but they steer however shakily towards the true harbour, while materialistic "progress" leads only to a yawning abyss and the Iron Crown of the power of evil.

In expounding this belief in the inherent *truth* of mythology, Tolkien had laid bare the centre of his philosophy as a writer, the creed that is at the heart of *The Silmarillion*.

Lewis listened as Dyson affirmed in his own way what Tolkien had said. You mean, asked Lewis, that the story of Christ is simply a true myth, a myth that works on us in the same way as the others, but a myth that *really happened*? In that case, he said, I begin to understand.

At last the wind drove them inside, and they talked in Lewis's rooms until three a.m., when Tolkien went home. After seeing him out into

> the High Street, Lewis and Dyson walked up and down the cloister of New Buildings, still talking, until the sky grew light.
>
> Twelve days later Lewis wrote to his friend Arthur Greeves: "I have just passed on from believing in God to definitely believing in Christ—in Christianity. I will try to explain this another time. My long night talk with Dyson and Tolkien had a great deal to do with it."[22]

In Lewis's autobiography, *Surprised by Joy*, he spends a lot of time expounding on his love for pagan mythology before becoming a Christian. As a teenager, he enjoyed myths the way young men now enjoy more intellectual fandoms. He even wrote what can only be referred to as fan fiction—a Norse myth he called *Loki Bound* in which Loki was a projection of Lewis himself.[23] Just as his friends Tolkien and Dyson pointed out, Lewis was moved by the idea of a pagan god that sacrifices himself. Humans always have and always will write stories that reflect the gospel—the only true myth.

There are myths that are strikingly similar to many other Bible stories as well, such as comparable creation or flood myths. Although imperfect, we can see general revelation in these stories since only humans who innately long for a God-man to come to earth and die on their behalf are capable of telling such stories. Yet there are also myths that more clearly reflect demonic supernaturalism and are likely inspired, at least in part, by fallen spirits. These are the myths rampant with themes of sexual immorality, human sacrifices, and appeasing the gods to gain more power.

Parents may feel tempted to restrict pagan mythology. After all, pagan myths are not true myths like Christianity. They tell deceptive stories of false gods who may represent actual demons. Wouldn't watching such things be contrary to Scripture? Yet we usually study these things in order to learn about other cultures and world history. When considering whether or not to expose children to these stories, there's room for nuance. Parents will likely need to pick and choose since some myths contain explicit content and may not be valuable to an education. As far as pop culture depictions, parents should ask themselves whether or not their children have the maturity to understand that characters like Hercules or Thor are not gods and that Jesus is the only true God-man. I've heard a former occultist urge people not to watch any Marvel movies because Thor is a false god and watching Marvel is a form of worship. But such restrictions are generally unnecessary for older children and teenagers. It may prove to be a stumbling block to people who previously worshipped idols, yet that isn't a majority consideration. I think it's safe to say that most people aren't tempted toward idolatry after watching Marvel's *Thor*.

When we begin to create regulations that prevent engaging with any stories involving mythologies or other religions, we end up cutting ourselves off from most of the world and gospel themes in pagan myths. When taken to its logical extreme, saying that someone can't watch or read stories about Thor would apply to *any* other religion. We would also have to say you can't watch anime because it will teach your children the false religion of Shinto. You can't watch *Mulan* (1998) because of ancestral worship. You can't read or watch indigenous fiction because of animism.

However, in a Christian environment, we can openly teach how those beliefs differ from Scripture or how they reflect special revelation through common grace. The careful teaching of it promotes understanding, empathy, and even a greater heart for evangelism. Talking about it openly, discipling with wisdom and clarity, and allowing engagement with mythology and other religions is unlikely to push people toward those practices. Instead, it's more likely it will draw them farther away from paganism and ground them more in Christ.

There may be times and certain stories that are restricted because their mythology is outright demonic or egregiously glorifies evil. How can we be certain about which myths are man-made and which were imparted by demons? There is no way to know for sure. However, Satan and his demons are highly intelligent, but they aren't original. Their deceptions are simultaneously sneaky in their appeal to our sinful flesh and also predictable in replicating Satan's lie in Genesis 3. Each lie is tailor-made to individual people groups and cultures. Yet they have the same values and principles—pride, lack of empathy, putting oneself above the good of others, and a total rejection of the upside-down kingdom logic. We can see this reflected in religions such as Hinduism that holds tightly to a caste system that dictates strict and abusive social hierarchy. Demons do not tell stories of self-sacrifice and real love.

Only humans, images of God, are capable of innately understanding the goodness and beauty of a God who lays down his life for the people he loves. This is why even pagan myths sometimes tell similar stories to the Bible. (The following contains spoilers.) It's why the television show *Loki* (2021–2023) ended the second season with Loki saying, "I know what kind of god I need to be," just before sacrificing himself to hold the multiverse together and save billions of lives. Stories filled with such common grace resound in the hearts of all humans—saved and unsaved—because our souls cry out for the love and acceptance of the one true king, Jesus. In that way, even pagan mythology is capable of "invention about truth."[24]

Chapter 11

Discerning Stories

We saw how each of the discernment questions appeared in Scripture, but what do they look like when applied to stories? How can we avoid being too compromising on Christian story ethics without making law? In fiction, we have talking animals, innate magic in humans, superheroes, and portals to other physical realms and dimensions. In reality, animals don't talk apart from the power of God, humans are never born with supernatural power, and the only other realm isn't physical but spiritual. But it's okay—even *good*—that we write about entirely fictional places and things. We're sub-creating with our Creator when we tell impossible stories.

Let's look at an example of what allowing for freedom in sub-creation looks like in practice. Fictional talking animals violate the distinction between a human's intellectual soul and animal life, since animals aren't God's image and can't talk apart from extremely rare moments of divine power (Num. 22:28–30). The intellectual soul is an important theological concept since it forms the basis of what it means to be the image of God. However, it would be foolish to refuse to allow preschoolers to watch cartoons about talking animals or to censor The Chronicles of Narnia from children on the basis that they might get the wrong idea about what it means to be God's image. Children and adults alike generally understand that just because a dog talks in a cartoon doesn't mean they can in real life.

More problematic concepts that appear in fiction include violations of essential theological issues such as distortions of God's nature and character, the gospel, biblical sexuality, or the presence of syncretism and Gnosticism. I previously gave the example that it's more important that an antagonist empowered by demons shouldn't see the future than it is that they shouldn't speak to the dead. Seeing the future is a more essential doctrine in this context because it points to the fact that God alone exists outside of time. This is more important in fiction than maintaining that only God has the authority to speak to the dead. From a literary standpoint, speaking to ghosts is not usually literal but metaphorical and used to convey a certain theme or message.

There is also a lot of grace to be given when analyzing whether a secular story aligns with divine supernaturalism. In searching a story written by a non-Christian, we aren't asking if the author overtly acknowledges God's power and presence. We're only asking if common grace has produced a story that is, in part, consistent with special revelation and God's natural law. All truth is God's truth (Ps. 19:1–4; Rom. 1:18–25). We can enjoy, celebrate, and learn from the pieces of common grace we find in secular stories while simultaneously separating truth from lies. And because of that common grace and general revelation, secular stories may not automatically align with the principles and values of demonic supernaturalism either.

As you read the following chapter, remember our discussion on the way we connect to stories and characters being primarily through our emotions. It can be difficult if not impossible to hear and internalize a criticism of a story you've formed an emotional connection to in the past. That bond can potentially remove your ability to be objective about a story's true value and message. As we discuss the following books and films, please know that my critiques aren't meant to restrict your enjoyment of that story. They are meant only to encourage you to think through it without being misled by an emotional bond. I am also not the ultimate authority on literary and film analysis. There may be many other opinions on these stories that are equally as good or better than my own. What I'm offering you below are merely examples of how you can use the five discernment questions. In fact, I encourage you to investigate these stories on your own and see if you come to a different conclusion than I did.

Question 1: Source

What is the source of the magic? Is it demonic or divine?

The categorical distinctions can be useful guidelines for helping us determine if a particular event in fiction more closely resembles the source of demonic or divine supernaturalism in reality. Yet since fictional magic rarely functions exactly the way real supernaturalism does, it may not always be clear. In secular fantasy, it can be difficult if not impossible to discern the source of supernatural power, especially if it doesn't align with mirrored magic in reality. It's also common in both secular and Christian fantasy for innate magic to appear as though the source is the self when it's really nature—the *supernatural as natural.*

Western materialists consider magic only as a work of fiction and often don't see a need to name or even consider that it might have come from somewhere outside the individual person. So although identifying the source of the power is the most obvious difference between the demonic and divine when we look at Scripture, the source is often not clear in fiction. Sometimes there is no source, or the source is nature or biology (innate magic), like in *X-Men*. Other times the source is the self, such as in *Eragon* by agnostic author Christopher Paolini.[1] In his world, the power to cast spells comes from the magician's own life force. However, innate magic usually looks more like superpowers. In secular stories, it's common that neither God nor any sentient higher power is mentioned at all. This is just one more symptom of invisible materialism seeping into our lives. When no source is mentioned in the story, we can still analyze the magic system using the four remaining questions. Even in secular works, the magic may end up aligning with divine supernaturalism when applying questions one through four since these are often reflected by common grace and general revelation.

In stories where religions are represented, the source could be a personal deity, but more often it's an impersonal power like "the Force" in Star Wars. The Force was based on Eastern thought, such as Buddhism, which was popularized in the 1970s by the New Age.[2] It's clear just how unlike Yahweh the Force and "midi-chlorians"[*3] are in a galaxy far, far away, since they empower both the Jedis (light) and the Sith (dark) equally, like the Chinese yin and yang. As we'll see in the next section, although the source doesn't reflect

* "Midi-chlorians were microscopic, intelligent life forms that originated from the foundation of life in the center of the galaxy and ultimately resided within the cells of all living organisms, thereby forming a symbiotic relationship with their hosts. The Force spoke through the midi-chlorians, allowing certain beings to use the Force if they were sensitive enough to its powers."

divine supernaturalism at all, the story still can reflect it in other ways. Talking through *Star Wars* with older children and teenagers could be a great way to introduce and disciple them through Eastern religious themes and the New Age as it appears in popular American culture.

Another common religious magic system is often found in Japanese anime (cartoons) and manga (graphic novels). Anime, like American cartoons, is diverse in its presentation of the supernatural, and it's unwise to categorize it as only one genre. Sometimes American parents find a problematic show or film and decide to restrict all anime as a result. This would be like discovering one inappropriate American cartoon or TV show and then restricting all of them. Anime can be any genre and is made for all demographics—from shows made for preschoolers all the way to pornography. It's equally unwise to assume all anime is appropriate for children simply because it's animated. There are many anime films and shows that are made exclusively for adults and are entirely unfit for children. I suggest considering each individual film, show, or manga on its own rather than restricting or allowing all Japanese media.

Is it possible to discern the magic's source in most anime? The complication in modern Japanese culture is that they are far more atheistic than religious. However, their Shinto roots are still reflected in cultural values such as *nagomi*—harmony. Shintoism frequently shows up in Japanese stories, since many view it as fictional mythology. Shinto is best understood as a blend of Buddhism and animism. The few Japanese people who actively practice Shintoism worship *kami* or nature spirits. They also believe in demon-like spirits, but these entities aren't always portrayed as purely evil as demons are in Christianity. The Japanese word *yōkai* can be translated as *demons*, *ghosts*, and more. These beings more closely resemble the fae in European mythology than biblical demons.

In the Japanese film adaptation of *Howl's Moving Castle* by director Hayao Miyazaki, the fire demon, Calcifer, is portrayed as mischievous and grumpy but lovable. At the end of the film, the protagonists reconcile and befriend the demon as well as a semireformed antagonist. This happens often in anime since the Japanese place high value on being in harmony with nature and other people, even their enemies.[4] Shinto-inspired anime presents a unique opportunity to analyze the difference between the biblical commands to forgive, reconcile, and "love your enemies" (Matt. 5:44) versus the Shinto concept of being in "harmony" with something or someone potentially evil. Each story is unique, and there are many instances of common grace where enemies come together after genuine forgiveness and reconciliation. Yet there is a fine line between the concepts of reconciliation and harmony, which younger children may not be able to understand.

Christian fantasy offers far clearer examples of how to discern the power source than other religions or atheist works. Yet even for believing authors, there is a wide variety in how they choose to go about conveying the source. One of the biggest factors in that decision is the challenge of marketing to a small audience. It's nearly impossible to sell books in that genre, which makes getting a publisher for openly Christian fantasy even more difficult. Many Christian speculative fiction authors choose instead to self-publish or publish into the general market (meaning they are not marketed as "Christian fiction").

However, publishing into the secular market greatly limits how explicit authors can be with their Christian themes and vocabulary. Like many secular authors, there may be times Christians won't mention a source of power. The themes of those books should and usually do reflect divine supernaturalism in the other four discernment categories. Their system's source may also align more with the distinctions of divine mirrored magic. They also typically include biblical themes steeped in metaphors. In more explicit stories, authors still usually name the *elohim* something unique to their world. Tolkien did this in The Lord of the Rings, sub-creating entire races such as the Valar (Maiar) that more closely resembled angels than humans.[5] He also named God "Eru Ilúvatar" in *The Silmarillion*.[6] Meanwhile Lewis had the Christlike Aslan and his father, the Emperor-beyond-the-Sea, in The Chronicles of Narnia.

Modern Christian authors use fictional terms for the members of the Trinity such as "Aedon"[7] in J. J. Fischer's The Nightingale Trilogy,* "Aodh"[8] in Gillian Bronte Adams's The Fireborn Epic,** and "White Light"[9] in Nadine Brandes's *Fawkes*.*** All of these books portray God as a sentient, personal, and all-powerful being without syncretism. Characters in Christian fantasy often interact with God in familiar ways—through prayer. However, White Light from *Fawkes* has a more unique and metaphorical role. (The following contains mild spoilers.) In Brandes's fantasy retelling of Guy Fawkes's Gunpowder Plot of 1605, the color-based magic system reflects the disparity between the Catholic and Protestant theology of speaking directly to God. While one side of the divide speaks only to one color to use their magic, those who speak directly to

* This series is noble dark fantasy and best for older teens and adults. It contains mild violence, references to trauma, and brief kissing.

** This series is best for teens and adults who enjoy epic war fantasy. It contains violence with some loss of limbs. Different countries have varying religious beliefs.

*** This book is best for teens and adults. It depicts historical racism as negative. There is brief, chaste kissing, and mild violence.

White Light—which contains the whole spectrum of color—can wield them all.

Serious doctrinal issues arise if an author violates the character and nature of God or the gospel through their fictional terminology. This may include portraying him as impersonal, referring to God as female like in *The Shack* by William P. Young,[10] or saying God is "in all of us" as though humans are divine like in Ted Dekker's Beyond the Circle series.[11] Dekker sometimes uses New Age concepts blended with Christianity to create syncretistic narratives. In his book *The 49th Mystic*, the protagonist, Rachelle, declares a kind of self-deification: "'Inchristi is me,' I said. 'And as one, we are in my earthen vessel. That's how Inchristi is me *and* in me.'"[12] In the sequel, *Rise of the Mystics*, Rachelle says that "most religion preaches a form of false law, blinding people to who they actually are as the light."[13] These statements about inner light and Rachelle *being* "Inchristi" are far more consistent with the New Age concept of "Christ consciousness" than orthodox Christianity.

Differences in mirrored magic are also to be expected. Yet within those categories, it's more problematic to depict demons as equal to or more powerful than God or portray demons with the authority to do such things as raising the dead, unless raising the dead is intended as an analogy. Minute nuance in every category would be too lengthy to discuss here, and we will all have our own preferences for how different or similar fantasy should be compared to Scripture. I encourage you to study supernaturalism in Scripture. Familiarize yourself with the nuance of language and the emphasis on the ultimate power of God. Then as you encounter fantasy, you and your family can discern fiction from reality on your own.

Question 2: Goal

What is the goal of the magic user? Do they desire the glorification of God (as the source) or of themselves? Do they love others or love themselves?

Although source is the first discernment question, the most important contextual clue is the telos or long-term goal of the magic user. If man's "chief end is to glorify God and to enjoy him forever,"[14] then the glory of God and our joy is the goal of all people. With divine supernaturalism, the long-term goal is to glorify God and love others, while demonic supernaturalism rejects this through self-glorification or the subjugation of others.

Since secular fiction won't have the goal of glorifying God, it will be easier to find the answer to this question by focusing on the secondary goal of loving others, which usually results in some form of self-sacrifice. Even in Christian fantasy, books are often published into the general market and may not discuss the glorification of God overtly. Regardless of the author's religious views, books in the general market will usually have antagonists with a demonic supernatural telos of self-aggrandizement or deification while the divine telos of glorifying God is absent, implied, or deeply buried. In overt demonic supernaturalism, the self is valued above everyone else and expects others to sacrifice for them alone.

For example, in Episodes I to III of Star War*s*, Anakin Skywalker (played by Hayden Christensen) originally seemed selfless when he primarily desired to protect Padmé (played by Natalie Portman). (The following contains spoilers.) But eventually, his character arc ends with him using the Force in self-serving villainy in *Star Wars: Episode III—Revenge of the Sith*[15] with the ultimate act of evil—murdering numerous children in the Jedi temple. The child that speaks to him in that scene bears a striking resemblance to the kindhearted boy Anakin once was in *Episode I: The Phantom Menace*,[16] reminding us just how far he'd fallen. Of course, audiences expected him to have a "negative change" arc since he was destined to become the antagonistic Sith lord, Darth Vader. Although Anakin was the protagonist in *Episode I*, his negative change arc wasn't a glorification of evil but served as a cautionary tale where evil was as grotesque as his marred appearance at the end of *Episode III*.

Allowing or encouraging others to sacrifice themselves is an act usually reserved for villains. The White Witch from *The Lion, the Witch and the Wardrobe* or Voldemort from Harry Potter are good examples. Both boldly murder and cheat others with their magic for their own gain. For a protagonist, that kind of selfishness usually manifests in the beginning or middle of their character arc while they're still on their journey toward the truth.

There is another way to display this kind of selfishness that has an appearance of goodness on the surface. Formally, it is an ethical system called "consequentialism," meaning the morality of an action is determined by the outcome or consequences alone. This system is more commonly known by the phrase, "The ends justify the means." This ethic is often applied to issues such as abortion (i.e., pro-choice advocates argue the benefits of aborting outweigh the loss of life) and is occasionally used in stories to justify sacrificing someone else's life for the "greater good" but is ultimately a rejection of the common good.* (The following contains spoilers.)

---

* The classical concept of the "common good" is a good where members of a whole together share possession of a single good, like teammates together possessing a single victory. The modern version sees the common good as a common means for individual gain, like trading goods and services. See 1 Cor. 12:7, 12, 27.

For example, in The Shadow and Bone trilogy by Leigh Bardugo,* the protagonist, Alina, kills her love interest, Mal, in order to defeat their enemy. Mal is a type of magical amplifier Alina needs to kill in order to boost her powers and defeat the villain. Mal eventually comes back to life, but at the time, Alina doesn't know that will happen. Based on the plot and confines of the magic system, there is no other way to accomplish their goal without murder. Although the antagonist of this series is a proper portrayal of demonic supernaturalism, the magic used by the protagonists doesn't fully align with divine supernaturalism since this death is reminiscent of human sacrifices. The author likely intended this scene to convey self-sacrifice since Mal was willingly dying and both of them were holding the knife. "With Mal's fingers guiding mine, I shoved the knife up and into his chest."[17] The convoluted moment of reluctant murder by Alina and partial suicide by Mal is still in alignment with consequentialism as well as pagan-like blood sacrifices.

More often, sacrificing others for the "greater good" is used by villains. (The following contains spoilers.) For example, the *Avengers: Endgame*[18] antagonist, Thanos (played by Josh Brolin), steals the Infinity Stones, places them in a gauntlet (metal glove), and then snaps his fingers to destroy half the universe's population. His argument for doing so is that the universe is overpopulated. For people to truly flourish, there must be fewer of them. He believes killing half of all life is a terrible but necessary sacrifice. Although this storyline stretches over multiple films, Thanos is eventually vanquished by the self-sacrifice of Tony Stark/Iron Man (played by Robert Downey Jr.), who uses the Infinity Stones to destroy

---

* This series contains violence, sensual kissing scenes, a brief sex scene, and gay/lesbian characters in the spin-off novels. I haven't personally read this series but only the concluding scenes referenced above.

Thanos and his army. Stark's selfless act ends his life, since the overwhelming power of the Infinity Stones was too great for a mere human to endure.

From this contrast of a self-serving villain against a self-sacrificing hero, it would seem Marvel understood that consequentialism is immoral. Yet in *Doctor Strange in the Multiverse of Madness*, we are given a story about a protagonist who is both actively fighting consequentialism and using it himself to reach his goals. Even from a secular standpoint, this film is thematically inconsistent as well as overtly demonic. In the first film, Doctor Strange (played by Benedict Cumberbatch) is taught real New Age practices such as astral projection and energy manipulation. Although this originally struck me as fantastical at the time, after my research into the New Age, I realized there was little about his training that was fictional. However, the second film is drastically worse.

The story begins with Strange's supposed nightmare of nearly killing America Chavez (played by Xochitl Gomez) because "in the grand calculus of the multiverse, your sacrifice is worth more than your life."[19] He is deeply disturbed by this vision and spends the rest of the film running from his fear that he or another version of himself from the multiverse might use his magic to sacrifice someone else for the greater good. This theme is so on-the-nose that Wanda Maximoff/the Scarlet Witch (played by Elizabeth Olsen) says early on in the film that America's "sacrifice would be for the greater good." To which Strange replies, "That's the kind of justification our enemies use."[20]

Strange manages to escape his fear of sacrificing America's life, but he doesn't escape consequentialism entirely. In the end, he's unable to hold onto the Book of the Vishanti (the book of light) that he needs to defeat the Scarlet Witch and, instead, uses the

Darkhold—the "Book of the Damned"—to raise another version of himself from a grave and defeat Wanda. This is portrayed as a victory since America survives, yet he is still forced to use overtly demonic magic and a zombie-esque resurrection to accomplish his goal of killing Wanda—the protagonist turned villain—*for the greater good.* The tragedy of this story is not only the graphic violence unfit for a family film and the glorification of demonic supernaturalism but also Strange's giving of himself to the very ethical system he'd been running from throughout the entire film.

Strange's goals don't perfectly align with either divine or demonic supernaturalism, so how do we think of this film within a scriptural framework? He seems to be just as confusing a figure as Balaam in Numbers 22. Strange is a character that doesn't desire to glorify God or himself. In fact, he seems to have admirable goals of protecting others and defeating the villain. If the protagonist is trying to do good, does it matter *how* they did it? As we discussed previously, when a character is willing to use *demanding* supernatural methods to reach their goals, they're not in alignment with good as much as they think they are. A character who forgoes morality for the sake of the greater good doesn't actually have proper goals and will not ultimately contribute to the common good.

Strange may have said he wanted to save lives and protect people, but resorting to something overtly evil to do so will only put more people in danger long-term. This is also a reflection of modern occultists who desire to be "light workers" and refuse to use black magic. Their stated goals may be to do good, but aligning with evil will never produce real, long-term goodness. Similarly, Strange and anyone who works with him will pay a high price for his consequentialist actions and blatant alignment with demonic supernaturalism in the long run.

In overt Christian fantasy, the primary and secondary goals of divine supernaturalism are often both present. However, the author will rarely state the goal of glorifying God outright since that would be too on the nose. Instead, it's woven into the fabric of the plot and characters. In *The Lion, the Witch and the Wardrobe*, the Pevensies take their thrones with the implied recognition that the true high king of Narnia isn't Peter but the great Lion himself.[21] Like David reigning under Yahweh, the Pevensies are merely the stewards of Aslan's kingdom. They all have active roles within the story, and their victory is celebrated in the end. This isn't a self-aggrandizement since they are humble in their new roles and are rightly honored by Aslan and Narnia for their success. Their crowning as kings and queens was also an act of obedience since it was the fulfillment of a prophecy from Aslan. The real hero of the story is as clear as day since the children could have done nothing to defeat the White Witch or rule Narnia without Aslan and his deeper magic.[22]

Question 3: Heart

What is the heart posture of the magic user? Is the user humble or proud before God, the source?

In the Sermon on the Mount in Matthew 5–7, Jesus taught that our heart, inner thought life, and posture toward God and others determines the presence or absence of virtue or vice. In divine supernaturalism, magic users should have a heart posture of humility before God where they recognize their power comes from him alone. In demonic supernaturalism, the heart is usually filled with some form of pride or false modesty and rejects God as the all-powerful source.

Humility will look different in Christian fantasy than in secular works. In Christian fiction that openly recognizes God (whether by his name or another in-world one), characters will need to have or learn a posture of humility before God. Either stated or implied, the character should be able to say, "I have accomplished this through the power of God alone, and not by my own strength." Humility can also be seen more simply in acknowledging the source of their power is from God and not themselves. This can be accomplished through something as simple as using prayer as a part of the magic system. Or the characters may view themselves as humble stewards of their magic.

Dream of Kings by Sharon Hinck* is a gender-swapped epic fantasy based loosely on the story of Joseph.[23] The Joseph character, Jolan, openly recognizes that dreams and her dream-telling gift come *from* God (named the Provider and Creator) and is *for* God and others. In only the first chapter, she says, "Yes, I lived in a wing of the palace, but I would always see myself as a servant to the high lord, the courtiers, and to the humblest villager. I'd seen what could happen to a dream teller who forgot that truth." In one simple sentence, Hinck establishes Jolan as a humble servant of God and her people—deeply aware of her place in the upside-down kingdom. Although this character still has a lot of growth in her arc, her humility in using her supernatural gift is one thing that never wavers.

Since some Christian fantasy is not always that overt, humility is often communicated in other ways. Authors usually give a metaphorical bowing of the knee to a creator or personal, singular deity by a brief display of dependency. This is a subtle way Christian

---

* This is best for teens and adults who enjoy biblical fantasy retellings. It contains mild violence and fully chaste kissing.

writers can tip readers off to the deeper, faith-filled meaning behind the book while still keeping it in the general market. However, Christian fiction should not encourage pride or align with worldly self-empowerment. If it does, the author may subscribe to some form of cultural syncretism or Disney-esque theology that teaches that you can do anything you set your mind to by your own strength and following your heart. It may also be an area of needed spiritual growth for the author. Just because someone publishes a Christian novel doesn't mean the author is always mature enough to disciple or teach others.

For secular fiction, having a heart posture of humility before Yahweh (as opposed to fictional deities) isn't usually possible unless the characters happen upon the idea that their power couldn't exist without him—although this is rare. More likely, a secular author with a background in Christianity may choose to use the religion of their childhood as a plot device in their work. For example, Michael in The Dresden Files by Jim Butcher is a knight of the cross who unashamedly acknowledges his power comes from God.[24] These books contain R-rated content and are decidedly secular despite overt references to Christianity.* Secular horror stories sometimes feature demons and Catholic priests who fight them off using a crucifix as though fighting off a vampire with garlic. This is a controversial storytelling tactic since some Christians feel that the cross of Christ is being co-opted by worldly horror authors for the sake of entertainment and inducing fear. Yet others accept this as a proper metaphor for Christ's authority over demons, which are rightly horrifying.

---

* This series contains swearing, explicit descriptions of women, graphic violence, sex scenes, bargaining with demons, and morally gray or black characters not portrayed negatively. I have not personally read this series.

Sometimes secular authors add "righteous" Christian characters, which has a similar effect as using a cross as a weapon against evil. This is not usually done skillfully since the effect of that character's faith is rarely understood rightly. Sometimes the writers are trying to criticize Christianity by portraying it as overly legalistic, or they might be simply attempting to add a wider variety of characters to the story for the sake of diversity.

In *Pirates of the Caribbean: On Stranger Tides*, a Christian missionary, Philip (played by Sam Claflin), is shipwrecked and dragged along on a journey to find the Fountain of Youth.[25] (The following contains spoilers.) When a siren-like mermaid (played by Astrid Bergès-Frisbey) is imprisoned by the pirates for her magical tears, Philip is the only one to take compassion on her. He insists she must be one of God's creatures and is worthy of protection. He eventually saves her life, falls in love with her, then permanently joins her in the ocean. This overt show of faith in God foreshadows the uneven and poorly resolved battle between Christianity and paganism despite the strange resolution of Philip's arc.

During the film's climax, Spanish soldiers join the pirate's crew at the Fountain of Youth in an attempt to stop them from drinking. Before destroying the fountain's "profane" temple, the Spanish captain declares, "Only God can grant eternal life, not this pagan water."[26] Despite his bold statement and the fountain's following destruction, Jack Sparrow (played by Johnny Depp) still manages to find a few meager swallows of water to achieve his goal of saving someone's life through overt pagan magic. The ending is a chaotic mishmash of themes and supernaturalism that leaves the audience wondering what the point of the movie might be or which side had truly prevailed.

More often, secular works don't mention God's existence at all. There's no real substitute in supernaturalism for humbling yourself before God or acknowledging that our power is his power. However, that doesn't mean non-Christian stories never have characters that portray humility in general. Just as common grace displays loving others as a goal or telos, so it can also display a posture of humility—albeit an incomplete one. Stories often have characters who refuse to use their power for selfish gain or reject a mindset of entitlement. Instead, they treat their magic or supernatural gifting as a tool to further the common good of all people. This is often seen with innate magic or superpowers where the character didn't work to earn their power. Superman is a clear example since his powers are a result of his alien DNA and the sun. There are times when he's shown to regret being different and would prefer to fit in with normal society rather than live with such a burdensome secret. He eventually learns to accept his origins and strength in order to help others and fight evil.

Pride usually plays a large role in the villain's motives. For example, Voldemort has no value for human life. He pridefully attempts to conquer death by killing others weaker than himself.[27] A more comedic example is from Disney's *The Incredibles* where Syndrome (voiced by Jason Lee) attempts to mimic superpowers through advanced technology.[28] In his bitterness with Mr. Incredible and his lack of innate powers, he murders Supers and releases a killer robot into the city. Once it's done some damage, he plans to swoop in and save the day alone. This would initially earn the respect of a Super before he eventually makes all people Super through his technology. When Mr. Incredible accuses Syndrome of pretending to be a Super, the villain replies, "Oh, I'm real. Real enough to defeat *you*!"

He isn't as evil as Voldemort who's attempting to become God by using dark magic, but he is trying to elevate himself to the status of a Super through murder and his grasp of science and technology. While this isn't exactly an example of demonic supernaturalism, it does shed light on how materialists have many of the same temptations as occultists. Through science, technology, and medicine, we try to control our environment, heal our wounds, and become enlightened about the material world. Another example of this is Mary Shelley's *Frankenstein* where the line between science and demonic supernaturalism is at its thinnest.[29]

A villain's pride isn't difficult to detect, but does the protagonist have similar motives that are portrayed as positive rather than negative? Protagonist pride is far more difficult to spot since they're usually buried beneath cultural ideologies like "loving yourself more" or "following your heart." In Disney's *Turning Red*, thirteen-year-old Meilin (played by Rosalie Chiang) is going through puberty.[30] She's experiencing age-appropriate mood swings and attraction to boys, which are suppressed by her overbearing mother. Her struggles are metaphorically portrayed through the generational blessing (or is it a curse?) of possession by the spirit of a red panda. Whenever they feel strong emotions, the women in her family physically turn into giant pandas. The magic in this film is overtly pagan ancestral worship. Their ancestor, Sun Yee, prayed to the gods for the spirit to be given to their family so she might protect her children while the men were away at war.

Had this been merely an example of modern-day Buddhism, it wouldn't be such an awful movie. Yet over and over we see clear examples of the glorification of evil. The night before Meilin receives the panda spirit, she has a terrifying nightmare of evil pandas with glowing red eyes. A while later, her mother tells her they must trap the spirit in a pendant because there is a darkness to it that will overtake Meilin if left unchecked. This has all the telltale signs of demon possession. But since this is supposed to be a metaphor for normal hormonal mood swings and budding sexuality that's demonized by an authoritarian parent, Meilin's arc doesn't go where it should. Unlike the healthy balance between an overbearing parent and a rebellious teenager in *The Little Mermaid*, *Turning Red* fails in a big way. The end of Meilin's arc includes her total rejection of her mother's advice, outright rebellion (including a physical boss battle with her raging Panda-mom where she twerks as part of the fight), and the eventual embrace of her panda spirit as part of herself. In the end, her mother tells her not to go out showing her ears and tail, and Meilin responds, "My panda, my choice."

I understand what the writers were trying to do with this movie. They obviously wanted to portray what it feels like to grow up in a strict, honor-based household as a Western teenager with uncontrollable emotional fluctuations. And there are moments during the film where Meilin is a sympathetic character. However, two extreme ideologies are at war here that we might miss without a proper understanding of the religious context. In Buddhism individuality is suppressed. Buddhists believe in the nonself where people are taught to break away from the concept that humans are permanent individual selves. Instead, all people are interconnected, nonpermanent beings. This is a different kind of Satanic lie that still manages to distort genuine humility through depersonalization, dehumanization, and relativism.

In Christianity, we're taught that wisdom is not turning "to the right or to the left" (Prov. 4:27). We shouldn't overcorrect problems but find the virtues between the two extremes. But what is Disney's answer to such a cultural clash within a single family? *Turning*

Red is an example of the world detecting problems and declaring the opposite extreme as the solution. So the answer we find to a total lack of unique, God-given individuality in Buddhism is the Western concept of individualism. In this ideology, the individual has greater value than the community, and families must sacrifice for the needs of each person's fluctuating desires and emotions. In *Turning Red*, the writers attempt to respect Chinese religious culture with the use of ancestral worship and the red pandas as a metaphor for puberty. Yet this falls flat by glorifying something that has the appearance of demon possession. They also end up rejecting the core ideologies of this religion through a rude, prideful, individualistic thirteen-year-old girl who learns her panda power and her emotional needs are more important than her role as a daughter.

Question 4: Setting

What is the setting of the magic? Is the relational setting upside-down or right-side up? Are vulnerable people honored or exploited?

In the Sermon on the Mount, Jesus establishes the importance of heart motives as well as an upside-down social ethos. In the Beatitudes specifically, he flips the Israelites' worldly perspective on its head when he begins with "Blessed are the poor in spirit, for the kingdom of heaven is theirs" (Matt. 5:3). This is a theme easily traced throughout the Bible with figures such as Jacob, Joseph, and David—younger brothers chosen over their elders. There were also lowly women such as Leah, Rehab, and Ruth who were chosen to be in Christ's lineage. In divine supernaturalism, the weak things of the world are chosen to shame the strong (1 Cor. 1:27). In demonic supernaturalism, power is given to the powerful, and weakness is exploited for selfish gain.

Most people, regardless of religion, naturally connect with the concept of the upside-down social setting in a story where the first is last and the last is first (Matt. 20:16). When an underdog character—like an abused or neglected orphan—is lifted out of their lowly station and placed in an entirely new environment, most people will feel seen or understood. This is why the "chosen one" trope in combination with Oliver Twist-like orphan stories will always be in demand (despite people complaining that it's overused). Wealthy people may also relate to these stories if they've ever been made to feel inferior for other reasons such as differences in intellect, appearance, ethnicity, gender, disability, or neurodivergence. This trope touches the most vulnerable parts of our own stories where someone sinned against us, bullied, or belittled us for something outside our control. When the stereotypical orphan child is given the chance to leave all that behind, we can't help but feel as though we're also moving on with them. We're leaving behind the people who made us feel as though we weren't good enough. Fantasy examples of this orphan narrative are Harry Potter, Peter and the Starcatchers by Dave Barry and Ridley Pearson,* and *By Darkness Hid* by Christian author Jill Williamson.[31]

Of course, any weak character can be used by God to "shame the strong" (1 Cor. 1:27), not just orphans. For example, in The Lord of the Rings and *The Hobbit*, Tolkien intentionally chooses the smallest, weakest race in Middle Earth to send on such treacherous

* Peter and the Starcatchers is a middle-grade general market fantasy series containing some mild innuendos, mild child abuse and child endangerment, alcoholism, mild language (such as d**n), and a few disturbing moments that may not be appropriate for some young readers.

adventures. All along the way, they are forced to beat the odds and rely on loyal friends to accomplish their goals. In *Dream of Kings* by Sharon Hinck, the Joseph-like character, Jolan, is repeatedly mistreated by slave traders and her slave masters before being wrongfully thrown into the king's prison. When she's eventually pulled from that place to interpret the king's dreams, she looks the part of a filthy, haggard criminal. Eventually she's given the highest responsibilities and honors by the king for her wisdom and ability to interpret dreams.

In demonic supernaturalism, many villains are fairly on the nose with their abuse of weak, vulnerable people. For example, the wicked stepmother in Snow White attempts to kill her mistreated and orphaned stepdaughter. On the surface, this appears straightforward enough. Yet even in this simple fairy tale, we see the layers of a villain's character. Often people who actively bully or work to hold others back are doing so because of their own insecurities, just as the stepmother was jealous of Snow White's beauty. Had she been secure in her own appearance, she wouldn't have felt threatened by someone else's.

In studying clinical narcissism, psychologists found that deep-seated feelings of inadequacy are at the heart of what appears to be pride on the surface.[32] These types of antagonists may also see themselves in the underdog narrative and others as their oppressors regardless of whether or not that's a true reflection of reality. From this comes a distortion of the upside-down narrative that resembles something more akin to blame shifting, gaslighting, and revenge. Lord Voldemort from Harry Potter is a good example of this since his tragic orphan backstory led him to do great evil and consistently harm and murder others due, in part, to seek revenge against Muggles (nonmagic people). Although his family history was one of hatred toward the nonmagical community, he was further disposed toward revenge since he grew up in a Muggle orphanage and his wealthy Muggle father abandoned his homely witch mother. In this, he sees himself as the victim of Muggle prejudice rather than the other way around. Although once an orphan victim like Harry, he grows up to become a far worse abuser than any he suffered from himself.

There's an even more deceptive way demonic supernaturalism's exploitative tendencies attempt to mimic the underdog narrative. When you find yourself connecting to the underdog protagonist who's out for revenge rather than justice and forgiveness, this should send up a red flag. Once that emotional bond forms, the audience then desires the protagonist to reach their goals even though they aren't moral, as we saw with *Inception*.* Although comical, a fantasy example of this is the orphaned Inigo Montoya from *The Princess Bride* whose only goal throughout the story is to duel the six-fingered man who killed his father. (The following contains spoilers.) When Inigo finally discovers the man, it feels satisfying to the audience that he semitortures his enemy before eventually stabbing him in the heart.

A much less comedic example is Netflix's *Damsel.* (The following contains spoilers.) Generations prior, a king attacked a local dragon, Khaevis, killing her three daughters. Khaevis retaliated by killing all but the king and forcing him to sacrifice his three daughters to her. In return, she spared the kingdom and demanded three

---

* Similarly, in romance, when a pitiable, sympathetic woman falls in love with a married man, the audience's emotions are often manipulated to desire the marriage to end. This is usually accomplished by giving the man a spouse that is cruel or unlikable. A more nuanced approach would be necessary if the spouse was an unrepentant abuser or adulterer.

more royal daughters from every following generation to satisfy the debt. Instead, the kingdom used a blood ritual with young women from other families to fabricate the requirement. By the time the protagonist, Elodie, is sacrificed, dozens of women had been eaten by the vengeful dragon. All the while, Khaevis believes she's receiving the sacrifices due her when she's actually being deceived by her enemy. Elodie discovers this deception and forces Khaevis to listen before she's eaten. In the end, the two team up to seek revenge against the royal family who'd tricked them both. Khaevis devours the entire family while Elodie escapes the cave and her death sentence.

Not only are most of the characters in *Damsel* devoid of admirable goals, but this is also a distortion of the upside-down kingdom narrative. The writers want you to sympathize with Khaevis and Elodie since they'd been deceived by a creepy, cultlike royal family. Elodie is especially sympathetic since she is a young female coerced into a marriage with a stranger then tossed into a pit where she's supposed to be eaten by a large dragon. It's also revealed later on that her father knew she would be sacrificed before blessing the engagement—something he comes to regret. Despite the fact that she's clearly a vulnerable young woman who's used as a disposable pawn in a political and semireligious game, her decision to have Khaevis kill her near murderers in response is not real justice but immoral revenge. This was intended to be an underdog story of female empowerment but instead ended with not one but three villainous parties out to kill one another for their own vengeful purposes.

Question 5: Methodology

What magical methodology is used? Is the method dependent on or demanding of the source?

Methodology is the least important discernment question, but it's not unimportant. Methodology is simply how the goal is accomplished. Most of the time, methods that *demand* magic from the source are indicative of demonic supernaturalism while methods *dependent* on the source indicate divine supernaturalism. God cannot be controlled or coerced, so methods that reflect our dependence on him are best when used by the protagonist. When villains (or a protagonist in a moment of weakness or sin) use demonic magic, it will likely have an appearance of being in total control over the source. That control may or may not be a deception within the context of the story. These rules of demanding and dependent methods don't usually apply in the case of the supernatural as natural since the characters can freely use their innate magic the same way we use our own natural talents.

Just as with the example of casting lots having the appearance of being demanding of God, so, too, will there be fictional magic that may initially appear demanding when it isn't. So long as the character or plot somehow states or implies that God is ultimately the source of that magic, it can still be categorized as divine. For example, in *The Lion, the Witch and the Wardrobe*, Lucy's magic cordial heals any injury at once and without the need for prayer. This becomes clear in the battle against the White Witch when Aslan hurries Lucy to use her cordial to heal others who are "at the point of death."[33] Although Aslan could have healed them with only his breath, he invites Lucy to use her gift to serve others. We also know that Aslan (and his father, the Emperor-beyond-the-Sea) is the source of the magic in the cordial since Father Christmas and his gifts were only allowed into Narnia when "Aslan was on the move."[34] Father Christmas also shows he's under Aslan's authority when he says, "Long live the true King!"[35]

In fantasy, most of the magic has the appearance of being demanding—even in Christian fantasy. As I mentioned when discussing magical sources, there are some Christian, Mormon, or other religious fantasy stories that might make a point of praying or showing overt signs of deference to God (or another deity) before using their magic. But that isn't common, especially in non-Christian fantasy. There are a few reasons for this. First, literature uses a lot of innate magic that doesn't require anything resembling spellcasting—the supernatural as natural. For example, Matilda doesn't cast spells but has the innate power of telekinesis due to her incredible intellect.

Second, some fantasy magic is a kind of literary device that's intended to be partially metaphorical or typological rather than a perfect reflection of real supernaturalism. For example, Aslan's Deep Magic is real within the world of Narnia, yet it's also representative of the law and the gospel. Third, fantasy methodology is sometimes based more on demonic supernatural methodology even if the rest of the magic system isn't. Authors often mimic things such as spellcasting, astrology, and other occult-esque methods simply because they've become somewhat stereotypical and normative even for fantasy magic.

When Westerners without knowledge of the occult think of casting spells, they're more likely to imagine Cinderella's fairy godmother singing "Bibbidi-Bobbidi-Boo" rather than real occult practices.[36] Yet that same fairy godmother is also using her spells to help an orphaned and abused young woman in need of freedom from her circumstances. Even though the methodology resembles real witchcraft, the rest of the story is more reflective of divine supernaturalism.

Disney magic is heavily critiqued by former New Agers and Christians who fear fictional magic specifically because of similar methodology. They feel that these stories are teaching children that occult magic is all fun and games and capable of being truly good like a fairy godmother. Although that doesn't seem to be statistically true, it's an understandable concern for someone who felt deeply deceived by how shiny and glittery the New Age first appeared. I've heard many former New Agers say that Satan is using Disney and Harry Potter to target their children with the concept of "good" magic. I sympathize with their position and concerns but must disagree. A story that aligns in the most essential ways with divine supernaturalism yet uses confusing methodology is unlikely to attract a child to the occult. If the methods in a Disney movie present a stumbling block, there is likely something else going on in that child's life—such as trauma or spiritual lust—that should be more closely examined.

What do we do with stories that include spellcasting, potion making, stargazing, or divination? These methods resemble occult methodology and are inherently demanding of the source rather than dependent on God. The methods in these stories aren't perfect. It's possible that some children may be confused about why it's okay for Cinderella's fairy godmother to cast spells but the Bible says not to in Deuteronomy 18:11. It's not my personal preference to write fiction with occult-like methodology, although I don't mind reading those books so long as the more essential aspects of divine supernaturalism are present. As we discussed, if the benefits of fantasy are extremely high for Christians, then restricting stories with imperfect methodology without exception could potentially throw the baby out with the bathwater.

There are also some methods that are more concerning than others. For example, necromancy (speaking to the dead) or something akin to blood rituals is a far weightier issue than Disney-esque spellcasting. That still won't always mean the story needs to be entirely restricted, but it may depending on the severity of the magic in a specific plot. In *Dungeons & Dragons: Honor Among Thieves*, the protagonists must raise a corpse and speak to it in order to complete their quest.[37] It's a brief exchange, but they definitely wouldn't have reached their goals without that step. Choosing whether to watch a film like *Dungeons & Dragons* comes down to personal preference for each individual person and family. Personally, I would be okay showing this film to teenagers and discipling them through the pros and cons of that moment as well as the entire D&D magic system.

In general, we need to give methodology a little less weight. If everything about the story and magic aligns with divine supernaturalism except the methods, then it's a moment for discipleship. For small children, you may choose to pause the movie when the fairy godmother pulls out her wand and simply tell the children that the Bible says spellcasting is wrong in real life. In those quick moments, I personally choose not to elaborate too much on why God says this or discuss all the nuances of discerning fantasy magic. That can wait until the movie is over and the children aren't waiting eagerly for you to hit play again. They're not going to be very good listeners when they're waiting for the movie to continue anyway. But it's okay to pause for a few seconds and give quick bits of wisdom that will help the child mentally sift what they're seeing as they watch. I've also found that these little interruptions usually don't ruin their enjoyment of the story.

In the animated series *Avatar: The Last Airbender*, the magic is based loosely on Buddhism, reincarnation, and elemental magic. The main character, Aang, is the Avatar—a reincarnated being with the special ability to "bend" all four elements where others in his world can only bend one. The Avatar spirit is reincarnated every generation and is intended to maintain harmony among the nations. Some parents might not be okay with their children watching this show because of its dependency on Eastern religious deceptions, and that's perfectly fine. Stories where the magic leans a bit left of center into the realm of New Age or paganism are great examples of using wisdom and Christian freedom. My husband and I decided to talk through the concepts of Buddhism and reincarnation with our children and then allow them to watch the show. But it's perfectly fine if other families choose to restrict this, especially for children who won't understand those spiritual distinctions. Or if a family has converted from an Eastern religion to Christianity, things like reincarnation may be too personally troubling or offensive to ever be regarded as entertaining.

Even though a lot of magical methodology can be discerned rather than restricted, there are still occult methods that are so demonic they should almost always be restricted. Such things are so obviously evil that they're unlikely to appear in lighthearted animated films intended for children. Yet they might show up in young adult or adult stories like the use of the Darkhold to raise a corpse into a zombie-puppet in *Doctor Strange in the Multiverse of Madness*.[38] Another example of overtly demonic methodology is blood sacrifices—human or animal. This appears in the Netflix original show, *Chilling Adventures of Sabrina*, which is overtly occult in nature. It's also an example of a show that can hardly be called fantasy at all and is far more similar to real-life depiction of the occult in fictional settings. Such stories overtly glorify evil in *both* methodology and other essential aspects of demonic supernaturalism.

It would also be a matter of discernment if the story created an intentional narrative of overt syncretism with Christian and pagan methodology. A seemingly Christian example is Ted Dekker's Beyond the Circle series I mentioned earlier in this chapter.[39] However, overt occult methods can also appear as a negative story element that aims to critique syncretism.

All of these examples barely scratch the surface of each story. What would it look like to apply the literary categories discussed as well as all five discernment questions to just one story?

Chapter 12

What about Harry Potter?

I want to be up-front with you about my personal investment in the Harry Potter series. As a child with ADHD, I rarely, if ever, read for fun outside of school. While my bookworm sister often stayed indoors consuming mass amounts of fiction, I only wanted to run around outside, climb trees, and get dirty. I was that raga-muffin '90s kid with skinned knees who rode her bike up and down the neighborhood and had little interest in anything else—besides movies, of course.

But in 1999, my uncle and aunt sent the first and third Harry Potter books to us for Christmas. My mom quickly ran out and bought the second to complete the set. I'm not sure why I read that first book when I had no interest in reading in general. In fact, I thought I was a bad reader, since I was so much slower than my sis-ter. But I did decide to read the first three Harry Potter books that year. I read them over and over again until the binding on book one started to crack. After that, I read many more books including the entire Chronicles of Narnia. Harry Potter had done what no other book could—it made a wild, nonreader fall in love with literature.

Not long after that, I took a class on creative writing and realized I loved that too. Without J.K. Rowling and Harry Potter, I wouldn't be the reader or the writer I am today.

Even with this history, I want you to know that nothing is more important to me than the truth. Despite any personal bias, I want to provide a balanced discussion of this series. I'll present you with both the pros and cons of the Harry Potter magic system based on the theological framework we've already discussed. Those of you who aren't interested in the Potter series specifically can still use this as another example of how to apply the five discernment questions.

Harry Potter Plot Summary

This chapter contains many spoilers for the Harry Potter series with emphasis on the ending of book seven, *The Deathly Hallows*.[1]

Harry is an orphan boy living with his maternal aunt, uncle, and cousin—the Dursleys. They are verbally and emotionally abusive and neglectful of Harry while spoiling his cousin, Dudley. The basic rules of the house are don't ask questions and don't have an imagination. All his life, Harry has been told that his parents died in a car crash. On his eleventh birthday, a friendly giant-man named Hagrid tells him he's a wizard and will be attending the magical boarding school, Hogwarts. Harry finally learns the truth his aunt and uncle hid from him all his life. His parents were actually murdered by a powerful dark wizard named Lord Voldemort (whose real name was Tom Riddle). Harry was also supposed to die, but he miraculously survived while Voldemort was supposedly killed. He's the only person ever known to have survived the killing curse.

Once at school, Harry becomes best friends with Ron Weasley and Hermione Granger. At the end of the first book, Harry comes face-to-face with Voldemort's spirit that possesses the body of one of the Hogwarts' teachers. After another failed attempt to kill "the boy who lived," Harry is left wondering why Voldemort was after him in the first place. He and his friends later learn that Voldemort has two goals throughout the series—conquer death and kill Harry, who is in the way of his conquering death. Yet since Harry's mother, Lily, had sacrificed her life in an attempt to save her son, a powerful counter-curse of love repeatedly protects him from death.

The series continues with Harry having adventures at school and Voldemort trying unsuccessfully to kill him. By the end of the fourth book, Voldemort is finally able to kidnap Harry, take some of his blood, and return to a physical body for the first time in fourteen years. The blood allowed Voldemort to make contact with Harry's skin without being burned—an effect of Lily's sacrificial protection. Voldemort doesn't realize that by taking Potter blood into his veins, he may be able to touch Harry, but he's also strengthening Lily's counter-curse. Harry escapes Voldemort's grasp when their spells connect and inhibit the killing curse again. Once back to full strength, Voldemort gathers his followers, known as the Death Eaters. In response, Harry and others who oppose Voldemort form their own group to fight back.

Eventually, Harry learns that there had been a prophecy made before he was born: "The one with the power to vanquish the Dark Lord approaches. . . . Born to those who have thrice defied him, born as the seventh month dies."[2] Voldemort killed the Potters only because they'd gotten in his way while trying to murder Harry. Yet when the Dark Lord cast the killing curse that night in an attempt to subvert the prophecy, he'd unintentionally splintered his soul and a piece of it had attached itself to Harry. That act had the opposite effect as the one Voldemort intended since it inevitably confirmed the prophecy would be fulfilled. This process of soul splintering was the darkest of all magic and required first-degree murder. Although it was unthinkable to murder and sever your soul in two, Voldemort split his into seven pieces and hid them inside precious objects. If he was ever destroyed like he had been the night he'd attempted to kill Harry, another piece of his soul would still exist in one of his "Horcruxes." In making seven Horcruxes, Voldemort felt he'd become immortal. Yet he unknowingly weakened himself and eventually fulfilled the prophecy by his own actions.

In the seventh book, Harry, Ron, and Hermione drop out of school, now run by Death Eaters, to hunt Horcruxes. Unaware that Harry himself became a Horcrux during infancy, they believe they'll be able to simply kill Voldemort like a mortal man once all his remaining soul fragments are gone. At the end of the seventh book, Voldemort and his Death Eaters descend on Hogwarts while Harry searches for the last Horcrux. Voldemort demands they give Harry to him or everyone will die. Once Harry learns he has a fragment of Voldemort's soul, he willingly goes to the Dark Lord. Without fighting back, he faces his enemy and gives up his life out of love for his friends. But instead of simply dying, Harry goes to a spiritual limbo where he is counseled by his mentor, Albus Dumbledore. In willingly giving up his life for his friends, Harry provides a counter-curse of love to protect them just as his mother had done for him. The fragment of Voldemort's soul inside of him was now gone, and Harry was free to return to the physical world. In the end, Voldemort and his Horcruxes are vanquished, and Harry is finally free of the killing curse that had been placed on him in his infancy.

Applying the Discernment Questions

Question 1: What is the source of the magic? Is it demonic or divine?

Like most general market fantasy, the source of the magic isn't ever stated. This is a case of *the supernatural as natural.* Although there is spellcasting in the books, which Scripture labels an abomination, only natural-born wizards (innate magic) are capable of casting spells. Wizards and witches also have other forms of magic in addition to spells. Being able to use magic is not a lifestyle choice like the occult but something characters are born with, similar to superpowers.

Other clues to a possible magic source are in book seven, *The Deathly Hallows.* There are two explicit Bible verses on the tombstones of Harry's parents and Dumbledore's mother and sister—1 Corinthians 15:26 and Matthew 6:21. Rowling also said in a 2007 interview that she is a member of the Church of Scotland and a professing Christian, albeit a liberal one.[3] Since the magic source isn't ever stated in the books or by Rowling, we can't place a definitive label of "divinely sourced" magic on this system. Both good and evil seem to draw on the same source of power when using innate magic. Yet that isn't unique to Harry Potter. I personally find more evidence for divine supernaturalism due to the use of *the supernatural as natural*, which implies magic may be used or abused for good or evil as it is in nature. Either way, this is an area of discernment and one parents will want to discuss with their children to avoid confusion.

Question 2: What is the goal of the magic user? Do they desire the glorification of God (as the source) or of themselves? Do they love others or love themselves?

We have to look for the secondary goal of divine supernaturalism since, again, this is a general market series and there is no direct goal of glorifying God. But is the secondary goal of loving others and self-sacrifice present? Absolutely, yes. In fact, this is a major theme throughout the series and the climax of book seven. In book one, it's revealed that Harry's mother, Lily, died trying to save his life from Voldemort. She didn't have to cast a spell in order for her death to trigger a powerful counter-curse of protection. "Your mother died to save you. If there is one thing Voldemort cannot understand, it is love. He didn't realize that love as powerful as your mother's for you leaves its own mark. Not a scar, no visible sign . . . to have been loved so deeply, even though the person who loved us is gone, will give us some protection forever."[4]

Self-sacrifice is a frequent theme throughout the series as Harry repeatedly puts himself in harm's way to save others. In the last book, *The Deathly Hallows*, Harry's self-sacrifice positions him as a Christ type. He goes to Voldemort willingly and without a fight in order to die on behalf of his friends and community, which is reminiscent of John 15:13: "No one has greater love than this: to lay down his life for his friends." Although he'd been fighting Voldemort and his Death Eaters for years, he puts down his wand in this scene because he knows he must die to defeat the Dark Lord. Inside him is a kind of curse—a splintered piece of Voldemort's soul. The only way Harry can defeat Voldemort is to give up his own life. And in doing so, his love casts a counter-curse of protection over his friends just as his mother's had done for him:

> "You won't be able to kill any of them ever again. Don't you get it? I was ready to die to stop you from hurting these people—"
>
> "But you did not!"
>
> "—I meant to, and that's what did it. I've done what my mother did. They're protected from you. Haven't you noticed how none of the spells you put on them are binding? You can't torture them. You can't touch them."[5]

Harry's willingness to die for those he loves allows him to return from spiritual limbo just as "death itself would start working backward" in Narnia.[6] The difference between Harry's death and Aslan's was that Aslan had taken the penalty for Edmund's sin, whereas Harry was dying to protect an innocent community from their enemy. The ending of the series certainly mirrors the gospel, which Rowling included intentionally.[7] In addition to his gospel-like sacrifice, the added element of Harry taking a curse not meant for him into his body typified the way Christ took our sin into his. Yet Lewis's Aslan is a sinless Christ type dying for a sinner rather than an imperfect one dying for innocent people, which is a more accurate depiction of penal substitutionary atonement.*

Harry's self-sacrifice also contrasts Voldemort and the Death Eaters who constantly hurt and kill people for their own gain. Voldemort is so deeply evil in desiring to be an immortal god that he splits his soul multiple times through multiple murders. A lesser-known evil wizard named Grindelwald also embodies this kind of selfishness by espousing consequentialism (i.e., the end justifies the

---

* *Penal substitutionary atonement* means that Jesus took our place on the cross and paid the price for our sins.

means). His motto is, "For the greater good," which he uses to justify the systemic subjugation of Muggles (nonmagic people). In this and many other ways, Voldemort epitomizes Satan, and both evil wizards properly reflect demonic supernaturalism.

Question 3: What is the heart posture of the magic user? Is the user humble or proud before God, the source?

As with the previous two, this question has to be answered in the general market sense because God is never explicitly mentioned. In fact, Harry seems to express confusion over what he should think about spiritual realities when faced with a tombstone that reads: "Where your treasure is, there will your heart be also" (Matt. 6:21 KJV).[8] This is also indicative of Rowling's own feelings toward the afterlife.[9] So we should know right off the bat that Harry isn't going to express humility before God.

Just as Superman is a humble, even regretful hero, does Harry likewise have that kind of humility? Does he slowly become puffed up with pride, or does he live only to use his power to serve others? Again, this is another prominent theme in the books. Harry is a kind of "everyman" hero. There's nothing particularly special about him other than being accidentally famous and being good at Quidditch (a wizard's sport). He's not funny like Ron or bookish like Hermione. In fact, the only thing special about him is his bravery in being willing to fight on behalf of others without any desire to seek his own glory. In his normalcy, he doesn't have a habit of envying others' talents or intelligence. He's only ever envious of other children who have loving parents and families.

In the second book, another famous wizard, Gilderoy Lockhart, is self-obsessed and constantly looking for opportunities to promote himself. The things he's famous for aren't even real, but only falsifications of his true magical aptitude. He sees Harry as a way to gain more fame and assumes Harry would desire the attention just as much as Lockhart does. Yet the opposite is true. Harry is always looking for ways to avoid him and the spotlight that comes with their interactions.

Voldemort stands in direct contrast to Harry's humility. Although Voldemort doesn't seek fame the way Lockhart does, he is the epitome of Satanic pride. This is emphasized more by his ability to speak to snakes and owning a large snake who also turned out to be a Horcrux. All his life Voldemort knew he was clever and a particularly adept wizard. Compared with Harry, he's smarter, stronger, and willing to do any evil to accomplish his goals. And it's his pride that comes before the fall. Like a true Satan-type, Voldemort is a narcissist—intelligent but utterly lacking in empathy and the ability to understand concepts like love. Since he can't grasp such selfless ideas, he doesn't see or understand how Harry is protected by Lily's love counter-curse or why he can't defeat him. Although he'd learned dark magic few people knew existed, he thought it beneath him to learn about the supernatural power of love. "'Is it love again?' said Voldemort, his snake's face jeering. 'Dumbledore's favorite solution, *love*, which he claimed conquered death.'"[10] And this prideful attitude that dark magic and not something as weak as love could conquer death is the very thing that destroys him in the end.

Question 4: What is the setting of the magic? Is the relational setting upside-down or right-side up? Are vulnerable people honored or exploited?

The upside-down kingdom where the first is last and the last is first is another major theme in this series. In fact, there are few books that do this as well as Harry Potter. The most obvious way we see this is in the neglected orphan as the "chosen one." His guardians are abusive and Rowling's idea of an authoritarian family. Harry is a clear underdog throughout the series, which makes him a deeply relatable character. Ron, poor and the youngest brother of five, feels overshadowed by his family and struggles with feelings of inferiority. Hermione, although intelligent, is a Muggle-born—someone born of nonmagical parents—and is looked down upon by many pure-blood wizards. A number of other prominent characters are from persecuted groups such as Hagrid (a half giant), Dobby (an enslaved house-elf), and Lupin (a werewolf, bitten as a child). There are too many other examples of this to mention them all.

There is also a strong antibullying message throughout the books that begins with Harry's school nemesis, Draco Malfoy, and ends with more dangerous figures like Voldemort. This culminates in the torture, subjugation, and murder of Muggles and Muggle-borns who Voldemort and the Death Eaters see as inferior. In the seventh book, Harry, Ron, and Hermione enter the Ministry of Magic (a government building) when the Death Eaters have taken control of the Ministry. Disguised as Ministry employees, they stand in front of a grotesque statue placed there by Voldemort's followers.

> "It's horrible, isn't it?" [Hermione] said to Harry, who was staring up at the statue. "Have you seen what they're sitting on?"
>
> Harry looked more closely and realized that what he had thought were decoratively carved thrones were actually mounds of carved humans: hundreds and hundreds of naked bodies, men, women, and children, all with rather stupid, ugly faces, twisted and pressed together to support the weight of the handsomely robed wizards.
>
> "Muggles," whispered Hermione. "In their rightful place."[11]

Question 5: What magical methodology is used? Is the method dependent on or demanding of the source?

This is where things get confusing. So far, the Potter series has aligned well with divine supernaturalism. Yet the magical methodology is a mixed bag of demanding and dependent methods and the reason this series is so deeply controversial. Although Rowling used a wide variety of methodology, much of which was entirely fictional, a good portion of it was borrowed directly from stereotypical occult practices such as spellcasting, potions, divination, and astrology. There's also the language of "witchcraft" that's still used by occultists today. Let's look at these occult-like methods in more detail and see just how much they align with real demonic supernaturalism.

Spellcasting is listed among the abominable practices in Deuteronomy 18. Rowling has been accused of using real spells and potions and even being a witch herself. Rowling is definitely not a witch or an occultist of any kind, and most, if not all, of her spells and potions are fictional.[12] However, the idea that it matters that her spells are "real" belies some level of ignorance about demonic supernaturalism since Satan will use any system of spells or rituals to deceive people. The power isn't in the words themselves but in the heart posture and the relationship formed between human and demon.

Yet that demonic source isn't reflected in Harry Potter. The power lies in their natural-born wizard and witch blood. A wizard or witch is the type of human that can perform magic. A Muggle isn't the kind of human capable of performing magic since the magic is not sourced directly from spiritual entities but from nature. This is emphasized by the presence of innately magical animals and plants in Rowling's alternate Earth. From this it seems the demanding nature of Harry Potter spells is in alignment with the supernatural as natural—meaning innate magic can be used on demand just as any naturally occurring talent. However, it still remains true that the initial appearance of the spells does look a lot like demanding occult magic.

Some people have accused Rowling of aligning with Wicca, which attempts to harness the energy of nature for supernatural purposes. Rowling outright denies this claim when asked why there weren't any Wiccan students represented at Hogwarts. "[Wicca is] a different concept of magic to the one laid out in the books, so I don't really see how they can co-exist."[13] Although the nuance of Rowling's magic system doesn't perfectly align with something like Wicca or other forms of demonic supernaturalism, I want to affirm that the use of spells and potions is confusing for Christians who are skeptical of the Potter series. On the surface it appears to be on-demand magic even if that isn't the true nature of Rowling's system.

Divination and astrology are difficult pills to swallow in the Harry Potter books since they are clearer depictions of occult practices. The distinction we need to make here isn't in the methods of divination and astrology but in Rowling's view of their validity, which comes out in the story. When the students begin divination classes in their third year, they meet a new and strange teacher for the first time—Sybill Trelawney. She's depicted as scatterbrained, overly dramatic, and seeing death omens around every corner. Trelawney is intended to be a pitiable, ridiculous, and humorous figure. When she's first introduced, "Harry's immediate impression was of a large, glittering insect."[14] This description is reminiscent of the gypsy-like attire attributed to a New Age psychic stereotype.

Although Harry and Ron are simultaneously disturbed and amused by Trelawney's antics, Hermione is exasperated, impatient, and highly skeptical of the validity of the subject matter in general. "I think Divination seems very wooly. . . . A lot of guesswork if you ask me."[15] After some little effort on her part to participate, Hermione eventually storms out of class and never returns. Rowling has stated in interviews that Hermione is an exaggerated version of her younger self.[16] This clear narrative of doubt and absurdity surrounding divination is a reflection of Rowling's own view of psychics as liars or con artists.

In book five, Trelawney is fired by an antagonist witch, and Dumbledore hires a centaur named Firenze as a divination professor instead. Centaurs had been previously known in book one as standoffish stargazers who track the future of major world events. Introducing Firenze is a minor plot point, and one that didn't make it into the film adaptation. When the centaur takes over the class, he expresses the same sentiment as Hermione about Trelawney.

> "Professor Trelawney did Astrology with us!" said Parvati excitedly. . . . "Mars causes accidents and burns and things like that, and when it makes an angle to Saturn, like now"—she drew a right angle in the air above her—"that means that people need to be extra careful when handling hot things—"
>
> "That," said Firenze calmly, "is human nonsense. . . . Trivial hurts, tiny human accidents. . . . These are of no more significance than the scurrying of ants to the wide universe, and are unaffected by planetary movements. . . . Sibyll Trelawney may have Seen, I do not know . . . but she wastes her time, in the main, on the self-flattering nonsense humans call fortune-telling. I, however, am here to explain the wisdom of centaurs, which is impersonal and impartial. We watch the skies for the great tides of evil or change that are sometimes marked there. It may take ten years to be sure of what we are seeing."[17]

It isn't until the end of book five that it's finally revealed why Dumbledore keeps Trelawney around at all—she was the one who gave the real prophecy about a boy born in July who would have the power to vanquish the Dark Lord. However, there is a drastic difference between Trelawney's inaccurate tea leaf-reading or crystal ball-gazing and her deliverance of an actual prophecy. Instead of appearing misty voiced and mysterious as usual, she goes into a kind of trance with a deep voice to deliver prophecies.

What's even more interesting is that there's also a shift in language. Firenze, although still doing a kind of divination, distinguishes between "astronomy" and "astrology" with the latter being more closely associated with Trelawney's New Age practices. A much more prominent language shift with Trelawney is from "divination" to "prophecy" when a real prediction of the future takes place. There's even a "Hall of Prophecies" within the Ministry of Magic where real predictions are recorded. Rowling seems to be separating what she sees as mere trickery—New Age divination—from something real that aligns with Scripture—prophecy.

Not all of the methodology resembles the occult in a way that requires caveats and discernment. There are also moments where Voldemort and his Death Eaters align so well with demonic methodology that it should serve as a warning against occult methods. Remember, something is only glorifying evil if the plot and characters are holding it up as a representation of goodness. The presence of darkness in the hands of the antagonist is usually a good thing since it doesn't glorify evil. An example of the occult being depicted as truly evil is Voldemort's disembodied spirit possessing a Hogwarts teacher in imitation of demon possession. That same teacher kills and drinks the blood of a unicorn in imitation of occult sacrifices and blood ceremonies. Another example is Voldemort's old diary—a Horcrux—talking to Ginny Weasley in imitation of a Ouija board. Her father says at the end of the book, "'*Ginny*!' said Mr. Weasley, flabbergasted. 'Haven't I taught you *anything*? What have I always told you? Never trust anything that can think for itself *if you can't see where it keeps its brain*. Why didn't you show the diary to me, or your mother? A suspicious object like that, it was clearly full of Dark Magic.'"[18] This is another way of saying you shouldn't talk to objects or let them talk to you.

Even though the methodology in the Harry Potter series isn't an accurate depiction of the occult, it's still legitimately confusing for Christians to distinguish the difference, especially since many of the skeptics haven't actually read the books. From the outside, Hogwarts looks like a school that teaches children real occult practices. Without a deeper understanding of the story and the gospel-like ending of the seventh book (which wasn't available until 2007, long after the controversy had begun), a primary focus on supernatural methods led many Christians to believe the stories promoted the occult.

So, why would Rowling depict divination and other near-occult practices when in so many other ways she appears to align with divine supernaturalism? Oddly enough, it's the same thing so many of us struggle with in our lived Christianity—Rowling is a materialist. She doesn't believe in magic or witchcraft. On the podcast, "The Witch Trials of J.K. Rowling," she states this emphatically. "There are two groups of people who think I'm wholeheartedly with them. One are people who believe passionately in the boarding school system, and the other group are practicing witches. I have to say, I'm not on either of their sides. . . . I don't believe in magic in that sense."[19]

For Rowling, magic is a literary device she used to convey certain truths about human nature.[20] She's likely unconcerned with the fact that some of her methodology looks occult-like because there's no real danger in the occult. It's all just "wooly" magic and fake psychics. She even references the Salem witch trials in books three and four as a historical event where some witches from her fictional world were burned at the stake. Again, she doesn't see a problem with using real historical events in her story because she doesn't believe witchcraft is a real danger.

It's not my preference to use occult-like methodology in fantasy, even as a literary device, because it creates confusion. Yet I do think it's possible for most children to learn the difference and not be attracted to the occult through this series if they're discipled well. Spiritual lust for the occult is a minority temptation, and even those with that temptation aren't often drawn into the occult through fantasy magic. For people who have that temptation, a history of trauma, or a background in the occult, there may be need for more caution, further education, or even restrictions when considering reading the Potter books. For most children, the extra step it takes to educate them on the true nature of things like spellcasting is well worth the effort since the benefits of reading the Harry Potter series are great.

It can be difficult to see any benefits of reading Harry Potter for parents who have never read the books and only see the spells and divination. Yet there have been many people who have been adamantly against the books, then changed their minds after taking the time to read the whole series rather than just bits and pieces. David Hogue is a Christian lawyer who represented the Cedarville, Arkansas, school district in a Harry Potter book ban case in 2002. He appeared as a guest on *The Witch Trials of J.K. Rowling* podcast with host Megan Phelps-Roper.

> Hogue: At first I took it seriously like a lot of people do, because, based on my own Baptist Christian raising and my study of witchcraft and demonology and so forth . . . and I found some things that matched sort of the real life stuff that I'd read about. . . .
>
> Phelps-Roper: David Hogue, for his part, eventually read the Harry Potter series in its entirety and changed his mind about it too.
>
> Hogue: They are good books. I think they do get a bit dark, but I don't see harm in those books.

> And if you have contact with J.K. Rowling, please thank her for the joy that those books are.[21]

Not all people will change their minds after reading this series, especially people who believe any amount of real or fictional witchcraft will "open doors" to Satan. However, those who are willing to engage with good but imperfect films and literature without fear that they will invoke demonic oppression will find this series well worth the effort.

Thematic Analysis

What happens when someone dies? Is there life after death? If only there were a way to conquer death—to become master of it. Then you would never have to know what came next. But death is not something a human can control, is it? It isn't a person to be ordered or threatened or throttled. Unless of course you're the kind of person who thinks you can take things that don't belong to you—things like power over life and death. Or perhaps you're the boy who lived, who conquered death, simply because someone else died to save you. Not just anyone, but the person who loves you most in the world—your mother.

Harry Potter is a story about the very struggle we've been discussing throughout the course of this book. Materialism or spiritualism? Science or the supernatural? Which will win out in the end—faith in life after death, in heaven and hell, in an invisible God who conquered death or leaving the material earth forever with no hope of life after death nor a heaven to store our treasures in? Rowling gave us a boy who lived, a man who longed to be master of death, the Deathly Hallows, Death Eaters, loss of parents, and much more because it was something that meant a great deal to her personally. After all, she lost her mother unexpectedly at a very young age only six months after she first had the idea for this story. "On any given moment if you asked me [if] I believe in life after death, I think if you polled me regularly through the week, I think I would come down on the side of yes—that I do believe in life after death. [But] it's something that I wrestle with a lot. It preoccupies me a lot, and I think that's very obvious within the books."[22]

This series is not just a story about a boy with magical powers; it's a story about a boy who lived when he should have died. It's not just about good versus evil but about one man who demands he should be the conqueror of death and one boy who conquers it only to save the lives of others. If there were a verse that summarized the theme of Harry Potter, it would be 1 Corinthians 15:26 (KJV): "The last enemy that shall be destroyed is death," which was carved into Harry's parents' gravestone. "'They're very British books, so on a very practical note Harry was going to find biblical quotations on tombstones,' Rowling explained. '[But] I think those two particular quotations he finds on the tombstones at Godric's Hollow, they sum up—they almost epitomize the whole series.'"[23] The second verse she's referring to is Matthew 6:21: "Where your treasure is, there will your heart be also." Even this verse is about something eternal since it follows the command to store up treasure in heaven.

The difference we see between Harry and Voldemort is that Harry must conquer death in order to save lives while Voldemort demands to conquer it by taking lives. Harry isn't perfect, but his position as a Christ type gives him the love, humility, and upside-down placement he needs to align with the core of divine supernaturalism. Meanwhile, everything about Voldemort—his pride, obsession with taking immortality for himself, and exploitation of the vulnerable—perfectly aligns him with demonic supernaturalism.

Again, we see that magical methodology isn't unimportant, but it isn't of primary importance. The heart of the character and theme are.

Rowling is constantly redirecting back to what a certain character, scene, or spell means about human nature. It isn't just about magic as magic for her. It's about what her books mean from a literary standpoint. The reason so many books have been written analyzing Harry Potter is because they are deeply metaphorical and philosophical in nature. This is one more example of Christians needing to consider the meaning of a story from a literary point of view rather than taking everything within the story literally. For example, this series is not mainly about a boy who goes to magic school but a neglected boy in an authoritarian home who is finally given agency for the first time in his life. It's not mainly a story about Horcruxes and counter-curses but about love having the power to conquer death. Without the ability to understand the meaning behind the magic, we'll miss the message in its entirety.

Does Harry contact and speak to the ghosts of his dead parents? Yes, and this is normally demonic methodology known as necromancy. If we only ask if the method is demonic, we miss what the ghosts mean from a *literary* standpoint. The Potters aren't just ghosts; they're an answer to Rowling's burning question born from her materialism: "Is there life after death?" And when Lily and James appear beside Harry, the answer is a resounding yes! When Sirius Black falls through a mysterious archway and passes suddenly into death, his voice joins that of all the others whispering "in there," just out of reach beyond the veil.[24]

Even the most doubt-riddled believer knows in their heart of hearts that a body is a thing that can break and die, but a soul is a thing that can never disappear into some unknown void. A human must go on living forever because that is the kind of thing we are created to be. Rowling doesn't believe in ghosts, and she would never tell her readers to literally speak to the dead. She's conveying something metaphorical—that the soul of a person who's gone must still exist. It means that her own mother didn't just disappear into a void because there is life after death.

Additional Concerns

I want to briefly mention two other potential problems with Harry Potter that Christians have raised. The first is the accusation that Rowling was "channeling" when she got the idea to write the Potter series. She has said many times in interviews that the idea just came to her, and she wasn't sure what the inspiration was. "I was on a train. I don't even know what I was thinking about, and the idea just came into my head."[25] This language of the idea just dropping into her head out of nowhere has been used by former occultists and hyperconservative Christians to prove the story came directly from Satan and is, therefore, evil. However, this is one more way in which Christians are unfamiliar with literary norms.

As a fiction writer myself, her description struck me as completely ordinary. I have personally had story ideas come to me in this manner, and I was quite sure I wasn't alone in that. I polled a group of Christian fiction writers on Facebook to see how many of them have had similar experiences. One hundred four people responded to the poll. Of these, 76 percent chose: "I've had at least one idea come to me out of nowhere"; 23 percent said, "All my ideas come to me out of nowhere." And only 1 percent said, "I always know exactly where my inspiration comes from." Is it impossible that a demon or even the Holy Spirit could drop story ideas into people's minds? Of course not. In fact, I'm sure it happens often. But to *assume* the story's mysterious origin proves Rowling was demonically inspired is baseless since her experience is entirely normal.

The second issue frequently raised by parents (whether Christian or otherwise) is the lack of consequences for rule-breaking at Hogwarts. Some parents feel that the books may encourage rule-breaking and rebellion against authority. There is some truth to this since there are times when Harry and his friends break rules and aren't caught or disciplined. Yet there are also times when they are caught and punished, sometimes severely depending on who caught them. There is also a magical map given to them by Ron's older, rule-breaking twin brothers. To use the map, they have to tap it with their wand and say, "I solemnly swear that I am up to no good." When they're done and they want to clear the parchment, they say, "Mischief managed." One of the map's original creators, Lupin, doesn't find the map nearly as funny as an adult, and he temporarily takes it from Harry. He eventually, with some hesitation, gives it back to him at the end of the school year.

There's a reason Rowling wrote the story this way. She said in an interview with Phelps-Roper, "I suppose the Dursleys are my epitome of a very authoritarian and conformist world that demands absolute obedience. And that's not the world you enter when you go to Hogwarts. . . . If there's one thing that I stand against more than any other, it is authoritarianism."[26] She's not saying she's against all authority, nor is there an entire disregard for it in her books. When rule-breaking goes unpunished in the Harry Potter series, Rowling is likely overcorrecting the problem of authoritarianism in her desire to give children agency.

What is authoritarianism, and how does it differ from healthy forms of authority? Authoritarianism is the demand for blind, strict obedience with total or little regard for personal agency, thoughts, or feelings of those under authority.* Although this is common in some Christian homes and churches, it should be regarded as a distortion of scriptural authority and one that often produces spiritual abuse. Extreme examples of this are often found in cults that require complete obedience at the expense of critical thinking. On the other hand, healthy authority figures gain trust and obedience through godly virtues such as love, grace, and a deep respect for the one under authority. These relational structures are also governed by the upside-down kingdom ethic where the last is first and the first is last. Christ's example of a servant leader who lays down his life for those under his rule is the standard all authority figures should hope to live up to.

It's a positive thing for Rowling to be opposed to authoritarianism and supportive of healthy forms of authority. She does portray many adults in a loving, benevolent, trusted position of authority over Harry and the other students. When teachers such as McGonagall, Dumbledore, and Lupin instruct the children not to do something, they usually listen because there is such a strong bond of trust. When they choose not to, things don't always go well. Yes, there are times when the children get away with rule-breaking, and this issue is another mixed bag in that way. However, the beauty of Harry's relationship with adults like Dumbledore, Lupin, and the Weasleys is an accurate depiction of a healthy authority figure that parents and leaders should aspire to imitate.

* For an example of what it looks like to remove personal agency from children, I recommend the science fiction series, Children of the Consortium by Christian author, Cathy McCrumb. Appropriate for teens (with some guidance) and adults.

Born of Imperfection

It may be tempting to think Harry Potter would have been a better series if Rowling wasn't a materialist. After all, Lewis and Tolkien gave us what they did because they were brilliant authors, as Rowling is, and they didn't have that same struggle. Yet as much as I discourage materialism, I think it's also important to appreciate what the Potter series became because of its imperfections. Without an author who's constantly asking herself if there's life after death, the series wouldn't have burned with that question as brightly as it did. Rowling's questions about death and the afterlife ended in the right place. In her battle between faith and materialism, the story concludes with the reality of the spiritual realm. Her fight to get to that ending subverts materialism even in a wizarding world built on its shoulders.

Chapter 13

Final Thoughts

"*Will my child be drawn to the occult if they read fictional magic?*" Although some Christians find this question ridiculous and superstitious, it's one born of genuine concern and a desire to obey God's Word. All too often, fantasy and film lovers have rejected this assertion without stopping to see if it's true. I wanted to honor the people with this uncertainty about fictional magic, so I took the time to investigate the occult and watch hundreds of spiritually dark testimony videos. Although some of you may still find me a biased source as a fantasy writer, it was important to me to be as intellectually honest with this issue as possible. That meant approaching my study of the occult ready to be proven wrong about books like Harry Potter. Yet it may be a comfort to you to know that although I write fantasy, I have no fiction books published or contracted for publication at the time of writing this. Had it become evident during my research that an overwhelming number of people are tempted by fictional magic, it would not have threatened any of my own fiction to admit that.

However, as we've seen, it is not the case that the majority of people are tempted in this way. Being drawn into the occult by fictional magic is a minority temptation and can usually be circumvented through education and discipleship. The tools we need to navigate fantasy magic are the contextual clues surrounding demonic and divine supernaturalism—source, goal, heart, setting, and methodology. That list may have felt overwhelmingly long, but with practice, these story elements will begin to jump out at you without much effort or digging in fiction as well as Scripture. This is likely a brand-new way of looking at a narrative, and time will help reshape the way you see both fantasy and spiritual warfare.

If you're feeling anxious or excited by the literary categories, discernment questions, or new information about spiritual realities, I encourage you to take time to let these ideas sink in. We're more prone to overcorrection, Satanic panic, or making rash decisions when we're in a new "cage stage"* of learning. After you close this book, read through some of the Scriptures we've discussed and investigate the surrounding contexts of the stories further. Take time to think through a few stories that are already familiar to you. I don't suggest you *immediately* create new rules or change the boundaries for your children unless it's urgent to do so. Discerning magic and media should be adapted to suit the needs of your own family. To adapt with prudence, let this information sink into your mind. Once you feel confident that you're not making rash lifestyle changes due to anxiety or enthusiasm, then it will be safe to broach this conversation with your children.

"Your adversary the devil is prowling around like a roaring lion, looking for anyone he can devour" (1 Pet. 5:8b). Satan, the accuser,

* A "cage stage" is a period of time when a person is overly passionate or dogmatic about a new system of belief.

wants to shipwreck our faith and drag us into hell alongside him. Fantasy is not the means by which he accomplishes this but the weapon we forge against him to shed light on the unseen realm and build up our faith in an all-powerful, invisible God. Stories built on the foundation of Christ—the ultimate Word of power—is one of the most human ways we weaponize the sword of the Spirit against our enemy. We don't need to live under a canopy of fear, panic, or superstition because Christ has already won. We can, with a clear view of supernaturalism in Scripture, engage with media in appropriate ways that will edify us and strengthen our faith.

Appendix

Further Resources

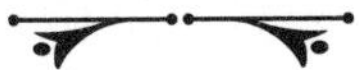

If you're now wondering where to turn for reliable reviews, articles, and fantastical community, here are resources for you or the fantasy lover in your life. I have a personal investment in only a few of these resources and cannot attest to the reliability of each review, article, or community.

- Join my Facebook group, On Magic and Miracles: Reader Community. I designed this group as a safe place for readers and parents to gather and discuss fictional magic and exchange book, film, and game recommendations.
- Visit Lorehaven.com to find reviews of Christian-made fantasy and science fiction novels for all ages. You will also find helpful articles that discuss topics related to faith and speculative fiction—some of which are written by me. Lorehaven also has their *Fantastical*

Truth podcast hosted by E. Stephen Burnett and Zackary Russell.

- Visit Redeemedreader.com for Christian reviews for all genres, book lists, and blogs.
- Visit Pluggedin.com/book-reviews or Pluggedin.com/games. Plugged In is a ministry of Focus on the Family and is primarily known for their film reviews. However, the site also has a variety of television, book, game, music, and YouTube channel reviews.
- Visit Christandpopculture.com for essays, articles, and podcasts that discuss how Christians can engage media and popular culture in Christ-honoring ways.
- Visit Lovethynerd.com for Christian content and community that exists to minister and love the nerds of the world.
- For the Christian Gamer Alliance, which provides community and discussion boards for gamers, visit cgalliance.org.
- Christ-Centered Gamer has Christian game reviews, blogs, and community forums at christcenteredgamer.com.
- To find fantasy books written by Christians, you can visit the publisher's website. Once you find a book that interests you, I encourage you to look at reviews at Lorehaven, Amazon, or Goodreads. Publishers of Christian-made fantasy include Enclave Publishing, Thomas

Nelson, Bethany House, Tyndale, Mountain Brook Fire, Descendant Publishing, Expanse Books, and Owl's Nest Publishers. (This list is not exhaustive.)

- Request your local Christian bookstore to carry more speculative fiction or a specific book.
- Request that your local library carry more speculative fiction from a specific Christian author, publisher, or request a specific book title.
- For Christians who write science fiction and fantasy, visit RealmMakers.com. Realm Makers is an annual conference for Christians who write speculative fiction for both the general and Christian markets. They also provide an online community in The RealmSphere.
- For the Christian Game Developers Conference, visit cgdc.org to find conference information, community, a blog, and other game development resources.
- You can sign up for my newsletter at majacobs.com, or follow me online. Instagram and Twitter: @majacobswrites and Facebook: http://www.facebook.com/majacobswrites.

Notes

Introduction

1. P. Matthijs Bal and Martijn Veltkamp, "How Does Fiction Reading Influence Empathy? An Experimental Investigation on the Role of Emotional Transportation," PLOS ONE, January 30, 2013, https://doi.org/10.1371/journal.pone.0055341.

Chapter 1

1. "How J. R. R. Tolkien Redefined Fantasy Stories," *Newsweek*, March 5, 2017, https://www.newsweek.com/legacy-lifetime-jrr-tolkiens-extended-impact-563520.
2. J. R. R. Tolkien, "On Fairy-Stories," in *The Monsters and the Critics, and Other Essays* (London: HarperCollins, 1997), 122.
3. J. R. R. Tolkien, *The Silmarillion* (New York: William Morrow, 2004), 26, e-book.
4. J. R. R. Tolkien, *The Fellowship of the Ring* (London: HarperCollins, 1991), 330, e-book.
5. C. S. Lewis, *The Lion, the Witch and the Wardrobe* (New York: HarperCollins, 1978), 163, e-book.
6. Narnia's Official Website, The Chronicles of Narnia, accessed April 21, 2023, https://www.narnia.com.
7. John Granger, *Looking for God in Harry Potter* (Carol Stream, IL: SaltRiver, 2006).
8. Richard Abanes, *Harry Potter and the Bible: The Menace behind the Magick* (Traverse City, MI: Horizon Books, 2001).
9. Megan Phelps-Roper, "Chapter 2: Burn the Witch," *The Witch Trials of J.K. Rowling,* February 20, 2023, published by The Free Press, podcast, MP3 audio, 51:59, https://podcasts.apple.com/us/podcast/chapter-2-burn-the-witch/id1671691064?i=1000600749979.

10. Linda LaFond, "What's the Harm in Harry Potter?" CBN, January 15, 2023, https://www2.cbn.com/articlc/not-selected/whats-harm-harry-potter.

11. "Harry Potter Author Reveals Books' Christian Allegory, Her Struggling Faith," *Christianity Today*, October 19, 2007, https://www.christiantoday.com/article/harry.potter.author.reveals.books.christian.allegory.her.struggling.faith/14052.htm.

12. Kristine McGuire, *Escaping the Cauldron: Exposing Occult Influences in Everyday Life* (Lake Mary, FL: Charisma House, 2012), 139.

13. C. S. Lewis, *Surprised by Joy* (San Francisco: HarperOne, 2017), 62, e-book.

14. Scott Rae and Sean McDowell, "Magic and the Christian Faith (with Joshua Ng)," Think Biblically: Conversations on Faith & Culture, podcast audio, July 20, 2023, https://podcasts.google.com/feed/aHR0cHM6Ly9jZG4uYmlvbGEuZWR1L3RoaW5rX2JpYmxpY2Fsb-HkvcG9kY2FzdC9mZWVkLnhtbA/episode/QnV6enNwcm91dC0xMjYzNzM2OA?ep=14.

15. Warren W. Wiersbe, *Be Delivered: Finding Freedom by Following God, OT Commentary: Exodus* (Colorado Springs, CO: David C. Cook, 1998), 37, e-book.

16. Sean McDowell, *Horrifying Story out of Witchcraft (w/ Julie Lopez),* video, 1:05:08, June 9, 2023, https://www.youtube.com/watch?v=I4-MQ4mXb5Y&t=2s&ab_channel=SeanMcDowell.

17. Brother A. D. A., *Ritual Magic for Conservative Christians* (Bradenton, FL: THAVMA Publications, 2016), 7, e-book.

18. McGuire, *Escaping the Cauldron*, 24.

19. Gustavo Benavides, "Magic," in *The Blackwell Companion to the Study of Religion*, ed. Robert A. Segal (Oxford: Blackwell Publishing, 2006), 317–30.

20. David E. Aune, "Magic in Early Christianity," in *Apocalypticism, Prophecy and Magic in Early Christianity*, ed. Jörg Frey (Tübingen, Germany: Mohr Siebeck, 2006) 368–420.

21. John M. Hull, *Hellenistic Magic and the Synoptic Tradition* (London: SCM Press Ltd., 1974), 45.

22. Hull, *Hellenistic Magic and the Synoptic Tradition*, 1.

23. Josephus, *Antiquities* II.274.

24. Hull, *Hellenistic Magic and the Synoptic Tradition*, 45.

25. Hull, *Hellenistic Magic and the Synoptic Tradition*, 45.

26. Joseph Ennemoser, *The History of Magic,* 1854 (Whitefish, MT: Kessinger Publishing, 2019), 204.

27. Hull, *Hellenistic Magic and the Synoptic Tradition*, 45.

28. T. Witton Davies, *Magic, Divination, and Demonology among the Hebrews and Their Neighbours* (Whitefish, MT: Kessinger Publishing, 2010), 1–2.

29. Richard Purtill, *Defining Miracles* (Downers Grove, IL: InterVarsity, 1997), 72, quoted in Lee Strobel, *The Case for Miracles* (Grand Rapids, MI: Zondervan, 2018), 32, e-book.

30. T. Witton Davies, *Magic, Divination, and Demonology among the Hebrews and Their Neighbours*, 1.

31. Lewis, *Surprised by Joy*, 62, e-book.

32. J. R. R. Tolkien, "On Fairy-Stories," in *The Monsters and the Critics, and Other Essays*, 122, e-book.

33. Allen Arnold, *The Story of With: A Better Way to Live, Love, and Create* (Colorado Springs, CO: Allen Arnold, 2016).

34. Sam Storms, *Understanding Spiritual Gifts: A Comprehensive Guide* (Grand Rapids, MI: Zondervan, 2020), 35, e-book.

Chapter 2

1. C. S. Lewis, "Sometimes Fairy Stories May Say Best What's to Be Said," in *Of Other Worlds* (San Francisco: HarperOne, 2017), 54, e-book.

2. Zachary Porcu, "Cosmological and Epistemic Presuppositions in Origen and the Early Fathers: Re-Framing the Discussion on Magic and Demonology in Late Antiquity," doctoral dissertation (Washington, DC: The Catholic University of America, 2021).

3. C. S. Lewis, *Surprised by Joy* (San Francisco: HarperOne, 2017), 202, e-book.

4. George H. Guthrie, *2 Corinthians: Baker Exegetical Commentary on the New Testament* (Grand Rapids: Baker Publishing, 2015), 983, e-book.

5. Guthrie, *2 Corinthians*, 983.

6. Jacob Cherian, "2 Corinthians," in *South Asia Bible Commentary* (Grand Rapids, MI: Zondervan, 2015), 1610.

7. *The Lord of the Rings: The Fellowship of the Ring*, directed by Peter Jackson (New Line Cinema, 2001).

8. *A Charlie Brown Christmas,* directed by Bill Melendez (CBS, 1965).

9. Adam Clarke, *Adam Clarke's Commentary on the Bible*, abridged by Ralph Earle (Nashville, TN: Nelson Bibles: 1989), 915.

10. Tim Chaffey, *Fallen: The Sons of God and the Nephilim* (Petersburg, KY: Risen Books, 2019), 43, Kindle.

11. For a more in-depth look at the *elohim*, sons of God, and the divine council, I recommend reading Tim Chaffey, *Fallen* or Kaspars Ozolins' essay, "The Divine Council" at Desiring God, June 7, 2022, https://www.desiringgod.org/articles/the-divine-council. Michael S. Heiser also covers these topics in his book, *The Unseen Realm: Recovering the Supernatural Worldview of the Bible* (Bellingham, WA: Lexham Press, 2019). Heiser's work is important in bringing this conversation to light. However, his disagreement with historical Christianity (i.e., "classical theology") regarding issues such as the image of God occasionally affects his hermeneutics, and his work should be read with discernment. The Eastern Orthodox Church also maintained the

doctrine of the divine council where it had been primarily lost to the Western branches of Christianity until recent years. To learn about these things from an Orthodox perspective, I recommend Andrew Stephen Damick, *The Lord of the Spirits: An Orthodox Christian Framework for the Unseen World and Spiritual Warfare* (Munster, IN: Ancient Faith Publishing, 2023), and chapter 3 in Stephen de Young, *The Religion of the Apostles: Orthodox Christianity in the First Century* (Munster, IN: Ancient Faith Publishing, 2021). Frs. Damick and de Young also cohost the informative podcast "The Lord of Spirits," which discusses the basics of these things in the first episodes. Keep in mind that the Eastern Orthodox Church doesn't hold to *sola scriptura* and considers writings from the early church as authoritative. Books such as 1 Enoch play a much larger role in their understanding of angelology and demonology.

12. Chaffey, *Fallen*, 38.

13. Daniel I. Block, *For the Glory of God: Recovering a Biblical Theology of Worship* (Grand Rapids: Baker Academic, 2014), 30, e-book.

14. John Piper, "The Surprising Role of Guardian Angels," Desiring God, April 4, 2017, https://www.desiringgod.org/articles/the-surprising-role-of-guardian-angels.

15. John Calvin, *Commentary on a Harmony of the Evangelists Matthew, Mark, and Luke* (Grand Rapids, MI: Eerdmans, 1949).

16. C. S. Lewis, *The Screwtape Letters* (San Francisco: HarperOne, 2015), 8, e-book.

17. See John Owen, *The Mortification of Sin* (Edinburgh: Banner of Truth Trust, 2016).

18. Jack Zavada, "Word of Faith Movement History," Learn Religions, December 10, 2018, https://www.learnreligions.com/word-of-faith-movement-history-700136.

19. Sam Storms, *Understanding Spiritual Gifts: A Comprehensive Guide* (Grand Rapids, MI: Zondervan, 2020), 299, e-book.

20. Leah Collins, "The Strange Origins of the Satanic Panic: How One Canadian Book Started a Worldwide Witch Hunt," CBC/Radio Canada, April 25, 2023, https://www.cbc.ca/arts/satan-wants-you-filmmakers-q-a-sean-horlor-steve-j-adams-1.6822213.

21. John Piper, "The Fall of Satan and the Victory of Christ" (sermon audio, Bethlehem Baptist Church, August 19, 2007).

Chapter 3

1. Adam Clarke, *Adam Clarke's Commentary on the Bible*, abridged by Ralph Earle (Nashville, TN: Nelson Bibles: 1989), 617.

2. William G. Blaikie, *An Exposition of the Bible*, vol. 2 (Hartford, CT: S. S. Scranton Company, 1908), 105, e-book.

3. Norman Geisler and Thomas Howe, *When Critics Ask: A Popular Handbook on Bible Difficulties* (Wheaton, IL.: Victor Books, 1992), 60.

4. James Montgomery Boice, *Ordinary Men Called by God: A Study of Abraham, Moses, and David* (Grand Rapids, MI: Kregel, 1998), 62.

5. Andrew E. Hill and John H. Walton, *A Survey of the Old Testament* (Grand Rapids, MI: Zondervan Academic, 2009), 116.

6. Clarke and Earle, *Adam Clarke's Commentary on the Bible*, 616–17.

7. Matthew George Easton, *Easton's Bible Dictionary*, 3rd ed., (N.p., 1897), e-book.

8. Clarke and Earle, *Adam Clarke's Commentary on the Bible*, 617.

9. J. R. R. Tolkien, *The Fellowship of the Ring* (London: HarperCollins, 1991) 330, e-book.

10. Clarke and Earle, *Adam Clarke's Commentary on the Bible*, 617.

11. Clarke and Earle, *Adam Clarke's Commentary on the Bible*, 617.

12. Kristine McGuire, *Escaping the Cauldron: Exposing Occult Influences in Everyday Life* (Lake Mary, FL: Charisma House, 2012), 35.

13. Philip Graham Ryken, *Exodus: Saved for God's Glory* (Wheaton, IL: Crossway, 2015), 294, e-book.

Chapter 4

1. Josh Peck and Steven Bancarz, *The Second Coming of the New Age: The Hidden Dangers of Alternative Spirituality in Contemporary America and Its Churches* (Crane, MO: Defender Publishing, 2018).

2. Stephen C Ministries, "From Luciferian to Jesus: Warning against the Occult and Satan's Tactics," YouTube video, 39:18, December 22, 2023, https://www.youtube.com/watch?v=37hkha-95kg&ab_channel=StephenCMinistries.

3. M. Stefon, "Anton LaVey," *Encyclopedia Britannica*, accessed March 6, 2024, https://www.britannica.com/biography/Anton-LaVey.

4. Blanche Barton, *The Church of Satan: A History of the World's Most Notorious Religion* (Poughkeepsie, NY: Hells Kitchen Productions, 1990), 107, e-book.

5. Peck and Bancarz, *The Second Coming of the New Age*, 11.

6. Peck and Bancarz, *The Second Coming of the New Age*, 12.

7. Peck and Bancarz, *The Second Coming of the New Age*, 74.

8. H. P. Blavatsky, *The Secret Doctrine* (Blackmore Dennett, 2018), 696, e-book.

9. C. S. Lewis, *The Lion, The Witch and the Wardrobe* (New York: HarperCollins, 1978),

10. *Cultish*, "Part 1: Navigating the New Age and the World of the Occult with Steven Bancarz," October 3, 2019, produced by Apologia Studios, podcast, MP3 audio, 48:07, https://podcasts.apple.com/us/podcast/part-1-navigating-the-new-age-the-world-of/id1440854210?i=1000431608865.

11. Delafé Testimonies, "From Hating God and Doing Witchcraft to Following JESUS!" YouTube video, 49:17, October 19, 2023, https://

www.youtube.com/watch?v=zF2_G9U_MvE&list=WL&index=4&ab_channel=Delaf%C3%A9Testimonies.

12. J. C. Ryle, *Expository Thoughts on the Gospel of Mark: A Commentary* (Abbotsford, WI: Aneko Press, 2020), 74, e-book.

13. C. S. Lewis, *Surprised by Joy* (San Francisco: HarperOne, 2017), 62, e-book.

14. Material taken from an email between author and Francesca Knapp, November 20, 2023.

15. Brother A. D. A., *Ritual Magic for Conservative Christians* (Bradenton, FL: THAVMA Publications, 2016), 13, e-book.

16. John Piper, "Did Israel's King Consult with a Witch?" Desiring God, June 9, 2017, https://www.desiringgod.org/interviews/did-israels-king-consult-with-a-witch.

17. Andrew E. Hill and John H. Walton, *A Survey of the Old Testament* (Grand Rapids, MI: Zondervan Academic, 2009), 115.

18. Benjamin Fearnow, "Number of Witches Rises Dramatically across U.S. as Millennials Reject Christianity," *Newsweek*, November 18, 2018, https://www.newsweek.com/witchcraft-wiccans-mysticism-astrology-witches-millennials-pagans-religion-1221019.

19. Sangeeta Singh-Kurtz and Dan Kopf, "The US Witch Population Has Seen an Astronomical Rise," *Quartz*, October 4, 2018, https://qz.com/quartzy/1411909/the-explosive-growth-of-witches-wiccans-and-pagans-in-the-us.

20. Mary Jackson, "Out of Darkness," *World Magazine*, April 18, 2024, https://wng.org/articles/out-of-darkness-1713232697.

21. Claire Gecewicz, "'New Age' Beliefs Common among Both Religious and Nonreligious Americans," Pew Research Center, October 1, 2018, https://www.pewresearch.org/short-reads/2018/10/01/new-age-beliefs-common-among-both-religious-and-nonreligious-americans.

22. Gecewicz, "'New Age' Beliefs Common."

23. Joseph MacKinnon, "Taxpayer-Subsidized Art Center in Minnesota Holds 'Playful Demon Summoning Session' for Families," Blaze Media, August 16, 2023, https://www.theblaze.com/news/taxpayer-subsidized-art-center-in-minnesota-holds-playful-demon-summoning-session-for-families.

24. *The Craft*, directed by Andrew Fleming (Columbia Pictures, 1996).

25. Kristine McGuire, *Escaping the Cauldron: Exposing Occult Influences in Everyday Life* (Lake Mary, FL: Charisma House, 2012), 139.

26. Sofia Quaglia, "Women Are Invoking the Witch to Find Their Power in a Patriarchal Society," Quartz, October 31, 2019, https://qz.com/1739043/the-resurgence-of-the-witch-as-a-symbol-of-feminist-empowerment.

27. Sady Doyle, “Monsters, Men and Magic: Why Feminists Turned to Witchcraft to Oppose Trump,” The Guardian, August 7, 2019, https://www.theguardian.com/lifeandstyle/2019/aug/07/monsters-men-magic-trump-awoke-angry-feminist-witches.

28. Naela Rose, “New Age to Jesus: Demon-Possessed Witch Saved by Christ #newagetojesus,” YouTube video, 2:11:27, September 5, 2023, https://youtu.be/fkSKMuyJk4Q?si=IwOnTibdNBvTFGMT.

29. Mary Jackson, “Out of Darkness,” *World* magazine, April 18, 2024, https://wng.org/articles/out-of-darkness-1713232697.

30. Delafé Testimonies, “From New Age Witchcraft to JESUS (Testimony),” YouTube video, 40:45, August 18, 2022, https://www.youtube.com/watch?v=fN6HbnA1QGI&list=PL8kzcMrFQ8x0MSFkg0ad7zRjz_dLwSYev&index=9&t=10s&ab_channel=Delaf%C3%A9Testimonies.

31. *Jesus Revolution*, directed by Jon Erwin and Brett McCorkle (Lionsgate, 2023).

32. “The Occult,” Christianity.org, accessed April 1, 2023, https://christianity.org.uk/article/the-occult.

33. Sean McDowell, “Horrifying Story out of Witchcraft (w/ Julie Lopez),” YouTube video, 1:05:08, June 9, 2023, https://www.youtube.com/watch?v=I4-MQ4mXb5Y&t=2s&ab_channel=SeanMcDowell.

34. G. Connor Salter, “What Is Thelema and Why Is It Dangerous?” Christianity.com, May 16, 2022, https://www.christianity.com/wiki/cults-and-other-religions/what-is-thelema-the-greek-word-and-the-occult-religion.html.

35. Catherine Beyer, “Understanding the Religion of Thelema,” *Learn Religions*, January 27, 2019, https://www.learnreligions.com/thelema-95700.

36. “What Is Magic? Aleister Crowley Explains,” Faena Aleph, accessed March 23, 2023, https://www.faena.com/aleph/what-is-magic-aleister-crowley-explains.

37. Sage Romano, “Neopagan New Age Priestess and Witch to Jesus—My Unfolding Story,” YouTube video, 23:31, February 14, 2023, https://www.youtube.com/watch?v=fCcTFeYyitc&t=455s&ab_channel=SageRomano.

Chapter 5

1. Eli Lizorkin-Eyzenberg, “Who Will Heal You? A Greek or a Jewish God? (John 5.2-5),” Israel Institute of Biblical Studies, February 19, 2013, https://blog.israelbiblicalstudies.com/jewish-studies/john-5-2-5-who-will-heal-you-a-greek-or-a-jewish-god.

2. *The Chosen*, “Did we get it wrong with Pool of Bethesda?” YouTube video, 10:10, Mar 13, 2022, https://www.youtube.com/watch?v=SdOYPcwNCio&ab_channel=TheChosen.

3. Pratap C. Gine and Jacob Cherian, *John*, South Asia Bible Commentary (Grand Rapids, MI: Zondervan, 2015), 1401.

4. Michael Heiser taught that Genesis 3 is not about a literal animal (see p. 74 in *The Unseen Realm: Recovering the Supernatural Worldview of the Bible* [Bellingham, WA: Lexham Press, 2019], and the serpent imagery for spiritual beings was a lot more common in the Bible than we know. He sees the being that guards God's throne, a "saraph," as related to the Mesopotamian description of a flaming cobra. Naked Bible, "Seraphim and Cherubim" YouTube video, 9:05, July 26, 2017, https://www.youtube.com/watch?v=xWvGVCPldkI&ab_channel=NakedBible.

5. Nathan W. Bingham, Sinclair Ferguson, "Why Are Some Demons Only Able to Be Cast Out by Prayer (Mark 9:29)?" Ligonier, August 25, 2022, https://www.ligonier.org/podcasts/ask-ligonier/why-are-some-demons-only-able-to-be-cast-out-by-prayer-mark-929?fbclid=IwAR1K9lY0DUjUQ0JUh7Zz2LDNiV-THvtzrhPPNqu76hx23ai_tHpehUbGQbk#:~:text=Jesus%20told%20His%20disciples%20that,(Mark%209%3A29).

6. Josh Peck and Steven Bancarz, *The Second Coming of the New Age: The Hidden Dangers of Alternative Spirituality in Contemporary America and Its Churches* (Crane, MO: Defender Publishing, 2018), 31.

7. R. D. Patterson and Hermann J. Austel, *1 & 2 Kings*, Expositor's Bible Commentary (Grand Rapids, MI: Zondervan, 1988), 177.

Chapter 6

1. Aristotle, *Physics* II.3 and *Metaphysics* V. 2.

2. Westminster Assembly (1643–1652); Hervey Wilbur, *The Assembly's Shorter Catechism, with the Scripture Proofs in Reference: with an Appendix on the Systematick Attention of the Young to Scriptural Knowledge* (Newburyport, MA:Wm. B. Allen & Co., 1816).

3. Lucinda White, "From a Self-Proclaimed Witch Tormented by Demons to Freedom in Jesus Christ. NEW AGE TO JESUS," YouTube video, 39:18, March 1, 2024, https://www.youtube.com/watch?v=tFd91OubfKQ&ab_channel=lucindawhite.

4. Dane Ortlund, *Gentle and Lowly: The Heart of Christ for Sinners and Sufferers* (Wheaton, IL: Crossway, 2020), 29.

5. Steven Bancarz and Josh Peck, *The Second Coming of the New Age: The Hidden Dangers of Alternative Spirituality in Contemporary America and Its Churches* (Crane, MO: Defender Publishing, 2018), 67, e-book.

6. John Piper, "What Is an Idol?" Desiring God, January 3, 2022, https://www.desiringgod.org/interviews/what-is-an-idol.

7. Havilah Dharamraj, *Judges*, South Asia Bible Commentary (Grand Rapids, MI: Zondervan, 2015), 319.

8. Jon Bloom, *Things Not Seen: A Fresh Look at Old Stories of Trusting God's Promises* (Wheaton, IL: Crossway, 2015), 125.

9. Bloom, *Things Not Seen*, 127.

10. David Murray, "Reflecting Sin: The Pedagogical Use of the Law," *Ligonier*, March 1, 2011, https://www.ligonier.org/learn/articles/reflecting-sin-pedagogical-use-law.

11. Walter Hooper, ed., *Collected Letters of C. S. Lewis, Vol. 2* (New York: HarperCollins, 2009), 955, e-book.

12. Michael S. Heiser, "Casting Lots in the Bible," YouTube video, 5:17, January 9, 2023, https://www.youtube.com/watch?v=wuP5rYJe-98&ab_channel=Dr.MichaelS.Heiser.

13. Relient K, "Down in Flames," track 4, *Anatomy of the Tongue in Cheek*, Gotee Records, 2001.

14. Jason Lisle, "What Was the Christmas Star?" *The New Answers Book 2: Over 30 Questions on Creation/Evolution and the Bible* (Green Forest, AR: Master Books, 2008) 157.

15. *Most Christians Don't Know THIS about the Christmas Star*, Answers in Genesis, YouTube video, 41:27, December 1, 2023, https://www.youtube.com/watch?v=EcPhaO3pY5Y&ab_channel=AnswersinGenesis.

16. Ortlund, *Gentle and Lowly*, 33.

Chapter 7

1. Thomas Aquinas, *Summa Theologiæ* (ST), trans. the Fathers of the English Dominican Province (New York: Benzinger Bros., 1948), I.93.2.

2. *Understanding the Cultural Mandate—Nancy Pearcey,* AccessTruth, YouTube video, 2:19, August 18, 2020, https://www.youtube.com/watch?v=MbJh3Mksi10&ab_channel=AccessTruth.

3. Leland Ryken, "Thinking Christianly about Literature," in *The Christian Imagination: The Practice of Faith in Literature and Writing*, ed. by Leland Ryken (Colorado Springs, CO: WaterBrook Press, 2002), 26.

4. C. S. Lewis, "Sometimes Fairy Stories May Say Best What's to Be Said," in *Of Other Worlds* (San Francisco: HarperOne, 2017), 53, e-book.

5. Lewis, "Sometimes Fairy Stories May Say Best What's to Be Said," 54.

6. C. S. Lewis, *Surprised by Joy* (San Francisco: HarperOne, 2017), 209, e-book.

7. Jasmine Fischer, "Why I Write Christian Fiction—Specifically Fantasy," The Gospel Coalition Australia, April 12, 2019, https://au.thegospelcoalition.org/article/write-christian-fiction-specifically-fantasy.

8. Merriam-Webster.com Dictionary, s.v. "imagination," https://www.merriam-webster.com/dictionary/imagination.

9. J. R. R. Tolkien, "On Fairy-Stories," in *The Monsters and the Critics, and Other Essays* (London: HarperCollins, 1997), 109–161.

10. Leland Ryken, *How to Read the Bible as Literature . . . and Get More Out of It* (Grand Rapids, MI: Zondervan, 1984), 216, e-book.

11. Tolkien, "On Fairy-Stories," 134.

12. C. S. Lewis, *The Lion, the Witch and the Wardrobe* (New York: HarperCollins, 1978), 2.

13. Tolkien, "On Fairy-Stories," 134, e-book.

14. Sam Storms, *Understanding Spiritual Warfare: A Comprehensive Guide* (Grand Rapids, MI: Zondervan, 2021), 30, e-book.

15. Tony Reinke, *Lit: A Christian Guide to Reading Books* (Wheaton, IL: Crossway, 2011), 105.

Chapter 8

1. Russell Moore, "J.K. Rowling's Witch Hunts Put Us on Trial," *Christianity Today*, May 11, 2023, https://www.christianitytoday.com/ct/2023/may-web-only/russell-moore-ct-jk-rowling-harry-potter-witch-hunt-trial.html.

2. R. C. Sproul, "3 Types of Legalism," Ligonier, July 17, 2019, https://www.ligonier.org/learn/articles/3-types-legalism.

3. Sproul, "3 Types of Legalism."

4. C. S. Lewis, *The Lion, the Witch, and the Wardrobe* (New York: HarperCollins, 1978), 163, e-book.

5. Jenn Edwards, "From Multi Million Dollar New Age Coach to Follow Jesus Christ. Lorna Testimony," YouTube video, 59:31, July 13, 2023, https://www.youtube.com/watch?v=10xYFbuagok&list=PL8kzcMrFQ8x0MSFkg0ad7zRjz_dLwSYev&index=99&t=2289s&ab_channel=JennEdwards.

6. Aristotle, *Nicomachean Ethics* II.6 (1107a1–11).

7. Jonathan Poletti, "A Sick and Twisted History of the Cabbage Patch Kids," Medium, September 15, 2023, https://medium.com/sexstories/a-sick-and-twisted-history-of-the-cabbage-patch-kids-cca151ac6f9f.

8. Randall J. Stephens, *The Devil's Music: How Christians Inspired, Condemned, and Embraced Rock 'n' Roll* (Cambridge, MA: Harvard University Press, 2018).

Chapter 9

1. *Doctor Strange in the Multiverse of Madness*, directed by Sam Raimi (Marvel Studios and Walt Disney Pictures, 2022).

2. Phil Vischer, "God Is Bigger," *VeggieTales: Where Is God When I'm S-scared?* (Big Idea Entertainment, 1993).

3. Delafé Testimonies, "Former Stripper Shares Powerful Testimony of Jesus!," YouTube video, 51:25, January 29, 2024, https://www.youtube.com/watch?v=X9nZMit7P44&list=PL8kzcMrFQ8x0MSFkg0ad7zRjz_dLwSYev&index=159&t=12s&ab_channel=Delaf%C3%A9Testimonies.

4. *Inception*, directed by Christopher Nolan (Warner Bros., 2010).

5. Darren Mooney, "10 Years Later: Inception Is a Movie about Movies, but It's Also Wary of Movies," *The Escapist*, July 15, 2020,

https://www.escapistmagazine.com/10-years-later-inception-about-movies-wary-of-movies.

6. E. Stephen Burnett, Ted Turnau, and Jared Moore, *The Pop Culture Parent: Helping Kids Engage Their World for Christ* (Greensboro, NC: New Growth Press, 2020).

7. Ted Turnau, *Popologetics* (Phillipsburg, NJ: P&R Publishing, 2012).

8. Burnett, Turnau, and Moore, *The Pop Culture Parent*, 9.

9. Burnett, Turnau, and Moore, *The Pop Culture Parent*, 8.

Chapter 10

1. K. M. Weiland, *Structuring Your Novel: Essential Keys for Writing an Outstanding Story* (Barnsley, South Yorkshire, UK: PenForASword Publishing, 2014).

2. K. M. Weiland, *Creating Character Arcs: The Masterful Author's Guide to Uniting Story Structure, Plot, and Character Development* (Barnsley, South Yorkshire, UK: PenForASword Publishing, 2016).

3. Weiland, *Structuring Your Novel*, 48.

4. Weiland, *Creating Character Arcs*, 32.

5. Weiland, *Structuring Your Novel*, 88.

6. Weiland, *Creating Character Arcs*, 41.

7. Weiland, *Structuring Your Novel*, 94.

8. Weiland, *Creating Character Arcs*, 43.

9. Weiland, *Structuring Your Novel*, 102.

10. Weiland, *Structuring Your Novel*, 114.

11. Weiland, *Creating Character Arcs*, 54.

12. Weiland, *Structuring Your Novel*, 124.

13. Weiland, *Creating Character Arcs*, 58.

14. Idina Menzel, "Let It Go," track 5, *Frozen* (Original Motion Picture Soundtrack, Walt Disney, 2013).

15. Jessica Paganini, "Frozen Was Very Different to the Snow Queen: Everything Disney Changed," *Screen Rant*, May 1, 2020, https://screenrant.com/frozen-movie-snow-queen-book-story-comparison-differences/#:~:text=Disney's%20Frozen%20is%20loosely%20based,The%20Snow%20Queen%22%20fairy%20tale.

16. ScreenSlam, "Frozen: Songwriters Kristen Anderson-Lopez & Robert Lopez Official Movie Interview | ScreenSlam," YouTube video, 7:07, October 31, 2013, https://www.youtube.com/watch?v=mzZ77n4Ab5E&ab_channel=ScreenSlam.

17. C. S. Lewis letter to Mrs. Hook, Narniaweb, December 29, 1958, https://community.narniaweb.com/index.php/community/the-man-behind-the-wardrobe/allegorical-aslan-c-s-lewis-quote.

18. J. R. R. Tolkien, *The Fellowship of the Ring* (New York: William Morrow, 2012), xv.

19. "Harry Potter Author Reveals Books' Christian Allegory, Her Struggling Faith," *Christian Today,* October 19, 2007, https://www.christiantoday.com/article/harry.potter.author.reveals.books.christian.allegory.her.struggling.faith/14052.htm.

20. Morgan L. Busse, *Mark of the Raven* (Grand Rapids, MI: Bethany House Publishers, 2018).

21. Merriam-Webster.com Dictionary, s.v. "myth," https://www.merriam-webster.com/dictionary/myth.

22. Humphrey Carpenter, *J. R. R. Tolkien: A Biography* (New York: Houghton Mifflin, 1977), 202–3.

23. C. S. Lewis, *Surprised by Joy* (San Francisco: HarperOne, 2017), 114.

24. Carpenter, *J. R. R. Tolkien: A Biography*, 203.

Chapter 11

1. Christopher Paolini, *Eragon* (New York: Alfred A. Knopf, 2003).

2. Daniel Burke, "The Spiritual Message Hidden in 'Star Wars,'" CNN, January 29, 2018, https://www.cnn.com/2018/01/26/us/star-wars-religion/index.html#:~:text=Lucas%20himself%20has%20been%20called,told%20Time%20magazine%20in%201999.

3. "Midi-chlorian," Wookieepedia, https://starwars.fandom.com/wiki/Midi-chlorian.

4. Ikigai Tribe, "Finding Peace with Your Enemy," July 14, 2022, https://ikigaitribe.com/vlog/finding-peace-with-your-enemy.

5. J. R. R. Tolkien, *The Silmarillion* (New York: William Morrow, 2004), 15.

6. Tolkien, *The Silmarillion*, 142.

7. J. J. Fischer, *Memoria* (Phoenix, AZ: Enclave Publishing, 2024).

8. Gillian Bronte Adams, *Of Fire and Ash* (Phoenix, AZ: Enclave Escape, 2022).

9. Nadine Brandes, *Fawkes* (Nashville: Thomas Nelson, 2018).

10. William P. Young, *The Shack* (Thousand Oaks, CA: Windblown Media, 2007).

11. Ted Dekker, *The 49th Mystic* (Grand Rapids, MI: Revell, 2018), e-book.

12. Dekker, *The 49th Mystic*, 397.

13. Ted Dekker, *Rise of the Mystics* (Grand Rapids, MI: Revell, 2018), 145, e-book.

14. Westminster Assembly (1643–1652). The Assembly's Shorter Catechism, with the Scripture Proofs in Reference: with an Appendix on the *Systematick Attention of the Young to Scriptural Knowledge*, by Hervey Wilbur (Newburyport, MA: Wm. B. Allen & Co., 1816).

15. *Star Wars: Episode III—The Revenge of the Sith*, directed by George Lucas (Lucasfilm Ltd., 2005).

16. *Star Wars: Episode I—The Phantom Menace*, directed by George Lucas (Lucasfilm Ltd., 1999).

17. Leigh Bardugo, *Ruin and Rising* (New York: Henry Holt and Co., 2014), chapter 17.

18. *Avengers: Endgame*, directed by Anthony and Joe Russo (Marvel Studios and Walt Disney Pictures, 2019).

19. *Doctor Strange in the Multiverse of Madness*, directed by Sam Raimi (Marvel Studios and Walt Disney Pictures, 2022).

20. *Doctor Strange in the Multiverse of Madness.*

21. C. S. Lewis, *The Lion, the Witch and the Wardrobe* (New York: HarperCollins, 1978), 41.

22. Lewis, *The Lion, the Witch, and the Wardrobe*, 86.

23. Sharon Hinck, *Dream of Kings* (Phoenix, AZ: Enclave Publishing, 2022).

24. Jim Butcher, *Storm Front* (New York: Roc Books, 2000).

25. *Pirates of the Caribbean: On Stranger Tides*, directed by Rob Marshall (Walt Disney Pictures, 2011).

26. *Pirates of the Caribbean: On Stranger Tides.*

27. J.K. Rowling, *Harry Potter and the Deathly Hallows* (New York: Scholastic, 2007).

28. *The Incredibles*, directed by Brad Bird (Walt Disney Pictures and Pixar Animation Studios, 2004).

29. Mary Shelley, *Frankenstein* (London: Penguin, 1985).

30. *Turning Red,* directed by Domee Shi (Walt Disney Pictures and Pixar Animation Studios, 2022).

31. *By Darkness Hid* (Blood of Kings series) is a Christian young adult fantasy series with some violence, mild depictions of child abuse, and brief kissing.

32. Chengquan Zhu, Su Ruiying, Xun Zhang, Yanan Liu, "Relation between Narcissism and Meaning in Life: The Role of Conspicuous Consumption," Heliyon, August 27, 2021, https://doi.org/10.1016%2Fj.heliyon.2021.e07885.

33. Lewis, *The Lion, the Witch, and the Wardrobe*, 158.

34. Lewis, *The Lion, the Witch, and the Wardrobe*, 97.

35. Lewis, *The Lion, the Witch, and the Wardrobe*, 97.

36. Verna Felton, "Bibbidi-Bobbidi-Boo," track 7, *Cinderella* (Original Motion Picture Soundtrack), Walt Disney Pictures, 1950.

37. *Dungeons & Dragons: Honor Among Thieves*, directed by John Francis Daley and Jonathan Goldstein (Paramount Pictures and eOne, 2023).

38. *Doctor Strange in the Multiverse of Madness.*

39. Ted Dekker, *The 49th Mystic* (Grand Rapids, MI: Revell, 2018).

Chapter 12

1. J.K. Rowling, *Harry Potter and the Deathly Hallows* (New York: Scholastic, 2007).

2. J.K. Rowling, *Harry Potter and the Order of the Phoenix* (New York: Scholastic, 2003), 841.

3. Shawn Adler, "'Harry Potter' Author J.K. Rowling Opens Up about Books' Christian Imagery," MTV, October 17, 2007, https://www.mtv.com/news/ggkjwf/harry-potter-author-jk-rowling-opens-up-about-books-christian-imagery.

4. J.K. Rowling, *Harry Potter and the Sorcerer's Stone* (New York: Scholastic, 1998), 216.

5. Rowling, *Harry Potter and the Deathly Hallows*, 738.

6. C. S. Lewis, *The Lion, the Witch and the Wardrobe* (New York: HarperCollins, 1978), 144.

7. Adler, "Rowling Opens Up about Books' Christian Imagery."

8. Rowling, *Harry Potter and the Deathly Hallows*, 326.

9. Adler, "Rowling Opens Up about Books' Christian Imagery.".

10. Rowling, *Harry Potter and the Deathly Hallows*, 739.

11. Rowling, *Harry Potter and the Deathly Hallows*, 100.

12. Megan Phelps-Roper, "Chapter 2: Burn the Witch," *The Witch Trials of J.K. Rowling*, February 20, 2023, published by The Free Press, podcast, MP3 audio, 51:59, https://podcasts.apple.com/us/podcast/chapter-2-burn-the-witch/id1671691064?i=1000600749979.

13. Patti Wigington, "How Wiccan Is Harry Potter?," Learn Religions, May 14, 2019, ttps://www.learnreligions.com/how-wiccan-is-harry-potter-2561839#:~:text=Harry%20Potter%20is%20a%20work,legends%2C%20and%20early%20occult%20writings.

14. J.K. Rowling, *Harry Potter and the Prisoner of Azkaban* (London: Bloomsbury Publishing, 1999), 79.

15. Rowling, *Harry Potter and the Prisoner of Azkaban*, 85.

16. Friday Night with Jonathan Ross, "JK Rowling on Crooked Security Guards That Stole the Manuscripts | Friday Night with Jonathan Ross," YouTube video, 14:36, August 3, 2019, https://www.youtube.com/watch?v=6t76yexCZCM&ab_channel=FridayNightWithJonathanRoss.

17. Rowling, *Harry Potter and the Order of the Phoenix*, 602–3.

18. J.K. Rowling, *Harry Potter and the Chamber of Secrets* (New York: Scholastic, 1998), 329.

19. Phelps-Roper, "Chapter 2: Burn the Witch."

20. Megan Phelps-Roper, host, "Chapter 1: Plotted in Darkness," *The Witch Trials of J.K. Rowling*, February 20, 2023, published by The Free Press, podcast, MP3 audio, 43:27, https://podcasts.apple.com/us/podcast/the-witch-trials-of-j-k-rowling/id1671691064?i=1000600750210.

21. Phelps-Roper, "Chapter 2: Burn the Witch."

22. Adler, "Rowling Opens Up about Books' Christian Imagery."

23. Adler, "Rowling Opens Up about Books' Christian Imagery."

24. Rowling, *Harry Potter and the Order of the Phoenix*, 774.

25. Friday Night with Jonathan Ross, "J.K. Rowling on Crooked Security Guards That Stole the Manuscripts."

26. Megan Phelps-Roper, host, "Chapter 3: A New Pyre," *The Witch Trials of J.K. Rowling*, February 28, 2023, published by The Free Press, podcast, MP3 audio, 58:33, https://podcasts.apple.com/us/podcast/chapter-3-a-new-pyre/id1671691064?i=1000602034798.